BUDGETING SENSITIVE TO DEMOGRAPHIC DIVIDEND

Principles, methods and applications

Latif DRAMANI

BUDGETING SENSITIVE TO DEMOGRAPHIC DIVIDEND

Principles, Methods and Applications

Preface by Dr. Sennen HOUNTON

Afterword by Prof. Barthélémy BIAO

Sénégal
L'Harmattan

10 VDN, Sicap Amitié 3, Lotissement Cité Police, DAKAR

http://www.harmattansenegal.com
senharmattan@gmail.com
senlibrairie@gmail.com

ISBN : 978-2-336-56620-7
EAN : 9782336566207

BRIEF CONTENTS

PREFACE

At a time when sub-Saharan Africa, and particularly the Sahel countries, are facing unprecedented demographic challenges, the Budgeting Sensitive to Demographic Dividend (BSDD) tool is designed as a strategic lever that should significantly contribute to transforming these challenges into development opportunities. This is the whole point of this book, which proposes strategic axes promoting a range of in-depth and multidimensional analyses of budgetary policies. Better still, based on these axes, countries now have solid levers to rethink these policies.

The book comprises nine chapters divided into two volumes. Volume 1 describes the analytical framework for Budgeting Sensitive to Demographic Dividend, the estimation of the demographic dividend profile, the demographic dividend monitoring index (DDMI), and its gender-specific version. This first volume comprises six chapters. Chapter 1 focuses on the economic analysis of the budget and serves as a framework for presenting the structure and components of the state budget. It also focuses on fiscal policy instruments. This chapter aims to demonstrate the effects of budget allocations on inclusive growth. Chapter 2 focuses on gender-sensitive budgeting and the demographic dividend. Starting with the definition of the concept of DD, it examines its integration into the public budget while ensuring gender sensitivity. Through this chapter, you will become familiar with the conceptual and methodological foundations of the DDMI. The objective is to promote integrated, equitable and effective budget planning.

Chapter 3 focuses on the Demographic Dividend profile. Here, the focus is on several West and Central African countries. Using socio-economic data and a rigorous and innovative methodology, this chapter conducts an analysis to identify the opportunities and challenges facing the countries.

Chapter 4 focuses on the Demographic Dividend Monitoring Index (DDMI). It serves as a framework to review the structure of the DDMI as well as its five (5) sub-indices (EDCI, QLEI, PESI, EHDI and NTSI). These make it possible to measure the capacity of countries to exploit the potential of DD. Better still, this chapter highlights regional disparities as well as demographic dynamics.

Chapter 5 focuses on the retropolation of the DDMI. It presents the methodology and, from there, the one that facilitates the production of time series while ensuring their consistency. Through this methodology, a great opportunity is offered to fill certain gaps related to the surveys and to carry out the temporal analysis of the DD.

Chapter 6 focuses on the profile of the Demographic Dividend. This chapter proposes a method that allows the transformation of the traditional state budget into a functional budget aligned with the functions of the DDMI. To this end, eight key functions have been identified: The objective being to win the challenge of the strategic and optimal allocation of public resources.

Volume two, which includes three chapters, begins with the notion of budgetary policy as a central element of government action and ends with the model of public policy simulations via a macro-budgetary model where the State is the main provider of collective well-being.

Chapter 7 presents an optimal public budget control model, applied to Budgeting Sensitive to Demographic Dividend (BSDD). The aim is to identify the best possible allocation of state budgetary resources in order to maximize the desired socioeconomic effects while respecting financial constraints. The methodological framework is based on the use of dynamic optimization tools, including Generalized Reduced Gradient (GRG) and the Kalman filter, applied to a system of eight sectoral structural equations representing the demographic dividend-sensitive budgetary functions (education, health, employment, governance, etc.). The approach consists of adjusting the budgetary parameters to minimize the gap between the target values of the DDMI index (Demographic Dividend Monitoring Index) and the results achieved by public policies. The chapter explores different solutions for optimized budget allocation, highlighting possible trade-offs between sectors to achieve maximum efficiency in capturing the demographic dividend. It emphasizes the need to consider overall budget constraints while adapting investment levels according to the specific elasticities of each sector.

Chapter 8 deals with the analysis of budget sensitivity in partial equilibrium and allows the analysis of the budget's sensitivity to the components of the DDMI by sector. This chapter focuses on the effectiveness of multi-sector public investments. The calculation of budget elasticities allows the identification of priority sectors. Thus, this chapter highlights the need to highlight strategic priorities to maximize the return on investment.

Chapter 9 focuses on policy simulations in global equilibrium. It serves as a framework for assessing the effects of various fiscal shocks on the performance of the DDMI. The resulting results allow us to anticipate the impact of policy choices in relation to demographic dynamics.

Anchored in the African Union Roadmap for Capturing the Demographic Dividend (DD) adopted in 2017, this book is a real contribution to the reflection on the future of countries. Its articulation with the four fundamental pillars, in particular: health and well-being, education and skills development, youth employment and entrepreneurship; governance and stability; reinforces the dynamics of structural transformation of countries. This book thus highlights the need to align budgetary choices with these priorities while emphasizing the importance of targeted investments in human capital, women's empowerment, and job creation for young people.

Through a rigorous approach, the author demonstrates that the BSDD goes beyond the technical distribution of resources and constitutes a real lever for public management reform. It is therefore important to ensure that each franc invested truly contributes to the well-being of the population and, above all, to maximize the economic, social, and structural benefits. This is why its articulation with the Demographic Dividend Monitoring Index (DDMI) provides an innovative tool for evaluating and monitoring public spending. The objective is to meet the challenge of efficient allocation of public resources.

This timely book is intended for policymakers, researchers, practitioners, and development stakeholders who want to understand the mechanisms and challenges of gender-responsive and sustainable development budgeting. It immerses the reader in comparative analyses and innovative methodological tools and offers concrete recommendations to support countries in implementing public policies that enable them to truly take advantage of the potential of sustainable development.

The book takes us on a journey of reflection on budgetary management and presents itself as a strategic tool for transforming our societies. It outlines the paths that allow each citizen to fully contribute to building a brighter and more equitable future.

Dr Sennen Hounton

Regional Director - UNFPA

West and Central Africa Regional Office (WCARO).

List of tables

List of graphs

Table of figures

Table of boxes

GENERAL INTRODUCTION

In a context where demographic challenges are intertwined with sustainable development ambitions, gender-responsive budgeting and the demographic dividend is a key strategy. By aligning economic priorities with social realities, this approach helps transform the aspirations of the African Union's roadmap into concrete actions for an inclusive and prosperous future.

Thus, the African Union's roadmap for capturing the Demographic Dividend (DD), adopted in 2017, reaffirms the commitment of Member States to transform the demographic dynamics of their populations into a lever for economic and social development. It is based on four strategic pillars that together aim to create the conditions for inclusive and sustainable growth. The first pillar, health and well-being, focuses on improving health services, particularly in reproductive, maternal and child health. The aim is to reduce infant mortality, increase life expectancy and ensure universal access to health care, all of which are essential conditions for a successful demographic transition. The second pillar, education and skills development, emphasizes the importance of quality education, especially for young people, to develop technical and vocational skills. Strengthening human capital is fundamental to preparing young people to contribute effectively to the economy and to meet the demands of an ever-changing labor market. The third pillar, youth employment and entrepreneurship, focuses on the economic empowerment of youth. It promotes the integration of young people into the formal labor market, encourages entrepreneurship, and aims to stimulate job creation, particularly in sectors with high growth potential. Finally, the fourth pillar, governance, peace and security, highlights the importance of democratic governance, the rule of law and political stability as prerequisites for the effective implementation of policies related to the demographic dividend. Peace and security are essential for creating an environment conducive to socio-economic development.

These four pillars are closely linked and are part of an integrated vision of long-term development. Their implementation aims to enable African countries to maximize demographic benefits and achieve their development goals by 2063, in line with the African Union's Agenda

2063. This ambitious strategy, based on the capture of the demographic dividend (DD), is based on the transformation of demographic dynamics into assets for economic and social development. But for this vision to become a reality, a concrete framework for action is needed, where gender-responsive budgeting and the demographic dividend (DD) plays a fundamental role.

In this regard, several countries have developed their own national roadmaps to achieve this goal. However, the realization of the demographic dividend is neither automatic nor guaranteed. It depends on the implementation of strategic and well-targeted investments in key areas such as education, health, youth employment, and women's empowerment. DD-sensitive budgeting, by integrating the specific needs of populations and ensuring an equitable distribution of resources, then becomes a crucial lever for directing public spending towards sectors that will maximize the benefits of the demographic transition.

In sub-Saharan Africa, particularly in the Sahel region, rapid popular-tion growth is leading to high dependency rates, increasing pressure on public and family resources. This often results in a fiscal imbalance, where a large portion of funds are allocated to meeting immediate social needs, to the detriment of long-term investments in human capital and job creation for young people. In this context, DD-sensitive budgeting makes it possible to reverse this trend by promoting a more rational and forward-looking management of financial resources, by aligning public spending with the priorities related to the demographic dividend.

The demographic transition nevertheless offers a unique opportunity to promote accelerated and inclusive economic growth. As the dependency ratio of young people declines, budgetary and family resources are freed up, allowing for their strategic reallocation in crucial areas such as the accumulation of human and physical capital. If these resources are invested effectively, the demographic dividend can be captured, with economic, social and structural benefits. A country's ability to maximize this dividend relies primarily on its ability to generate enough jobs for the cohorts of young people entering the labor market each year, underscoring the importance of a coherent and responsive budget allocation.

The benefits of the demographic dividend are not limited to the economic field alone. They also influence sectors such as improving living conditions, poverty reduction, territorial mobility and social inclusion. The use of tools such as the Demographic Dividend Monitoring

Index (DDMI), a composite index based on generational economic theories, makes it possible to monitor and evaluate progress in capturing the demographic dividend. This index provides a clear view of progress made or gaps that need to be filled, identifying sectors that need increased investment to create an enabling environment for dividend optimization and the achievement of the Sustainable Development Goals (SDGs).

In this context, budgeting sensitive to demographic dividend becomes a strategic instrument to ensure that allocated resources are effectively directed to the sectors capable of triggering these transformational changes. The role of the national budget is crucial. As the main tool for allocating resources, it determines the success of public policies aimed at maximizing the demographic dividend. Its size and composition directly affect a country's ability to finance multisectoral programs in education, health, employment, and the empowerment of youth and women. Budgeting that is sensitive to the demographic dividend implies not only efficient and equitable management of public resources, but also an integrated approach that prioritizes key sectors. This ensures that investments made today deliver the transformative effects expected in the long term, including in terms of human development, job creation and overall well-being.

Thus, gender- and demographic dividend-sensitive budgeting is not limited to a simple technical readjustment of financial resources. It represents a real overhaul of public management, oriented towards inclusive, equitable and sustainable development. To better understand the challenges of this strategic redesign, it is essential to understand the key concepts behind it, including the demographic dividend, demographic dividend-sensitive budgeting, and the inclusive and equitable approach of gender-responsive budgeting.

➢ Concepts and Foundations of the Demographic Dividend

The demographic dividend refers to economic growth resulting from the transformation of the age structure of the population (Bloom et al., 2007). For this potential to be realized, this transformation must be accompanied by investments in human capital (health and education), job creation, and good governance. This concept is central to the analysis of a country's economic and social development. It comes from the demographic transition, where a young and dependent population evolves into a population with a higher proportion of people of working age compared to dependent people, such as children and the elderly.

This transition can open a window of opportunity for rapid economic growth, provided that adequate policies are put in place to take advantage of this potential.

It is important to emphasize that the demographic dividend does not automatically materialize with the change in demographic structure; It requires strategic investments in several key areas. First, investments in human capital are essential. This includes improving maternal and child health, providing access to quality education at all levels, and strengthening the skills and capacities of the workforce. Strong human capital is crucial to maximizing the economic potential of workers. In addition, job creation is fundamental to capturing the demographic dividend. While rapid population growth can put pressure on the labor market, policies that promote job creation can turn this abundant labor force into an engine of economic growth. This requires policies that encourage entrepreneurship, promote investment in productive sectors, and boost innovation and productivity.

Finally, good governance is essential to achieve the demographic dividend. Effective and transparent institutions, prudent fiscal and fiscal policies, and adequate regulatory and supervisory mechanisms are needed to ensure an efficient and equitable allocation of resources, and to ensure an inclusive distribution of the benefits of economic growth. The process of capturing the demographic dividend can be measured by using the Demographic Dividend Monitoring Index (DDMI). This index makes it possible to monitor positive or negative changes in its dimensions and to identify sectors requiring increased investment to create conditions conducive to optimizing the demographic dividend and achieving the Sustainable Development Goals. To optimize the capture of the demographic dividend, it is crucial that countries strengthen the effectiveness of their fiscal policies by restructuring their budgets to align them with the dimensions of the DDMI (Demographic Dividend Monitoring Index). Improved strategic fiscal planning will make the state budget responsive to the demographic dividend.

➢ Concepts and Foundations of Demographic Dividend-Sensitive Budgeting

Demographic dividend-sensitive budgeting is an approach to public financial management that focuses on maximizing the economic and social benefits associated with changes in a country's population structure. This dividend refers to the potential economic gains that occur when the proportion of the working-age population increases relative to dependents (children and seniors). By integrating these considerations into the budget process, governments can better plan and allocate resources to stimulate economic growth and improve social well-being, while ensuring gender equality.

This integration of the demographic dividend into the budget process is of critical importance for several reasons. First, it makes it possible to take full advantage of the opportunities offered by a growing labor force, which can boost economic growth. By investing in education, health and employment, governments can strengthen the skills and productivity of the workforce. Second, it helps anticipate and address the challenges associated with demographic changes, such as an aging population. By planning, governments can develop social protection policies and health systems that are fit for future needs. Third, demographic dividend-sensitive budgeting promotes intergenerational equity by ensuring that resources are allocated in a way that benefits all age groups of the population, while considering the specific needs of men and women. This approach thus contributes to social stability and national cohesion. Finally, this approach improves long-term planning and the sustainability of public finances. By considering demographic trends, governments can avoid fiscal crises and ensure more stable and predictable management of public resources. This book aims to provide an in-depth understanding of the principles and factors influencing the demographic dividend, with a particular focus on gender aspects. It shows how demographic objectives, including gender equity, can be aligned with national and local fiscal policies, illustrating the integration of the demographic dividend into the budget process.

➢ Gender-Responsive Budgeting: An Inclusive and Equitable Approach

Integrating a gender perspective into budgeting is essential to meet the aspirations and needs of the entire population, whether men, women, boys or girls. A gender-focused budget allocates government funds based on their impact on different groups, considering social dynamics, gender roles, and access to resources. This approach aims to ensure fair benefits for all. Gender-responsive budgets respond to the diverse needs of all sectors of society, thereby improving the effectiveness of budgeting choices. Gender-neutral policies can lead to divergent impacts on women and men due to their distinct roles in the economy and society. Effective public management requires understanding these differentiated impacts and adjusting policies to equitably meet the expectations of all socio-economic groups. Gender-sensitive budgets help to increase economic efficiency and promote social welfare. Ignoring the specific roles of women in the economy and society, as well as their needs, undermines the effectiveness of certain public policies. Gender inequalities, in addition to their injustice, entail significant economic costs, affecting productivity, skills development and overall well-being. Thus, gender-responsive budgeting aims to optimize the use of resources to improve the quality of life of all individuals.

These budgets aim to reduce gender gaps and inequalities, highlighting the distinct but crucial contributions of women and men to the economy, including in the field of care. They encourage innovative solutions to recognize, value and equitably distribute women's unpaid work, leading to a fairer allocation of resources. Gender-sensitive budgets are more effective in the fight against poverty, recognizing that women and men experience poverty differently and require specific approaches. To be fair and effective, poverty reduction strategies, policies and budgets must take these differences into account. In addition, these budgets help governments meet their equality commitments, as set out in the Beijing Platform for Action, the Convention on the Elimination of All Forms of Discrimination against Women and the Sustainable Development Goals. They also strengthen the role of parliament in the budget process, improving resource allocations to poor women and men, and strengthening the links between economic and social outcomes.

Integrating a gender perspective into the budget process enhances transparency and accountability, allowing for more rigorous control of spending and better allocation of resources to meet the needs of society. By controlling spending against gender and development commitments, the transparency of the budget process is improved. Mechanisms and tools to develop gender-responsive budgets are essential for effective and equitable budget management, ensuring that available resources are used to improve the quality of life of all citizens. Adopting this approach represents a crucial step towards a more just and prosperous society. The foundations of gender budgeting are based on key principles such as inclusive participation, transparency and accountability, which are reflected in practices to ensure equity and effectiveness in public policies.

Inclusive participation involves the active engagement of women and men in the budget process. According to Diane Elson, a leading figure in feminist economics, the inclusion of women in budget discussions allows for better identification and consideration of their specific needs. In South Africa, for example, the involvement of women's groups in the formulation of the national budget has led to a more equitable distribution of resources in the health and education sectors. According to Budlender (2005), this approach has allowed for a fairer distribution of resources, thus meeting the distinct needs of women and men.

Budget transparency ensures that financial decisions are made in an open manner and accessible to all citizens. Transparency International points out that the publication of gender-disaggregated budget data allows citizens to monitor and assess the impact of public spending. In Sweden, for example, annual budget reports include detailed analyses on the impact of economic policies on women and men, thereby strengthening public trust in government institutions (SIDA, 2016). This practice promotes equity and holds public decision-makers accountable. Accountability requires governments to be accountable for the use of public funds and their impacts on different genders. According to Elson (2002), accountability in gender budgeting requires decision-makers to consider the consequences of their policies on gender equality and to adjust their actions accordingly. For example, Australia has implemented gender audits to assess the impacts of fiscal and fiscal policies on women, leading to meaningful reforms to improve equity (Sharp, 2003). These audits have made it possible to uncover hidden inequalities and to promote fairer policies. Methodologies and analytical tools for gender-responsive budgeting are essential for assessing the impact of fiscal policies. A gender audit, as proposed by Budlender and Sharp (1998), is a systematic evaluation of policies, programs and budget allocations aimed at identifying gender inequalities and proposing adjustments. In the United Kingdom, gender audits have revealed significant disparities in the funding of reproductive health services, leading to budget reallocations in favor of women's services (UN Women, 2015).

Continuous monitoring and evaluation of gender-focused fiscal policies is essential to assess their effectiveness and impact. Tools such as gender indicators and dashboards are used to monitor progress and make necessary adjustments. For example, in India, the use of gender dashboards has been used to monitor investments in girls' education, leading to a notable increase in enrolment and retention rates (UNDP,

2014). These monitoring and evaluation tools allow for continuous adaptation of policies to meet the changing needs of society.

Thus, the principles of inclusive participation, transparency and accountability, supported by rigorous methodologies and analytical tools, are crucial for effective gender-responsive budgeting. These principles aim to create more equitable public policies and improve the social and economic well-being of all people. Thus, these core principles of inclusive participation, transparency, and accountability are not limited to gender-responsive budgeting alone. They also play a central role in Budgeting Sensitive to Demographic Dividend (BSDD), supporting public policies geared towards maximizing economic and social benefits. By leveraging rigorous methodologies and advanced analytical tools, BSDD aligns financial resources with strategic priorities, contributing to sustainable and inclusive development. It is with this in mind that the implementation of BSDD is part of a structured process, which we will detail in the following steps.

- **Implementing Demographic Dividend-Sensitive Budgeting**

The implementation of Budgeting Sensitive to Demographic Dividend (BSDD) is based on a multi-step structured process, each corresponding to a specific work package. This process integrates an analytical and methodological approach based on National Transfer Accounts (NTAs), the creation of specific indices, fiscal transformation and the optimization of public resources. Each module contributes to the Building of a coherent fiscal strategy, aligned with the objectives of capturing the demographic dividend and inclusive development.

– ***Module 1: Development of NTA Profiles***

The first module consists of developing the profiles of the National Transfer Accounts (NTAs) for the available survey years. This methodology makes it possible to analyze the distribution of economic resources between different age groups, measuring what each individual produces, consumes, saves and transfers throughout his or her life cycle. These NTA profiles are essential for understanding social demand across age groups and are a key planning tool for policymakers. Process steps include Building NTA profiles for years when surveys are available. The estimation of these profiles for the non-survey years, making it possible to constitute a continuous time series of at least 20 years. Estimation of the Economic Dependency Coverage Index

(EDCI) over the last 20 to 25 years, with a time series analysis to identify economic trends related to the life cycle.

– ***Module 2: Development of the DDMI Indices***

The second module focuses on the development of Demographic Dividend Monitoring Indices (DDMI) over a period of 20 to 25 years. These indices track progress in capturing demographic dividend through key indicators, such as levels of investment in education, health and employment. Key actions include Calibration of DDMI indices for survey years. The estimation of the indices for the years without a survey, to constitute a coherent time series. These indices provide a clear view of the efforts made by governments to maximize the demographic dividend and identify sectors in need of adjustment.

– ***Module 3: Functional Budget Transformation***

In this module, the objective is to transform the classic budget into a functional budget, in line with the objectives of the BSDD. This transformation takes place over a period of at least 20 years, with a harmonized nomenclature by the economic sector. The sectors concerned by this transformation are: Economic Affairs, Civil engineering and Energy, Education, Health, Institutions, Security, Social Network, Professional Network. This fiscal reorganization allows for a better allocation of resources to sectors critical to the demographic dividend, facilitating a more functional and transparent management of public finances.

– ***Module 4: Determining the Optimal Budget Allocation***

The fourth module focuses on optimizing budget allocation using optimal control techniques, such as the Kalman Filter and the Generalized Reduced Gradient (GRG). The goal is to minimize the gap between the DDMI's forecasts and budget constraints, while maximizing economic benefits. The system to be checked includes eight sectoral structural equations, all subject to a wider envelope of budgetary equations. This approach helps determine the levels of sector investment that generates the most well-being, helping to maximize the demographic dividend.

– ***Module 5: Alignment and Estimation of Sectoral Elasticities***

The fifth module aims to calculate sectoral budget elasticities, i.e. the effect of the increase in the budget in each sector on the overall well-being produced by that sector. These elasticities make it possible to identify the sectors where increased investment generates the greatest economic and social impact.

– ***Module 6: Economic Policy Simulations***

Finally, the sixth module consists of carrying out economic policy simulations, analyzing the direct and induced effects of an increase in the budget in a particular sector. These simulations make it possible to examine the transmission channels of shocks between sectors and to assess the potential consequences of different investment scenarios.

➢ **Outline of the structure**

The introduction precedes a detailed analysis, structured around several key chapters, which aim to deepen the fundamental concepts related to the demographic dividend and its integration into budget management. Each chapter looks at specific aspects of this phenomenon, ranging from the characterization of the demographic dividend, to monitoring tools such as the DDMI (Demographic Dividend Monitoring Index) and the GDDI (Gender Demographic Dividend Index), to the implementation of optimal budgetary strategies. This structure will provide a better understanding of how public policies and financial resource management can be aligned to maximize the economic and social benefits arising from the demographic transition. The objective is to provide a coherent and rigorous overview of the mechanisms underlying the capture of the demographic dividend, while providing concrete avenues to guide governments' budgetary decisions, particularly in the context of rapid population growth. Each chapter offers a precise methodological approach and analytical tools to assess existing policies, identify areas in need of adjustment, and explore ways for a more efficient allocation of public resources for inclusive and sustainable growth.

Chapter 1 will focus on the economic analysis of the national budget by presenting the structure and composition of the State budget, the fiscal policy instruments and their roles in economic stability and the social impact of fiscal policy.

Chapter 2 will address the principle of gender-responsive budgeting and the demographic dividend with a particular focus on the key concepts and foundations of the demographic dividend, its implement-tation process, and the principles that frame the restatement of budget expenditures according to the Demographic Dividend Monitoring Index (DDMI).

In Chapter 3, we will study the concept of the demographic dividend profile, the research methodology and the presentation of the profiles of West and Central African countries.

Chapter 4 will examine the results of the DDMI index as well as the GDDI in West and Central African countries.

Chapter 5 will present the methodology of the DDMI back-casting, the analysis of the back-expelled DDMI series from West and Central African countries as well as the discussion of the results.

In Chapter 6, we will study in detail the methodology of the transformation of the classic State budget into a functional budget according to the sub-components of the DDMI.

Chapter 7 will introduce an optimal control model for the allocation of the state budget, proposing methods for optimizing public resources to maximize the benefits of the demographic dividend.

In Chapter 8, the focus will be on the sectoral alignment of the budget with the DDMI, with an analysis of the sensitivity of the State budget to the demographic dividend index in a partial equilibrium model.

Finally, Chapter 9 will propose simulations of economic policies in a context of global equilibrium, illustrating the potential effects of different strategies on capturing the demographic dividend and balancing the budget.

CHAPTER 1

ECONOMIC ANALYSIS OF THE NATIONAL BUDGET

Introduction

In recent years, new terms such as "national budget" or "national budget" have appeared, mainly in Anglo-Saxon countries, the Netherlands and Sweden. These expressions, used both in addition to and in opposition to the classic notion of the "state budget", refer to a forecasting process encompassing all the anticipated economic results of the Nation, including revenues and expenditures (J. Marczewski, 1948). This process, which is the act organizing and validating the expenditure and revenue of a public entity for a period of one year, is mainly based on forecasts anticipating expenditure and revenue for the following year. Prepared by the executive branch, this budget is then adopted by a democratically elected representative institution, such as Parliament (Moysan, 2017). Approval of the budget by vote gives the executive the authority to implement expenditures and collect projected revenues, thus establishing a sequence where budget authorization systematically precedes its execution.

The budget is therefore the essential tool of the government's economic policy. Much more than a simple list of revenues and expenditures, it is presented as the guiding framework for social and economic policy for each budget year. The national budget reflects the Government's intentions and objectives, setting out its funding programmes over a defined period and establishing the main national priorities. Beyond the numbers, the budget represents a concrete action plan, determining the areas of government investment needed to achieve development goals. It specifies which economic sectors will be used to finance these initiatives, how the Government will respond to short-term economic fluctuations, and who will directly or indirectly benefit public services. In short, the budget concerns the entire population and must meet the expectations of the majority. It enables the Government to articulate its strategies for the well-being of the people, in accordance with the Constitution, national bills of rights, as well as various international instruments and standards, such as development agendas. It also reflects the government's overall policy directions.

As the main guiding framework for the Government's economic and social policy, the national budget guides decisions on public expenditure and resource allocation. As the work of John Maynard Keynes (1936) and Paul Samuelson (1948) has shown, by defining and prioritizing national objectives in crucial areas such as economic development, education, health, and infrastructure, the budget effectively structures government efforts. It is also of paramount importance in financial planning, making it possible to forecast revenues and expenditures for the coming year, as demonstrated by Richard Musgrave (1959) and James M. Buchanan (1962). This forecast facilitates proactive management of public finances. By carefully planning the allocation of resources, the government ensures that the necessary funds are available for priority projects and essential services, thereby ensuring an efficient administration that meets the needs of society.

The national budget strengthens accountability and transparency of government actions. Submitted to Parliament for approval and made public, it allows for democratic control of public finances. In addition, it facilitates the audit and evaluation of expenditure, ensuring that public funds are used in accordance with the objectives set and allowing for the detection and correction of possible inefficiencies. The national budget plays a key role in regulating the economy. Through spending and revenue, the government can influence aggregate demand, fight economic cycles, and stabilize the economy. In times of economic crises or cyclical fluctuations, the budget can be adjusted to provide stimulus or stabilization measures, thereby supporting the country's economic resilience.

The budget is an essential tool for promoting social equity. It allocates funds to social programs, reduces inequalities and supports vulnerable groups. By integrating gender considerations, the budget can also contribute to gender equality, by financing initiatives that improve women's access to education, health and employment. By directing investments towards strategic sectors, the budget promotes inclusive and sustainable growth, contributing to balanced development. By considering the demographic dividend, it can also maximize the economic benefits of a young working-age population, by investing in education, skills training and job creation. The national budget is crucial for the implementation of public policies. It provides the necessary resources for government programs and policy initiatives. Through supplementary or amending finance laws, the budget allows the government to adapt to new priorities or unforeseen economic constraints, thus ensuring the flexibility and effectiveness of public policies. In this chapter, we will conduct an in-depth economic analysis of the national budget. This analysis will be structured in three points. Part 1: Structure and Composition of the National Budget will focus on examining the distribution of resources and expenditures, as well as the classification of the different budget items. Part 2: Fiscal Policies and Economic Stability will address the various fiscal policies implemented to maintain economic stability, assessing their effectiveness and impacts on the national economy. Finally, Part 3: Social Impact of Fiscal Policies will analyze the effects of fiscal policies on society, focusing on different demographic groups and the implications in terms of well-being and social inequalities.

Section 1: Structure and Composition of the National Budget

This section will focus on the analysis of the distribution of resources and expenditures, as well as on the classification of the various budget items.

Recipes

The main sources of revenue for the national budget are tax and non-tax revenues. Tax revenue is generated by taxes and duties imposed on individuals and businesses and is subdivided into two categories: direct taxes and indirect taxes. Direct taxes, such as income tax and corporate tax, are levied directly on income and wealth. Indirect taxes, such as VAT and excise duties, are levied on the consumption of goods and services. Taxes, such as property taxes and road taxes, represent mandatory contributions collected by the government to fund specific services. Tariffs, imposed on imports and sometimes exports, are intended to protect domestic industries and generate revenue for the state. In addition, non-tax revenues come from state-owned enterprises, investment dividends, fines and penalties, as well as income from state assets, generated by activities and assets held by the government.

Tax revenue

Tax revenue refers to the funds collected by a country's government through the taxation of individuals and companies. These funds are collected in the form of taxes, duties and other compulsory levies. Tax revenues are essential to finance public spending, such as government services, infrastructure, education, health, and security.

In the literature, the constraints of tax mobilization have recently been revitalized by taking into account factors such as corruption and the limited skills of tax administration in tax management. Traditionally, economic studies have focused on tax policies, leaving aside a detailed examination of the effectiveness of tax administration in mobilizing tax revenues. However, this trend has changed, especially with the creation in 2015 of the Journal of Tax Administration, a scientific journal dedicated to this field. This evolution has made it possible to incorporate political and administrative dimensions into the analysis of tax systems, highlighting the importance of understanding how taxes are collected and managed.

In response to an increased awareness of tax inefficiencies, many reforms have been put in place to enhance the efficiency of tax and customs administrations, particularly in developing countries. One of the main initiatives has been the reorganization of the tax services, through the creation of specific divisions such as the Directorate of Large Enterprises (DGE), intended to better target taxpayers according to their turnover or sector of activity. However, despite the potential benefits of these reforms, recent studies show that challenges remain, including the tax avoidance strategies used by some companies to evade increased scrutiny.

Another significant reform was the allocation of tax revenue collection to semi-autonomous agencies. Although this method is costly, it has been adopted by many countries and has led to significant improvement in domestic revenue mobilization. These agencies, through their autonomy, demonstrate a government commitment to more efficient and equitable tax collection.

In addition, research, such as that conducted by Best et al. (2015), has explored innovative solutions to counter tax evasion, such as the introduction of a minimum turnover tax. These studies, both theoretical and empirical, help to guide tax and administrative policies, highlighting the need to design tax systems that are not only efficient but also fair for all citizens.

Indirect taxation

Indirect taxation, often referred to as "indirect taxation", is based on the taxation of the consumption of goods and services rather than on the income of individuals or companies. Unlike direct taxation, which taxes taxpayers based on their income or profits, indirect taxation is mainly achieved through taxes on products and services purchased by consumers. An emblematic example of this form of taxation is VAT (value-added tax), which is considered a key element of the initial tax reform in developing countries (Baunsgaard and Keen, 2010; MAAE, 2011). VAT was introduced with the aim of diversifying revenue sources and reducing dependence on direct taxes. Its widespread adoption across the globe has been envisioned as a solution to improve tax efficiency. However, recent studies have revealed a significant gap between theoretical forecasts and the practical implementation of VAT in developing countries. This research highlights the discrepancies between "effective" VAT, as applied, and "ideal" VAT, which would theoretically be more efficient and fairer (James, 2015; Gendron, 2016).

After more than five decades of application, VAT systems are now better understood in economic and budgetary terms. Analysts are now interested in various aspects such as VAT rates, tax bases, tax thresholds and the efficient management of systems, including the refund of VAT credits (Bodin, 2012; Keen, 2012). VAT assessment tools have evolved to include these dimensions, allowing VAT effectiveness to be broken down into two components: the policy gap, which measures the difference between the theoretical basis of VAT and the actual basis due to policy decisions, and the compliance gap, which assesses the impact of administrative failures and fraud on tax revenues.

Initially developed in OECD countries, VAT gap assessments are now also used in developing countries. These analyses complement tax expenditure estimates, providing a more complete view of the effectiveness of tax systems and facilitating the identification of necessary reforms (Barbone et al., 2013). However, the implementation of VAT in developing countries often faces unique challenges, such as limited administrative infrastructure, high tax evasion, and a low tax compliance culture among taxpayers. Despite these obstacles, VAT remains a potentially powerful tool to improve government revenues and support economic development, provided that reforms are put in place to strengthen tax administration and reduce compliance gaps.

Public expenditure

Government spending can be broken down into two broad categories: current spending and capital spending. Current expenditure includes the costs essential to the day-to-day management of public administration, including civil servants' salaries, the operating costs of public services, the acquisition of goods and services, and subsidies and social transfers. In contrast, capital spending is directed towards infrastructure investments such as the Building of roads, bridges, schools, and hospitals, aimed at boosting long-term economic growth.

Social expenditure includes the financing of educational institutions such as schools and universities, as well as subsidies and training programs. They also include funding for health care institutions such as hospitals, public health initiatives and health insurance. Military and defense expenditures include costs associated with the armed forces, including salaries and benefits for members, acquisition and maintenance of military equipment, and expenditures related to military operations and missions abroad. Finally, public debt servicing includes the repayment of maturing loans and the payment of interest on existing debt. These payments are essential to maintain the government's solvency and its ability to borrow on favorable terms in the future.

Tax expenditure refers to a transfer of public resources resulting from a reduction in tax liabilities relative to a predefined standard, rather than a direct expenditure (OECD, 2010). This definition highlights two conditions characterizing a tax expenditure: (1) a decrease in government revenues, and (2) a deviation from the established tax standard, also known as the reference system. Tax expenditures offer an alternative to public spending.

The evaluation of tax expenditures and their publication as an annex to the budget law strengthen fiscal transparency (IMF, 2007) and streamline the tax system, thereby improving domestic revenue mobilization. It is important to recognize that some derogatory measures, which constitute tax expenditures, are the result of discretionary decisions, often unknown to the public. The analysis of these tax expenditures also contributes to broadening the tax base, promoting a more equitable distribution of tax burdens and considering the specific needs of different population groups, including by integrating gender and demographic dividend perspectives.

To assess tax expenditures, a three-step method is generally followed: defining a reference tax system (LICO), examining all derogatory measures in relation to this LICO in force in the country, and estimating the cost of these measures. It is also essential to incorporate tax gap analysis, which assesses the difference between actual and projected revenues, to ensure the efficient use of public resources while promoting social inclusion and the equitable participation of all citizens in economic and social development.

Tax expenditures can be categorized according to their objectives: to encourage investment or to support household consumption. The former includes investment incentives, while the latter emphasizes equity and redistribution. It is critical that these measures are designed to foster women's economic empowerment, by facilitating their access to education, health, and other basic social services, to maximize the potential of the demographic dividend. In addition, it is crucial to ensure that the design of tax policies does not reinforce gender inequalities, but on the contrary, contributes to mitigating them and promoting equal opportunities for all.

A budget deficit occurs when government spending exceeds revenue over a period, requiring borrowing or the use of reserves to make up the difference. Conversely, a budget surplus occurs when revenues exceed expenditures, allowing the government to reduce its debt, increase its reserves, or invest in new projects.

Social spending

Social spending, at the heart of fiscal policies, includes a variety of measures such as cash benefits, goods and services provided directly, and tax breaks for social purposes. They are intended for different demographic groups such as low-income households, the elderly, people with disabilities, sick or young people. These social programs involve a redistribution of resources among households or mandatory participation. Social benefits are classified as public when the administrations, whether central, local or linked to social security, control the financial flows. On the other hand, data not provided by public administration is considered private. Note that private transfers between households are not included in this category.

According to Harris (2013), total net social spending includes both public and private spending, considering the effects of direct and indirect taxation as well as social tax breaks. This spending is often measured as a percentage of GDP or in US dollars per capita. Investing in social spending is crucial to ensure equitable access to basic services and promote the general well-being of the population, as Andrews et al. (2012) also point out.

For example, health spending ensures access to medical care and improves its quality, thereby helping to reduce morbidity and mortality rates. Similarly, spending on education is essential to provide quality education to all citizens, fostering the development of individual skills and paving the way for equitable economic and social opportunities (Harris, 2013).

Social spending also plays a crucial role in reducing inequality and poverty. Ortiz (2017) and Samson and Charrier (2009) highlight the importance of social protection programs, such as direct cash transfers, family allowances, superannuation, and food security programs, which aim to mitigate the effects of poverty and provide financial support to the poorest households. By ensuring a decent standard of living and fostering social inclusion, these initiatives strengthen social cohesion and promote sustainable development.

Thus, sustained commitment to social spending is essential to build inclusive, resilient and prosperous societies, as Ortiz (2017) also notes. Governments must continue to invest in these priority areas, ensuring an efficient and equitable allocation of resources to meet the diverse needs of the population. By strengthening social spending, governments can make a significant contribution to achieving the Sustainable Development Goals and building a better future for all.

Deficits and Public Debt

In developing countries, fiscal policy and macroeconomic management face medium- and long-term sustainable financing challenges. These nations face a variety of obstacles, including a limited tax base, limited tax-collecting capacities, over-reliance on monetary financing, and high levels of public debt. Unlike industrialized countries, they have fewer opportunities to attract foreign savings to finance their public deficits and face difficulties in issuing domestic debt due to limited local savings and underdeveloped financial markets (Baunsgaard and Keen, 2010). These constraints increase their use of seigniorage, i.e., money creation, exposing them to greater macroeconomic and financial instability (Keen and Lockwood, 2010). In addition, high public debt puts pressure on real interest rates, thereby increasing economic volatility.

This situation has prompted liberal and neoliberal theorists to criticize deficit fiscal policies, advocating minimal state intervention in the economy, limited to sovereign functions such as maintaining law and order (Crawford et al., 2010). For developing countries, which are often dependent on assistance from the Bretton Woods institutions, this translates into injunctions aimed at a sustainable balance between public revenues and expenditures.

However, other schools of thought, such as Keynesian and post-Keynesian approaches, argue that government spending can boost the economy in the short run and promote growth in the medium to long term (Berthomieu and Ehrhart, 2000). Neo-structuralist analyses share this perspective by highlighting the crucial role of public spending in promoting economic growth (Berthomieu, Ehrhart and Hernandez Bielma, 2005, 2006). In this theoretical context, research on the financing of fiscal deficits in countries that cannot access external financing focuses mainly on two options: money creation and borrowing on the domestic market. However, for many developing countries that follow the recommendations of the IMF and the World Bank, and have adopted the principle of central bank independence, domestic savings remain the main source of financing (Martinez-Vasquez, 2010).

State intervention in the economy through public borrowing can have a variety of effects on the private sector. For example, crowding out can reduce private investment, while the ripple effect can stimulate economic activity (James, 2015). An increase in the budget deficit can thus influence other macroeconomic variables such as the interest rate and the volume of output. Fluctuations in bank credit and public investment also play a crucial role in private sector investment decisions, highlighting the complexity of economic interactions related to budget deficit management (Gendron, 2016).

Section 2: Fiscal Policies and Economic Stability

Fiscal policies refer to the government's decisions on public spending and tax revenues. According to Keynes (1936), they play a crucial role in the regulation of the economy, the allocation of resources, and economic stabilization. These policies can be expansionary, aimed at stimulating the economy by increasing spending or reducing taxes, or restrictive, aimed at curbing an overheating economy by cutting spending or raising taxes.

Role of Fiscal Policies in Economic Stability

Fiscal policies play a crucial role in stabilizing the economy in the short term and promoting sustainable growth in the long term. In times of recession, expansionary measures, such as increased government spending or tax cuts, can boost aggregate demand and boost economic activity, as demonstrated by Auerbach and Gorodnichenko (2012). Conversely, in times of economic shock, restrictive fiscal policies, aimed at reducing aggregate demand, can help control inflation. The work of Blanchard and Perotti (2002) shows that such interventions can mitigate business cycles and promote macroeconomic stability.

Governments use fiscal policies to direct resources to strategic sectors such as education, health, infrastructure, and research and development. According to Barro (1990), these investments are essential for a country's long-term development and economic competitiveness. In addition, fiscal policies play a crucial role in reducing economic and social inequalities. Social protection programs, targeted subsidies, and progressive tax systems help redistribute income and provide a safety net for the most vulnerable segments of the population (Atkinson, 2015).

Fiscal policy instruments include public expenditure and tax revenues. Government expenditure is divided into current expenditure and capital expenditure. By adjusting these expenditures, the government can influence the level of aggregate demand and economic activity (Romer, 2012). Tax revenue comes mainly from direct and indirect taxes. By changing tax rates and broadening the tax base, the government can regulate revenues and, therefore, aggregate demand.

In addition, fiscal policies can be used to stimulate innovation and increase economic competitiveness. Injections of funds into research and development, encouraged by tax incentives such as research tax credits, have the potential to boost technological innovation and foster long-term economic growth (Hall and Soskice, 2001). Similarly, tax benefits for firms that invest in the training and development of their employees can improve productivity and strengthen competitiveness in global markets. Thus, fiscal policies are important levers for creating an environment conducive to innovation and sustainable economic growth. In addition, these policies can be designed to promote gender equality and harness the demographic dividend by specifically encouraging investments in women's training and skills development, thereby helping to reduce gender disparities in the labor market and strengthen women's economic empowerment.

Resource Allocation and Equity

The effectiveness of fiscal policies can be undermined by a variety of challenges. Often, there is a lag between the implementation of these policies and their economic effects, making it difficult to perfectly synchronize measures with business cycles. In addition, some public expenditures, such as pensions or interest on public debt, are difficult to adjust quickly because of their mandatory nature, which limits the flexibility of fiscal policies. High levels of public debt can also hamper the government's ability to adopt expansionary fiscal policies during recessions. Analysis considering gender and the demographic dividend reveals that fiscal policies can have differentiated implications for men and women, as well as for different age groups of the population. For example, public spending directed towards sectors such as education and health can disproportionately benefit women and youth, thereby enhancing their economic and social inclusion. Similarly, prudent management of public debt is essential to ensure that fiscal policies do not undermine future economic opportunities for generations to come.

History offers illuminating examples of the impact of fiscal policies on economic stability. The New Deal in the United States in the 1930s demonstrated the effectiveness of expansionary fiscal policies in stimulating economic recovery. On the other hand, the restrictive fiscal policies adopted by some European countries after the 2008 financial crisis have sometimes slowed economic growth. These cases underscore the importance of designing fiscal policies that are tailored to specific economic circumstances and adjusting them to society's changing needs.

In summary, fiscal policies are essential tools for macroeconomic management. Their development and implementation must consider the specific economic, social and demographic realities of each country. A prudent and strategic approach is needed to ensure that these policies contribute to sustainable economic stability and inclusive development, considering the needs and prospects of all segments of the population.

Section 3: Social Impact of Fiscal Policies

This section examines the impact of fiscal policies on society with a focus on diverse demographic groups and the consequences for social well-being and inequality.

Understanding the Social Impact of Fiscal Policies

The social impact of fiscal policies encompasses the various consequences and repercussions they have on society and its various demographic components. This includes changes in living conditions, economic opportunities, access to essential social services such as education and health, as well as levels of poverty and inequality. It is crucial to recognize that fiscal decisions made by the state go beyond their immediate economic impacts, profoundly influencing the social structure and well-being of citizens. Thus, social impact analysis aims to assess how these decisions affect the living conditions and prospects of various segments of the population, especially the most vulnerable.

The state, as a major economic player, exerts a significant influence on the economy and society through its budget. Understanding the social impact of fiscal policies is crucial for several reasons. First, these policies can have a disproportionate impact on different social groups due to factors such as income level, place of residence, gender and age. It is therefore essential to assess whether these policies contribute to reducing or worsening social and economic inequalities.

In addition, budget decisions directly affect citizens' quality of life, including by affecting their access to essential social services such as education, health and housing. Understanding the impact of these policies on the well-being of citizens makes it possible to direct budgetary choices towards measures aimed at improving the quality of life of the population. Finally, fiscal policies can also have an impact on social stability, influencing aspects such as unemployment, social cohesion and trust in public institutions. A social impact analysis makes it possible to anticipate possible negative effects on social stability and to put in place preventive measures to remedy them.

Budget Reallocation Strategies for Enhanced Social Protection

The reallocation of public spending to strengthen social protection is a widely adopted strategy to tailor government budgets to society's priority needs. This approach is mainly deployed in two parts. First, it involves the transfer of resources initially allocated to less critical sectors to the financing of social protection programs. Second, it aims to increase the efficiency of the collection of resources or expenditures, thus making it possible to optimize the use of available funds and to free up additional resources for social protection. This improvement in efficiency can include measures such as the fight against corruption and a reassessment of public spending through in-depth analyses.

Despite its potential benefits, the reallocation of budget expenditures faces a variety of challenges. It can be difficult to prioritize spending based on its social impact, especially in developing countries where public spending is often non-discretionary. This constraint makes reallocation to sectors such as social protection more complex.

Several countries have already successfully implemented budget reallocation strategies for social protection. For example, Costa Rica and Thailand cut military spending after the 1997 Asian financial crisis to invest in universal health programs. Similarly, Egypt has set up a special unit within its finance ministry to review fiscal priorities after the Arab Spring.

Along with the reallocation of spending, the removal of poorly targeted subsidies is another strategy to strengthen social protection.

For example, in Senegal, widespread food and fuel subsidies have been criticized for their ineffectiveness in reaching the most vulnerable populations. A redirection of these resources towards more targeted social protection programs, considering the specific needs of women and young people, could have a more significant impact on reducing poverty and inequality.

Conclusion

In this chapter, we have explored in depth the essential role of the national budget as the guiding framework for the government's economic and social policy. Through its various dimensions, the national budget plays a central role in the organization of public finances, the definition of national priorities and the promotion of general welfare. We have seen how it guides decisions on public spending and the allocation of resources, thus directly influencing the country's economic and social dynamics. In analyzing the structure and composition of the national budget, we examined the distribution of resources and expenditures, as well as the classification of the different budget items. This first step allows us to understand how funds are allocated, and which sectors are receiving priority funding.

In the second section, we discussed fiscal policies and their impact on economic stability. By evaluating different approaches, we examined how these policies can influence economic growth, inflation, and other aspects of national economic health. Finally, in the third section, we analyzed the effects of fiscal policies on society, with a particular focus on different demographic groups and the implications in terms of well-being and social inequality. By integrating gender and demographic dividend considerations, we explored how the budget can be used to promote social equity and maximize the economic benefits of a diverse population.

In conclusion, the national budget remains an essential tool to guide public policies, promote economic and social growth, and ensure long-term stability. Its in-depth analysis is crucial to understanding how it can be used effectively to meet society's needs and achieve the Sustainable Development Goals.

Bibliographical references

Émilie Moysan In The Essentials of Public Finance Law (2017), pages 11 to 16. Fact sheet 1. The notion of budget

Bloom, D. E., Canning, D., & Sevilla, J. (2003). The Demographic Dividend: A New Perspective on the Economic Consequences of Population Change. RAND Corporation.

Becker, G. S., Glaeser, E. L., & Murphy, K. M. (1999). Population and Economic Growth. American Economic Review, 89(2), 145-149.

Cleland, J., Bernstein, S., Ezeh, A., Faundes, A., Glasier, A., & Innis, J. (2006). Family planning: the unfinished agenda. Lancet, 368(9549), 1810-1827.

Acemoglu, D., Johnson, S., & Robinson, J. A. (2001). The Colonial Origins of Comparative Development: An Empirical Investigation. American Economic Review, 91(5), 1369-1401.

Arnstein, S. R. (1969). A Ladder of Citizen Participation. Journal of the American Institute of Planners, 35(4), 216-224.

Barro, R. J., & Sala-i-Martin, X. (1995). Economic Growth. McGraw-Hill.

Behn, R. D. (2003). Why Measure Performance? Different Purposes Require Different Measures. Public Administration Review, 63(5), 586-606.

Becker, G. S., Glaeser, E. L., & Murphy, K. M. (1999). Population and Economic Growth. American Economic Review, 89(2), 145-149.

Bloom, D. E., Canning, D., & Sevilla, J. (2003). The Demographic Dividend: A New Perspective on the Economic Consequences of Population Change. RAND Corporation.

Bloom, D. E., & Williamson, J. G. (1998). Demographic Transitions and Economic Miracles in Emerging Asia. World Bank Economic Review, 12(3), 419-455.

Bloom, D. E., & Canning, D. (2000). The Health and Wealth of Nations. Science, 287(5456), 1207-1209.

Bongaarts, J., & Casterline, J. (2013). Fertility Transition: Is Sub-Saharan Africa Different? Population and Development Review, 38(Supplement), 153-168.

Cleland, J., Bernstein, S., Ezeh, A., Faundes, A., Glasier, A., & Innis, J. (2006). Family Planning: The Unfinished Agenda. Lancet, 368(9549), 1810-1827.

Gertler, P. J., Martinez, S., Premand, P., Rawlings, L. B., & Vermeersch, C. M. (2011). Impact Evaluation in Practice. The World Bank.

Hanushek, E. A., & Kimko, D. D. (2000). Schooling, Labor-Force Quality, and the Growth of Nations. American Economic Review, 90(5), 1184-1208.

Kolsaker, A., & Lee-Kelley, L. (2008). Citizens' Attitudes Towards E-Government and E-Governance: A UK Study. International Journal of Public Sector Management, 21(7), 723-738.

Lee, R., & Mason, A. (2006). What is the Demographic Dividend? Finance and Development, 43(3).

Mishan, E. J. (1982). Cost-Benefit Analysis: An Informal Introduction. George Allen & Unwin.

Power, M. (1997). The Audit Society: Rituals of Verification. Oxford University Press.

Smith, J. P. (2004). Unraveling the SES-Health Connection. Population and Development Review, 30(Supplement), 108-132.

Weil, D. N., & Galor, O. (1999). From Malthusian Stagnation to Modern Growth.

Acemoglu, D., Johnson, S., & Robinson, J. A. (2001). The Colonial Origins of Comparative Development: An Empirical Investigation. American Economic Review, 91(5), 1369-1401.

CHAPTER 2

THE PRINCIPLE OF GENDER-RESPONSIVE BUDGETING AND THE DEMOGRAPHIC DIVIDEND

Introduction

Demographic dividend-sensitive budgeting is an approach to public financial management that focuses on maximizing the economic and social benefits associated with changes in a country's population structure. This dividend refers to the potential economic gains that occur when the proportion of the working-age population increases relative to dependents (children and seniors). By integrating these considerations into the budget process, governments can better plan and allocate resources to stimulate economic growth and improve social well-being, while ensuring gender equality.

This integration of the demographic dividend into the budget process is of critical importance for several reasons. First, it makes it possible to take full advantage of the opportunities offered by a growing labor force, which can boost economic growth. By investing in education, health and employment, governments can strengthen the skills and productivity of the workforce. Second, it helps anticipate and address the challenges associated with demographic changes, such as an aging population. By planning, governments can develop social protection policies and health systems that are fit for future needs. Third, demographic dividend-sensitive budgeting promotes intergenerational equity by ensuring that resources are allocated in a way that benefits all age groups of the population, while considering the specific needs of men and women. This approach thus contributes to social stability and national cohesion.

Finally, this approach improves long-term planning and the sustainability of public finances. By considering demographic trends, governments can avoid fiscal crises and ensure more stable and predictable management of public resources. This chapter aims to provide an in-depth understanding of the principles and factors influencing the demographic dividend, with a particular focus on gender aspects. It shows how demographic objectives, including gender equity, can be aligned with national and local fiscal policies, illustrating the integration of the demographic dividend into the budget process.

Section 1: Gender-responsive budgeting

Gender, like social class, represents an essential social dimension. Gender analysis is an indispensable tool in planning to meet the needs of society, considering women and men. Gender equality translates into equitable access to resources, opportunities, and representation. Despite the importance of women's and men's contributions to the economy, they often hold different positions and receive different remuneration (Esther Duflo and Abhijit Banerjee, 2019). When looking at the participation of men and women in economic activity, three main sectors can be distinguished. First, the formal economy encompasses paid activities in the public and private sectors, where men generally dominate. Second, the informal economy includes small-scale activities, often characterized by unpaid work performed by women and men. Finally, the care economy focuses on the tasks of reproduction, maintaining the workforce, and caring for the family and community, work that is primarily carried out by women and often unpaid.

The distinction between work in the public sphere (market economy and public sector) and work in the private sphere (domestic and community work) creates an artificial division that obscures the importance and contribution of the care economy. This division often deprives women of recognition for their efforts and leads to inefficient allocation of resources. It is essential to recognize that the budget is not neutral. The strategic directions that guide it reflect the interests and concerns of society, including men, women, boys and girls. Integrating gender-responsive budgeting helps address these inequalities and promote a more equitable distribution of resources and opportunities.

Gender-Responsive Budgeting: An Inclusive and Equitable Approach

Integrating a gender perspective into budgeting is essential to meet the aspirations and needs of the entire population, whether men, women, boys or girls. A gender-focused budget allocates government funds based on their impact on different groups, considering social dynamics, gender roles, and access to resources. This approach aims to ensure fair benefits for all.

Gender-responsive budgets respond to the diverse needs of all sectors of society, thereby improving the effectiveness of budgeting choices. Gender-neutral policies can have divergent impacts on women and men due to their distinct roles in the economy and society. Effective public management requires understanding these differentiated impacts and adjusting policies to equitably meet the expectations of all socio-economic groups. Gender-sensitive budgets help to increase economic efficiency and promote social welfare. Ignoring the specific roles of women in the economy and society, as well as their needs, undermines the effectiveness of certain public policies. Gender inequalities, in addition to their injustice, entail significant economic costs, affecting productivity, skills development and overall well-being. Gender-responsive budgeting aims to optimize the use of resources to improve the quality of life for all individuals.

These budgets aim to reduce gender gaps and inequalities, highlighting the distinct but crucial contributions of women and men to the economy, including in the field of care. They encourage innovative solutions to recognize, value and equitably distribute women's unpaid work, leading to a fairer allocation of resources. Gender-sensitive budgets are more effective in the fight against poverty, recognizing that women and men experience poverty differently and require specific approaches. To be fair and effective, poverty reduction strategies, policies and budgets must take these differences into account.

These budgets help governments meet their equality commitments, as set out in the Beijing Platform for Action, the Convention on the Elimination of All Forms of Discrimination against Women and the Sustainable Development Goals. They also strengthen the role of parliament in the budget process, improving resource allocations to poor women and men, and strengthening the links between economic and social outcomes.

Integrating a gender perspective into the budget process enhances transparency and accountability, allowing for more rigorous control of spending and better allocation of resources to meet the needs of society. By controlling spending against gender and development commitments, the transparency of the budget process is improved. Mechanisms and tools to develop gender-responsive budgets are essential for effective and equitable budget management, ensuring that available resources are used to improve the quality of life of all citizens. Adopting this approach represents a crucial step towards a more just and prosperous society.

Guiding Principles for Gender Responsive Budgeting

The foundations of gender budgeting are based on key principles such as inclusive participation, transparency and accountability, which are reflected in practices to ensure equity and effectiveness in public policies.

Inclusive participation involves the active engagement of women and men in the budget process. According to Diane Elson, a leading figure in feminist economics, the inclusion of women in budget discussions allows for better identification and consideration of their specific needs. In South Africa, for example, the involvement of women's groups in the formulation of the national budget has led to a more equitable distribution of resources in the health and education sectors. According to Budlender (2005), this approach has allowed for a fairer distribution of resources, thus meeting the distinct needs of women and men.

Budget transparency ensures that financial decisions are made in an open manner and accessible to all citizens. Transparency International points out that the publication of gender-disaggregated budget data allows citizens to monitor and assess the impact of public spending. In Sweden, for example, annual budget reports include detailed analyses on the impact of economic policies on women and men, thereby strengthening public trust in government institutions (SIDA, 2016). This practice promotes equity and holds public decision-makers accountable.

Accountability requires governments to be accountable for the use of public funds and their impacts on different genders. According to Elson (2002), accountability in gender budgeting requires decision-makers to consider the consequences of their policies on gender equality and to adjust their actions accordingly. For example, Australia has implemented gender audits to assess the impacts of fiscal and fiscal policies on women, leading to meaningful reforms to improve equity (Sharp, 2003). These audits have made it possible to uncover hidden inequalities and to promote fairer policies. Methodologies and analytical tools for gender-responsive budgeting are essential for assessing the impact of fiscal policies. A gender audit, as proposed by Budlender and Sharp (1998), is a systematic evaluation of policies, programs and budget allocations aimed at identifying gender inequalities and proposing adjustments. In the United Kingdom, gender audits have revealed significant disparities in the funding of reproductive health services, leading to budget reallocations in favor of women's services (UN Women, 2015).

Gender-differentiated cost-benefit analyses assess the costs and benefits of public policies in terms of their impact on men and women. A World Bank report (2012) highlights the importance of such analyses to ensure that public investments benefit all genders equitably. In Canada, for example, analysis of parental leave policies has shown that parental leave shared between mothers and fathers promotes gender equality in the labor market and within the home (OECD, 2016). These analyses help guide policies to maximize benefits for all members of society.

Continuous monitoring and evaluation of gender-focused fiscal policies is essential to assess their effectiveness and impact. Tools such as gender indicators and dashboards are used to monitor progress and make necessary adjustments. For example, in India, the use of gender dashboards has been used to monitor investments in girls' education, leading to a notable increase in enrolment and retention rates (UNDP, 2014). These monitoring and evaluation tools allow for continuous adaptation of policies to meet the changing needs of society.

Thus, the principles of inclusive participation, transparency and accountability, supported by rigorous methodologies and analytical tools, are crucial for effective gender-responsive budgeting. These principles aim to create more equitable public policies and improve the social and economic well-being of all people.

Long-Term Impacts on Sustainable Development

The long-term impacts of gender budgeting on sustainable development are broad and multidimensional. An equitable distribution of resources not only promotes gender equality, but it also catalyzes sustainable economic growth, reduces poverty and strengthens the resilience of communities.

Ensuring an equitable distribution of resources is a key element in promoting gender equality, ensuring that women and men benefit equitably from public investment. This includes access to services such as education, healthcare, employment, and infrastructure. For example, investing in girls' education has significant multiplier effects: according to UNESCO, each additional year of a girl's schooling can increase her future income by 10 to 20%, which directly affects overall economic growth. In addition, gender-responsive budgeting promotes sustainable economic growth. Research shows that when women are fully integrated into the economy, the benefits are significant. According to the McKinsey Global Institute, gender economic equality could add up to $28 trillion to global GDP by 2025. A concrete example is Sweden, where integrated gender-focused policies have led to a significant increase in women's participation in the labor market, contributing to a stronger and more resilient economy.

Moreover, poverty reduction is intrinsically linked to gender equality. Women make up a disproportionate share of the world's poor, and fiscal policies that target the specific needs of women and girls are crucial to fighting poverty. A case in point is the Bolsa Familia program in Brazil, which used conditional cash transfers to improve children's health and education, with a particular focus on mothers. A similar program is carried out in Senegal with family security scholarships.

Finally, gender-responsive budgeting strengthens the resilience of communities by recognizing and valuing the role of women in resource management and local decision-making, making them more able to cope with economic and environmental shocks. For example, in many rural communities in Africa, women often play a central role in the management of natural resources. Initiatives to integrate gender perspectives into water management have led to a more sustainable and efficient use of this vital resource.

In summary, gender-responsive budgeting, by incorporating equitable perspectives into the distribution of public resources, not only promotes gender equality, but also helps strengthen economies, reduce poverty, and make communities more resilient. Inclusive and transparent fiscal policies are essential to achieving the Sustainable Development Goals and ensuring a prosperous future for all members of society.

The Benefits of Gender-Responsive Budgeting

The World Bank calls gender equality a "smart economic strategy." Expanding economic opportunities for women and girls' benefits not only them, but whole society. Gender-responsive budgeting has many benefits in enabling people who are discriminated against to access economic opportunities more equitably. One of the main benefits is the increase in women's participation in the labor market and the improvement of their incomes, which reduces poverty and stimulates economic growth. Research shows that effective gender mainstreaming can accelerate the annual growth rate of GDP.

In addition, gender-responsive budget analysis creates opportunities to reform public financial management, thereby strengthening planning and budgeting systems. It also requires a detailed presentation of budgets and activities, thereby improving budget transparency and strengthening financial accountability for public expenditure. This approach requires gender-sensitive performance indicators and results-based management. Finally, effective gender mainstreaming has a positive impact on improving the living conditions of men and women, increasing their longevity. With better budget allocation, targeted populations benefit from better nutrition, access to quality water, and better control of communicable diseases, among other positive effects.

Major Constraints in Gender-Responsive Budgeting

Implementing gender budgeting requires a shift in perspectives and practices, which inevitably creates barriers to overcome. While introducing this approach is relatively straightforward, the real challenge lies in maintaining and sustaining it.

One of the main obstacles is the inefficiency of budgeting and planning systems, which often lack the data needed for in-depth gender analysis. Gender-disaggregated data and baseline statistics for many indicators are often lacking. In addition, expertise in gender analysis and integration is limited. Even though gender-responsive budgeting is frequently discussed, its implementation remains complex. It requires well-trained staff with specific skills in this area.

Gender-responsive budgeting requires sustained and consistent efforts. In many government agencies, staff mobility can hinder the continuity and effectiveness of this initiative. Practices and attitudes that have been ingrained for decades, if not centuries, are not changing quickly. The main challenge is to transform mindsets and perceptions of gender power relations. Without the decisive support of the leadership team, buy-in to gender equality remains elusive.

Collaboration with strong institutional mechanisms for gender is crucial to transforming mindsets. In the absence of such institutions or if they are weak, the effectiveness of gender-responsive budgeting suffers. This budgeting should be integrated into planning and budgeting functions, ideally within the Ministry of Finance and Planning. A lack of coordination can create confusion and weaken efforts. The lack of accurate and relevant data limits the ability to effectively evaluate and guide policies. To avoid problems related to the mobility of focal points, it is necessary to create stable gender cells.

In conclusion, while gender-responsive budgeting offers significant benefits for gender equality and socio-economic development, it requires robust systems, adequate expertise, and ongoing efforts to overcome the challenges inherent in its implementation.

Section 2: Concepts and Foundations of the Demographic Dividend

In this section, we'll dive into the foundations of the demographic dividend by examining its definition and developing an in-depth understanding of its nuances.

Defining and understanding the demographic dividend

The demographic dividend refers to economic growth resulting from the transformation of the age structure of the population (Bloom et al., 2007). For this potential to be realized, this transformation must be accompanied by investments in human capital (health and education), job creation, and good governance. This concept is central to the analysis of a country's economic and social development. It comes from the demographic transition, where a young and dependent population evolves into a population with a higher proportion of people of working age compared to dependent people, such as children and the elderly. This transition can open a window of opportunity for rapid economic growth, provided that adequate policies are put in place to take advantage of this potential.

It is important to emphasize that the demographic dividend does not automatically materialize with the change in demographic structure; It requires strategic investments in several key areas. First, investments in human capital are essential. This includes improving maternal and child health, providing access to quality education at all levels, and strengthening the skills and capacities of the workforce. Strong human capital is crucial to maximizing the economic potential of workers.

In addition, job creation is fundamental to capturing the demographic dividend. While rapid population growth can put pressure on the labor market, policies that promote job creation can turn this abundant labor force into an engine of economic growth. This requires policies that encourage entrepreneurship, promote investment in productive sectors, and boost innovation and productivity.

Finally, good governance is essential to achieve the demographic dividend. Effective and transparent institutions, prudent fiscal and fiscal policies, and adequate regulatory and supervisory mechanisms are needed to ensure an efficient and equitable allocation of resources, and to ensure an inclusive distribution of the benefits of economic growth.

The process of capturing the demographic dividend can be measured using the Demographic Dividend Monitoring Index (DDMI). This index makes it possible to monitor positive or negative changes in its dimensions and to identify sectors requiring increased investment to create conditions conducive to optimizing the demographic dividend and achieving the Sustainable Development Goals.

To optimize the capture of the demographic dividend, it is crucial that countries strengthen the effectiveness of their fiscal policies by restructuring their budgets to align them with the dimensions of the DDMI. Improved strategic fiscal planning will make the state budget responsive to the demographic dividend.

Budgeting Sensitive to Demographic Dividend (BSDD) is a five-step planning process aimed at achieving this goal. First, we proceed with the back-polling, calibration and calibration of the DDMI (Demographic Dividend Monitoring Index). Then, the restructuring of the classic budget into a functional budget is carried out. Each budget function is then aligned with the dimensions (or sub-dimensions) of the DDMI. The third step consists of a budget sensitivity analysis to assess fiscal elasticities and identify the ancillary functions needed for optimal budget allocation. Finally, the programming in the national budget adjusts the budgetary functions so that they become sensitive to the demographic dividend.

The Foundations and Pathways of the Demographic Dividend

The potential for the demographic dividend is based on a multitude of interconnected factors that influence a society's ability to take advantage of changes in its age structure. These factors include demographic transition, investments in human capital, access to reproductive health services, employment and social protection policies, and core public infrastructures.

The demographic transition marks the beginning of the process of exploiting demographic dividend. This process involves a shift from a high birth and mortality regime to a low birth and mortality regime, thus leading to a change in the age structure of the population. According to Bloom et al. (2007), this change can reduce the dependency ratio, i.e., the number of inactive people relative to the active population, thus creating a higher proportion of people of working age.

Investments in health and education play a crucial role in maximizing the demographic dividend. Becker, Glaeser, and Murphy (1999) point out that improvements in public health, particularly maternal and child health, increase life expectancy and labor force productivity. Similarly, quality education strengthens the skills of the workforce, making workers more adaptable and innovative.

Increased access to reproductive health services, such as family planning, helps to control birth rates and improve the overall health of populations. Cleland et al. (2006) show that the availability of these services promotes the reduction of family size, allowing parents to invest more in each child and society to benefit from a better-educated and healthier working-age population.

Job creation is essential to absorb the increase in the working-age population. Bloom and Canning (2004) indicate that employment-friendly policies, such as tax incentives for firms, promotion of entrepreneurship and vocational training programs, are essential to realize the economic potential of the demographic dividend. In addition, robust social protection systems provide workers with a safety net, thereby reducing poverty and inequality.

Well-developed economic infrastructure, such as transport networks, communication systems and financial services, are needed to support a dynamic economy. According to Bloom et al. (2012), improving this infrastructure promotes increased productivity, facilitates trade, and stimulates innovation, all of which are crucial to maximizing the benefits of the demographic dividend. Governance and institutions also play a central role in realizing the demographic dividend. Effective and transparent institutions are needed to create an environment conducive to investment and economic growth. Acemoglu, Johnson, and Robinson (2001) emphasize that the quality of institutions is one of the most important determinants of economic development. Prudent fiscal and fiscal policies, effective regulation, and adequate oversight mechanisms are essential to ensure efficient resource allocation and inclusive growth.

In summary, achieving the demographic dividend depends on an integrated approach that encompasses investments in human capital, reproductive health policies, job creation, strong economic infrastructure, and effective governance. By combining these elements, societies can transform demographic changes into drivers of economic growth and sustainable development.

Section 3: Implementing Demographic Dividend-Sensitive Budgeting

Implementation Process and Steps

Within the parameters of the demographic dividend, eight key budget convergence functions, divided into four distinct components, have been established to align the traditional budget with the DDMI.

Table 1: Budget Component and DDMI Functions

Budget component	Budget function/DDMI
Human Capital	Education
	Health
Governance	Institution
	Security
Structure of the economy	Economic Affairs
	Building & Energy
Professional and social networks	Social network
	Professional network

Source: CREG 2023

According to the functional approach of the budget, three (03) categories of nature of expenditure have been defined:

1. Capital expenditure (INV): Capital expenditure is the value of the amounts of a producer's fixed asset acquisitions during the accounting period, plus some specific expenses spent on services that add value to non-produced assets. In the case of DDMI, debt charges are counted as capital expenditures.

2. Operating Expenditures (FON): Operating expenditures are measured by the value of goods and services and the value of compensation paid to employees in the process of a good or service.

3. Transfers & Subsidies (TRF): A transfer or subsidy is an operation in which one institutional unit provides goods, services, or asset to another unit, without receiving a direct counterpart.

The definition of the various DDMI functions is recorded in the following table:

Table 2: Defining DDMI Functions

Components	DDMI Functions	Definition
Human Capital	Education	All expenditures on the production of goods and services for skills building
	Health	All expenses that serve people's health
Governance	Institution	Expenditure on the production of goods and services determining the legal and institutional environment in which the individual is attached
	Security	Expenditure on the production of goods and services to ensure the peace of mind of the individual and the people
Structure Economy	Building and Energy	Expenditure related to the production of market and non-market goods and services
	Economic Affairs	Budgetary expenditure contributing to the production of market goods and services
Networks	Professional Network	Spending on behavior change interaction
	Social network	Expenses related to the production of any good and service aimed at cementing social relations

Source: CREG 2023

Principles

According to the process of transition from the traditional state budget to the functional budget, the assignment of a DDMI main function to an institution is based on its main mission. In other words, where the institution's wording covers multiple domains, the first domain mentioned guides the designation of the corresponding DDMI function. For example, the Ministry of Land Affairs, Housing and Urban Planning is assigned to the main function of DDMI "Economic Affairs", as is the Ministry of Petroleum and Energy.

Procedures

At the end of the grooming work, a list of Institutions and sub-Institutions was obtained. It was used to assign the main functions of the DDMI to the Institutions.

Figure 1: Illustration of how the DDMI main function is assigned

List of State institutions and sub-institutions	Mission/Main Function/DDMI
NATIONAL ASSEMBLY	Institution
Chief of Staff	Institution
Questure	Institution
General Secretariat	Institution
NATIONAL HUMAN RIGHTS COMMISSION	Institution
Chief of Staff	Institution
General Secretariat	Institution
CONSTITUTIONAL COUNCIL	Institution
Chief of Staff	Institution
General Secretariat	Institution
ECONOMIC, SOCIAL AND CULTURAL COUNCIL	Institution
Chief of Staff	Institution
Questure	Institution
NATIONAL TRANSITIONAL COUNCIL	Institution
Questure	Institution

The main function of the DDMI

Source: CREG 2023

Secondary functions of the sub-institutions (budget chapters)

Principles

In this phase of the functional transformation of the budget in its stage 2, it is a question of assigning to each budget line the corresponding DDMI function according to the purpose of the expenditure.

For example, the main bodies that are the General Secretariat, Cabinet Directorate, DAAFM, General Inspectorate, Human Resources Directorate are directly attached to the main function of the supervisory institution. Case-by-case treatment is carried out for the rest of the sub-institutions or chapters. Indeed, regardless of the institution or sub-institution, the allocation of the DDMI secondary function to each budget expenditure line is based on the purpose of the expenditure. In other words, the DDMI function may not necessarily be the main function of the institution, it is in line with the budget line of the sub-institution.

Example: within the framework of the Ministry of Defense, through the chapter "General Directorate of Military Administration", for the expenditure line "Medical evacuation", it will be assigned the secondary function DDMI "health" and not "Security". The following table illustrates the transition between budget lines and DDMI sub-functions.

Table 3: Transition grid between budget lines and DDMI sub-functions

No.	Budget lines	DDMI Functions
01	Medical evacuation, surgical and medical equipment, medical expenses, laboratory supplies, etc.	Health
02	Family allowances, CNRT & CNPS, social security contributions, death benefit, scholarships and celebrations and ceremonies, aid and relief	Social Network
03	Communication & Telecommunication, Various Presses	Professional Network
04	Military remuneration, National Security Agency (ANS), Security, General Staff, Global Institutional Food Premium (PGIA), Military equipment	Security
05	Training Internship, Schools, Institutes and Universities	Education
06	Building, Rehabilitation, Structure, Building, Building	Building & Energy

Source: CREG 2023

Procedure

Filtering techniques are used in this case to match each expense line to a DDMI subfunction. The goal is to identify expense lines that may correspond to a given DDMI subfunction. For example, the column "Budget lines label" is filtered to systematically identify all budget expenditure lines corresponding to a fixed DDMI secondary function.

Table 4: Classic budget transition table to functional budget

Functions defined in the Budget	ECONOMY AFFAIRS	BUILDING AND ENERGY	EDUCATION	INSTITUTION	PROFESSIONAL NETWORK	SOCIAL NETWORK	HEALTH	SECURITY
Acquisition of Medical-surgical Equipment								
ADP * Family Allowances								
ADP * Death allowance								
External Scholarships								
External Scholarships								
Death benefit								
Fuels and lubricant								
COA * Building of hydraulic structures								
Communications and Telecommunications								

	DA * CNPS social charges								
	DA * CNRT social security contributions								
	DA * Basic remuneration per Decision-makers								
	Direction de Cabinet								
	Water and Electricity								
	Military warehouses								

Source: CREG 2023

Section 4: Budgetary Expenditures by Economic Nature

Principle

As part of the Demographic Dividend Sensitive Budgeting process, several steps must be followed, including the classification of budget expenditures according to their economic nature. This implies the use of a grid to move from budgetary expenditure to its functional nature DDMI. In general, in this process of functional transformation, budgetary expenditures (such as personnel costs, goods and services, transfers and subsidies, and investments) are divided into three categories of DDMI:

– Operation

– Investment

– Transfer & Subsidy

In this context, expenditure on "personnel" and "goods and services" are classified under the "operating" category, transfers and subsidies under "transfer", and investment and equipment expenditure under "investment". In addition, all debts, including financial charges, are considered investments.

Table 5: Correspondence between the nature of expenditure category of the classic budget and the nature of the DDMI

Number	Budgetary nature	Nature DDMI
01	Financial Expenses	Investments
05	Investments	
02	Personnel	Operation
03	Goods and Services	
04	Transfers and subsidies	Transfers

Source: CREG 2023

Procedures

The procedure involved going from five (05) types of expenditure in the budget nomenclature to three types of DDMI. In the column "Title of expenditure", financial expenses (code 1) and investments (code 5) have been grouped under the DDMI type of expenditure "Investment". Personnel costs (code 2) and goods and services have been classified in the "Operating" category DDMI. Finally, transfers and subsidies have been grouped under the "Transfer" category DDMI. The expenditure lines designated "Supplies, small office equipment" were considered as investments for a certain level of expenditure (above 10 million). All debts, both principal and interest, were systematically considered as investment expenditures. This process is represented in the table below:

Table 6: Passage table budget classification according to budgetary nature

Budget Expenditures	Nature DDMI		
	FON	**INV**	**TRF**
Acquisition of Land Vehicles		■	
Acquisition of Medico-Technical Equipment		■	
Computer Hardware Acquisition		■	
Scholarships			■
Death benefit			■
Fuels & Lubricants	■		
COA * Building Telephone Lines		■	
COA * Building Building		■	
Water Consumption	■		
Gas consumption	■		
Overall Expenses (Student Transportation)	■		
EI * Miscellaneous Equipment		■	
Office Equipment Maintenance and Repair	■		
FE * Basic remuneration of civilian staff	■		
FF * Insurance premiums	■		
Mission expenses	■		
Clothing	■		
Interest – Multilateral external debt		■	
Interest - Domestic debt		■	
Base Salary of Civilian Personnel - Government Contract Personnel	■		
SUB * Overall Expenditure			■
SUB * Student transport			■

Source: CREG, 2023

Conclusion

Demographic dividend-sensitive budgeting is a promising approach to maximizing the economic and social benefits of demographic change. By including gender considerations in this process, governments can not only foster gender equity but also increase the effectiveness and impact of fiscal policies. However, this integration of gender into demographic dividend-sensitive budgeting faces several challenges. Persistent gender stereotypes, disparities in access to resources and opportunities, as well as rigid socio-cultural structures, can hinder the effective implementation of these policies. In addition, the lack of sex-disaggregated data and the lack of institutional capacity to analyze differentiated impacts on men and women may be additional barriers.

Despite these challenges, gender mainstreaming in demographic dividend-sensitive budgeting opens important opportunities. By recognizing and addressing the specific needs of men and women in the planning and allocation of resources, governments can help reduce gender inequalities, promote women's empowerment, and strengthen social cohesion. In addition, a gender-sensitive approach can foster more inclusive and sustainable economic growth, harnessing the full potential of the entire workforce.

In conclusion, gender mainstreaming in demographic dividend-sensitive budgeting is essential to fully realize the benefits of this approach. This requires a continued commitment from governments to overcome barriers and promote an inclusive and equitable approach to public financial management. By investing in women's empowerment, eliminating gender discrimination, and strengthening gender analysis in the budget process, countries can truly harness the potential of demographic dividend for sustainable and equitable development.

Bibliographical references

Émilie Moysan In The Essentials of Public Finance Law (2017), pages 11 to 16. Fact sheet 1. The notion of budget

Bloom, D. E., Canning, D., & Sevilla, J. (2003). The Demographic Dividend: A New Perspective on the Economic Consequences of Population Change. RAND Corporation.

Becker, G. S., Glaeser, E. L., & Murphy, K. M. (1999). Population and Economic Growth. American Economic Review, 89(2), 145-149.

Cleland, J., Bernstein, S., Ezeh, A., Faundes, A., Glasier, A., & Innis, J. (2006). Family planning: the unfinished agenda. Lancet, 368(9549), 1810-1827.

Acemoglu, D., Johnson, S., & Robinson, J. A. (2001). The Colonial Origins of Comparative Development: An Empirical Investigation. American Economic Review, 91(5), 1369-1401.

Arnstein, S. R. (1969). A Ladder of Citizen Participation. Journal of the American Institute of Planners, 35(4), 216-224.

Barro, R. J., & Sala-i-Martin, X. (1995). Economic Growth. McGraw-Hill.

Behn, R. D. (2003). Why Measure Performance? Different Purposes Require Different Measures. Public Administration Review, 63(5), 586-606.

Becker, G. S., Glaeser, E. L., & Murphy, K. M. (1999). Population and Economic Growth. American Economic Review, 89(2), 145-149.

Bloom, D. E., Canning, D., & Sevilla, J. (2003). The Demographic Dividend: A New Perspective on the Economic Consequences of Population Change. RAND Corporation.

Bloom, D. E., & Williamson, J. G. (1998). Demographic Transitions and Economic Miracles in Emerging Asia. World Bank Economic Review, 12(3), 419-455.

Bloom, D. E., & Canning, D. (2000). The Health and Wealth of Nations. Science, 287(5456), 1207-1209.

Bongaarts, J., & Casterline, J. (2013). Fertility Transition: Is Sub-Saharan Africa Different? Population and Development Review, 38(Supplement), 153-168.

Cleland, J., Bernstein, S., Ezeh, A., Faundes, A., Glasier, A., & Innis, J. (2006). Family Planning: The Unfinished Agenda. Lancet, 368(9549), 1810-1827.

Gertler, P. J., Martinez, S., Premand, P., Rawlings, L. B., & Vermeersch, C. M. (2011). Impact Evaluation in Practice. The World Bank.

Hanushek, E. A., & Kimko, D. D. (2000). Schooling, Labor-Force Quality, and the Growth of Nations. American Economic Review, 90(5), 1184-1208.

Kolsaker, A., & Lee-Kelley, L. (2008). Citizens' Attitudes Towards E-Government and E-Governance: A UK Study. International Journal of Public Sector Management, 21(7), 723-738.

Lee, R., & Mason, A. (2006). What is the Demographic Dividend? Finance and Development, 43(3).

Mishan, E. J. (1982). Cost-Benefit Analysis: An Informal Introduction. George Allen & Unwin.

Power, M. (1997). The Audit Society: Rituals of Verification. Oxford University Press.

Smith, J. P. (2004). Unraveling the SES-Health Connection. Population and Development Review, 30(Supplement), 108-132.

Weil, D. N., & Galor, O. (1999). From Malthusian Stagnation to Modern Growth.

Acemoglu, D., Johnson, S., & Robinson, J. A. (2001). The Colonial Origins of Comparative Development: An Empirical Investigation. American Economic Review, 91(5), 1369-1401.

CHAPTER 3

THE PROFILE OF THE DEMOGRAPHIC DIVIDEND

Introduction

The youth dividend, or demographic dividend (DD), is defined by United Nations experts as the economic growth that occurs when there are more people of working age, between the ages of 15 and 64, than inactive, under the age of 14 and over 65. It is the rapid economic growth resulting from the decline in mortality and fertility in a given country and changes in the population age pyramid. In other words, it is a transitional advantage that a country has during the demographic transition with a large working population and few children and the elderly.

The demographic dividend is, according to the PRB (Population Reference Bureau), the acceleration of economic growth that can result from a rapid decline in a country's fertility and the subsequent evolution of the age structure of the population. To put it another way, this corresponds to a demographic phase in which the children of the demographic boom have become adults, have fewer children, and are not yet elderly: the full class of the age pyramid corresponds to the active population between 18 and 65 years old. The term dividend is to be understood here in the financial sense as the benefit, the economic fruit, of the increase in the share of the active population. It represents the economic opportunity offered by the situation in which a country would reach its optimum in the ratio between the "non-dependent" (active) population and the "dependent" population (the youngest and the oldest).

According to the UN, DD is the ideal time to "invest in health and education", i.e. in "human capital", at a time when the ratio of beneficiaries of health and education systems is the lowest for those who finance it. But the demographic dividend is also a challenge: that of creating jobs for the working population, without which the hopes for development that it raises can only remain in vain.

According to UNFPA, it is described as an increase in economic productivity that occurs when the ratio of the labor force to the number of dependents increases. At a time when the age pyramid in Africa is reaching this stage, it is important not to miss the rendezvous between demography and the economy. Because capturing this demographic dividend will make it possible to achieve sustainable and inclusive development throughout the continent, and more particularly in the Sahel region, the most vulnerable. UNFPA's Regional Office for West and Central Africa (WCARO) has worked tirelessly to make it a central part of the "African Common Position" framework in the post-2015 development agenda. This recognition resulted in its inclusion in the United Nations 2030 Agenda for Sustainable Development as well as the 2063 Agenda for Africa's Transformation before being unanimously adopted at the AU summit in Addis Ababa; the 54 African heads of state also concretized the modalities of its implementation.

There are different definitions of the demographic dividend, including the one given by the African Union (AU) in its Roadmap: Reaping the Full Advantage of the Demographic Dividend, as "the benefit that is likely to emerge when a country enjoys a relatively large proportion of its population of working age due to declining fertility rates, and invests effectively in its health, empowerment, education and employment through public action and private sector engagement."

According to demographers, the dividend is likely to occur in a country when there is a decline in fertility rates. This is followed by a transition phase in which the proportion of the population of working age (15-64 years) begins to increase. Typically, this only happens once, in a period of about 30 to 50 years. As such, it is also referred to as the "demographic window of opportunity." During this period, individuals and families have more resources to improve their living conditions and invest in their children's health and education (human capital), as well as in equipment and buildings that produce goods and services (physical capital).

Thus, a demographic dividend refers to rapid economic growth resulting from the decline in mortality and fertility in each country, and from changes in the age structure of the population. The decline in the annual birth rate leads to changes in the age distribution of a population; There are fewer dependent young people compared to the working-age population, which means that less investment is needed for these dependent young people. This creates an opportunity for faster economic growth provided that appropriate social and economic policies and investments are implemented.

Changes in the structure of the population and the corresponding changes in the dependency ratio have economic consequences. The entry of a high proportion of young people into the labor force can increase per capita output and saving in relation to the size of other age groups as well as behavioral effects. These advantages constitute the first demographic dividend.

The dividend does not end with the absorption of a young workforce. As this working-age population matures, the prospect of retirement can provide greater motivation to save for financial security. Depending on the number of other dependents, the additional savings can either be spent or used to prolong economic growth. This last stage of economic growth has been called the second demographic dividend.

The demographic dividend occurs when a country manages to derive an economic benefit from its age pyramid. To achieve this, the ratio of the working population to the number of dependents must increase.

Section 1: The pillars of the demographic dividend

For decades, the relationship between demographic change and economic growth has been studied and debated widely, with a focus on population size and growth. However, the debate has not paid sufficient attention to the critical issue of the age structure of the population, which can change dramatically as fertility and mortality rates change. The change in the age structure can have significant effects on economic growth depending on the proportion of children and elderly (dependents) in the working-age population that contributes directly to economic productivity.

The demographic dividend refers to the economic benefit that comes from a significant increase in the proportion of working-age adults to young dependents, resulting from the rapid decline in fertility if this change is accompanied by sustained investments in education and skills development, health, job creation, and good governance. When fertility and mortality decline significantly, the age structure changes so that there are more working-age adults than young dependents in the population. This shift can accelerate economic growth through increased productivity of the relatively large working-age population if the economy generates enough decent jobs, well-trained, skilled and healthy workers. A new impetus for economic growth is being generated by increased household savings and investment, which results from the reduction in the costs of the basic needs of fewer children and a relatively smaller young population. Studies of the socio-economic development experienced by East Asian countries such as Malaysia, South Korea and Thailand have shown that between a quarter and a third of the economic growth these countries experienced between 1970 and 2000 can be attributed to the demographic dividend (Bloom & AMP; Williamson, 1998; Mason, 2001).

It is essential to emphasize that DD is neither automatic nor guaranteed, even for countries with a well-known decline in fertility. In order to reap the demographic dividend, countries should implement policies that not only accelerate the decline in fertility but also ensure that the resulting surplus labor force is educated, skilled, healthy, and economically active, and ensure accountability and efficiency in the use of public resources and in the delivery of public services. The comprehensive reforms that countries need to adopt and implement to harness the demographic dividend can be grouped under the five pillars or wheels illustrated below:

Figure 2: The Five Pillars of the Demographic Dividend

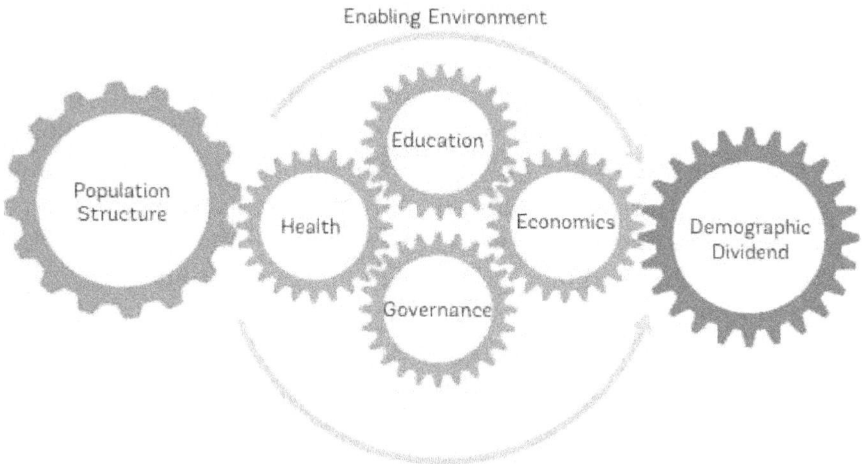

Source: Population Reference Bureau

The essential point is that all five strategic pillars or wheels are interdependent; they reinforce each other; and should be implemented simultaneously to lead the country towards economic prosperity that can come from the demographic dividend. Like the elements of a gear, each of the wheels contributes to the functioning and success of the others. If one breaks down or is dysfunctional, all other wheels will be slowed down, limiting a country's ability to harness the demographic dividend. In addition, the demographic dividend is not an event that occurs or is achieved in any given year. It is an accumulation of economic gains that benefit the country for many years as the age structure of the population shifts in favor of the working-age population and the necessary investments are made for human capital development and employment-oriented economic reforms.

The demographic dividend refers to the economic growth that can result from changes in a country's age structure. It occurs when there is an increase in the number of people of working age relative to the number of dependents, leading to increased productivity and economic growth. However, this demographic dividend can only be achieved if there are appropriate policies in place to ensure that the working-age population is healthy, educated and employed.

The economic benefits of the demographic dividend can be appreciated at the microeconomic level with households and individuals and at the macroeconomic level with countries. Both are rooted in the same economic growth.

– **Benefits at the microeconomic level**

A growth in the working-age population, an explosion in the youth population, implies greater economic returns and income per household, if everyone who reaches working age is productively employed. In addition to the low costs of maintaining dependent people, households may see their disposable incomes increase. Growth in household income affects both expenditure and savings related to human capital. With fewer children per household and an increase in disposable income, each household has the capacity to invest the additional income in education, nutrition and health care for each child. Over time, growth in household income could lead to growth in savings, especially when heads of household are in the 40 to 65 age group. Investments on the account of older children could be replaced by savings due to retirement prospects and the decline in the ability to rely on less offspring for support in old age. There will be an increase in investment due to better health and longevity of adults.

– **Macroeconomic benefits**

At the country level, when growth in the working-age population is sufficiently utilized as a labor force, this induces growth in output per capita for the country. Growth in household savings has national ramifications. Private household savings are often invested, thus contributing to a national accumulation of capital, which could be used to finance economic growth. An increase in savings creates a financial environment favorable to external investment, i.e. Foreign Direct Investment (FDI). As a result, growth in savings generates economic growth and acts as a stimulus for external financing. Finally, as much as households can invest in more resources per child, at the national level, a lower dependency ratio and increased productivity of workers allow the state to use savings to invest in quality human capital or to redirect their spending to other sectors of the economy.

Section 2: Literature Review

The detailed review of the literature on the demographic dividend has identified the policies and strategies that have enabled some countries to exploit the demographic dividend. The aim is to identify good practices that a country can adopt to harvest DD. To contextualize the literature on DD, we also examined national development policies and strategies to understand short-, medium- and long-term development goals and objectives, key bottlenecks, recommended solutions, and how all of this is aligned with the issue of DD capture and the achievement of the SDGs. We also explored international experiences on policy and program options that could drive progress and possible transformations.

Secondary indicators and data were compiled, and further analyses of existing data were conducted to fill gaps in previous studies to identify trends in different demographic and socio-economic phenomena. These trends, as well as the current policy framework and the demographic and socio-economic indicators of the countries with which Senegal wants to compare, have been used to determine the development goals that Senegal should strive to achieve to harness DD. The data used is mainly derived from national data series and official statistics. They were supplemented by international data compiled from United Nations (UN), World Bank and International Labor Organization (ILO) statistics when national data were not available. National data are obtained from population and housing censuses, demographic and health surveys, economic reports and other official sources.

– Demographic Dividend Modeling

To assess the DD potential in Senegal and identify the multi-sectoral policies and investments required to exploit it, the DemDiv modelling tool was used. DemDiv is developed by the Health Policy Project (HPP) with funding from USAID to the Futures Group (HPP & USAID, 2014). It is structured as a two-pronged model that projects and incorporates demographic and economic changes. The model is based on projections and scenarios aimed at showing the different possible development trends according to the public policy options adopted. DemDiv allows for the design of several scenarios showing how the combination of investments in family planning, health, education, and the economy can help generate DD.

The DemDiv model can make projections for a period of forty years with the ability to extract estimates for each year during that period. Therefore, this model is adapted to provide insight into the demographic dividend since DD mining is not a one-time event or a short-term investment from which a country can expect a quick return on investment. In fact, the full returns on investments in the education and health sectors are achieved over longer periods of time that can take as long as a generation or more. Thanks to the DemDiv tool, a projection and analysis of scenarios over a period of forty years can inform on the strategies that the country needs to put in place immediately to maximize the dividend over a long period. These projections are in line with long-term development visions and plans such as the PSE, which African countries are implementing through medium-term development plans. The African Union's Agenda 2063 is a long-term vision for the continent that projects the continent's situation in 50 years' time. We recognize, however, that the accuracy of the projections is reduced the longer the duration of the period. On the other hand, estimates for each year between the base period and the last year of the projection can be extracted to inform possible trends for each scenario. For this study, the base year is 2013 and the last year is 2053. For the main results, estimates were presented for both 2053 and 2035, the latter being the target year of the PSE.

In Senegal, one example is the National Transfer Accounts (NTA) methodology, which has been used to analyze the impact and consequences of economic life cycles on sustainable development. This work was mainly implemented by the Centre for Research in Applied Economics and Finance in Thiès (CREFAT).

Section 3: Methodology

National Transfer Accounts (NTAs) are a tool for analyzing trade between individuals in the same society. The objective of the NTAs is to measure how, at each age, economic resources are acquired and used (Lee and Mason, 2011). The NTAs are based on a unified international approach that consists of introducing age into the national accounts. They are intended to understand how economic flows circulate between different age groups of a population for a given country and for a given year. They indicate at each age the different sources of income and the different uses of this income in terms of consumption, whether private or public, and savings (d'Albis et al. 2015). They thus make it possible to study the consequences linked to changes in the age structure of the population.

The NTA approach is basically only a way of schematizing the life cycle, while allowing it to be quantified. It is based on a fundamental identity that states that, for a given age, all outflows of income are equal to all inflows of income. It is based on this equation that Lee (1994) introduced the life-cycle deficit indicator, which is becoming the central element in the NTA methodology.

Fundamental equation of NTAs and the notion of life cycle deficit

The NTAs are based on an accounting equation that states that, at each age, resources must be equal to the uses made of them (United Nations, 2013):

$$\underbrace{Y^l(a) + Y^a(a) + \tau^+(a)}_{\text{Inflows}} = \underbrace{C(a) + S(a) + \tau^-(a)}_{\text{Outflows}}$$

The left-hand side consists of all the current inputs for age group a: labor income Y^l (a), capital income Y^k (a), wealth income Y^p (a) and transfers received τ+(a). The right-hand side consists of all outflows of age group a: consumption C(a), savings S(a) and transfers paid τ^- (a). Thus, according to this equation, the sum of labor income, capital income, wealth income and transfers received must be equal to the sum of consumption, savings and transfers paid. This identity is obtained for both aggregate and per capita values at each age. The above equation shows all values indexed by age a, but the identity is also valid for national aggregates, in other words, all age groups combined.

By rearranging the terms of inflows and outflows to match the conceptual foundations of NTAs, the equation helps to highlight the economic life cycle and the economic mechanisms used to reallocate resources across ages. The economic life cycle is represented on the left-hand side (of the equation below) by the life cycle deficit which corresponds, for a given age a, to the difference between consumption and labor income ($LCD(a)=C(a)-Y^l(a)$). This life-cycle deficit gives rise to reallocation of resources between ages in the form of either net public or private transfers ($\tau(a)=\tau+(a)+\tau^-(a)$) or asset reallocations ($Y^k(a)+Y^p(a)-S(a)$). This has materialized to the right of the following equation:

NB: Each flow in the equation is disaggregated to distinguish between public and private.

Economic support ratio and demographic dividend

$$C(a) - Y^l(a) = Y^a(a) - S(a) + \tau^+(a) - \tau^-(a)$$

Life Cycle Deficit (LCD)	Assets Based Reallocations	Net Transfer
	Age Reallocations	

In addition to the economic life cycle analysis, the NTAs make it possible to determine the economic support ratio (ESR) and to measure the demographic dividend. The ESR is an indicator designed to capture the weight that workers feel from the consumers to be taken care of (United Nations, 2013). It is determined by dividing the number of actual employees (L) by the number of actual consumers (N):

$$ESR = \frac{L}{N} = \frac{\sum_{\alpha} \varphi(\alpha) * P(\alpha)}{\sum_{\alpha} \rho(\alpha) * P(\alpha)}$$

Section 4: Results

- **Economic dependency coverage ratio**

The age-dependent ratio is the ratio between people whose age qualifies them as dependent (under 15 and over 65) and people in the economically active groups (15 to 64 years) of the population. The age-dependency ratio is an important indicator for assessing the economic burden of the productive segment of the population. Figure 3 compares the evolution of this indicator between West Africa, Africa and the world. By 2020, the age-dependency ratio in West Africa is expected to be 85. A ratio of 85 dependent people per 100 people aged 15 to 64 means that 1.2 people of working age take care of one dependent person. This ratio is expected to fall to 64.26 in 2050 and then to 52.26 in 2100.

Figure 3: Evolution of the demographic dividend in West Africa and in the world

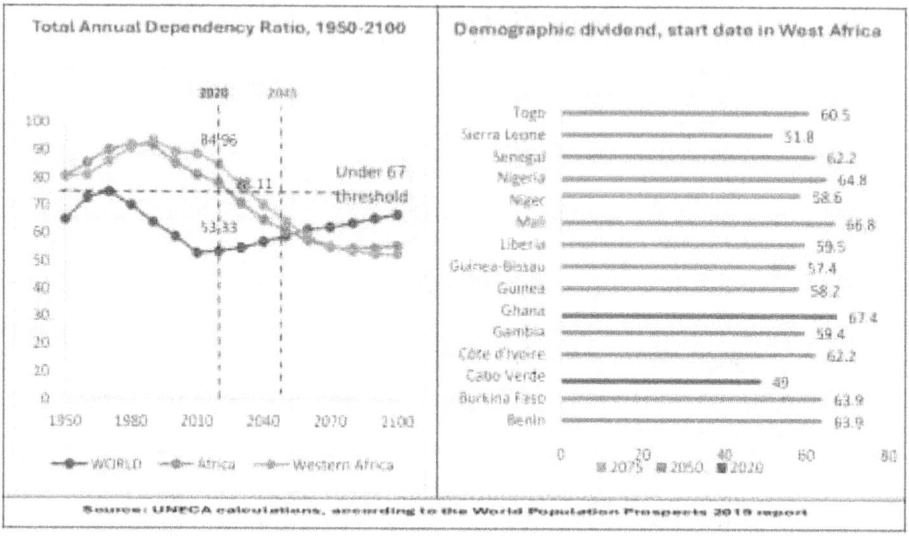

According to some studies, the demographic dividend occurs when the total dependency ratio does not exceed 67 dependents per 100 people of working age. In this case, at least 3 people of working age take care of 2 dependent people (Hayes and Setyonaluri, 2015). It can therefore be deduced that the window of opportunity for West Africa will open as early as 2045, when the dependency ratio drops to 67. Figure III-1b shows that Ghana and Cabo Verde are already realizing their demographic dividend, while most countries in the subregion will have to wait until 2050. Compared to many West African countries, Niger will take 25 years longer to reach the start date of its demographic dividend.

- **RESULTS OF AVERAGE AND AGGREGATE PROFILES (CONSUMPTION, INCOME, LCD) OF SENEGAL**

❖ **SENEGAL**

Average Total Consumption Profile

The consumption profile shows a strongly increasing pace among young people ranging from 300,000 FCFA to more than 760,000 FCFA for the 0 – 24 age group. This shows a strong need for consumption among young people and therefore requires significant resources to take care of their level of consumption. Beyond the age of 24, the consumption profile takes a relatively downward trend until the age of

60, corresponding to the retirement age in Senegal, then rises to 71 years before resuming the downward trend for the rest of the life cycle.

Graphic 1: Average Total Consumption Profiles

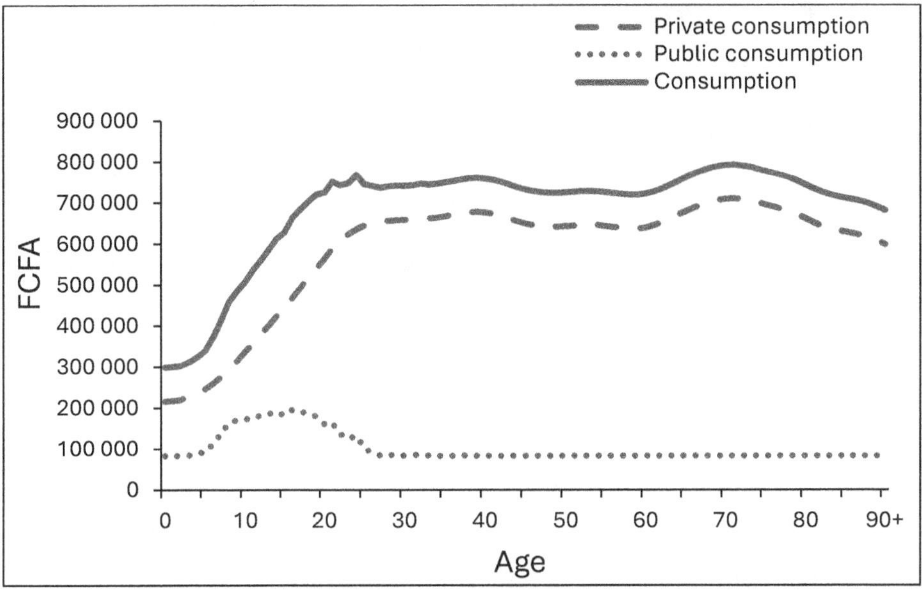

Source: National Team and CREG 2022 calculations

Aggregate Total Consumption Profile

The aggregate consumption of children aged 0 years increased from 112 to 140 billion from 2011 to 2019; On the other hand, it ranges from 78 billion for individuals aged 40 to 109 billion from 2011 to 2019, and from 34 billion for people aged 60 to 54 billion from 2011 to 2019.

It should also be noted that the 12-22 age group, which had the highest level of aggregate consumption in 2011 with a level of around 160 billion francs for each age, was replaced by the 8-14 age group in 2019, ranging from 217,209 to 236,608 billion.

Graphic 2: Aggregate Total Consumption Profiles

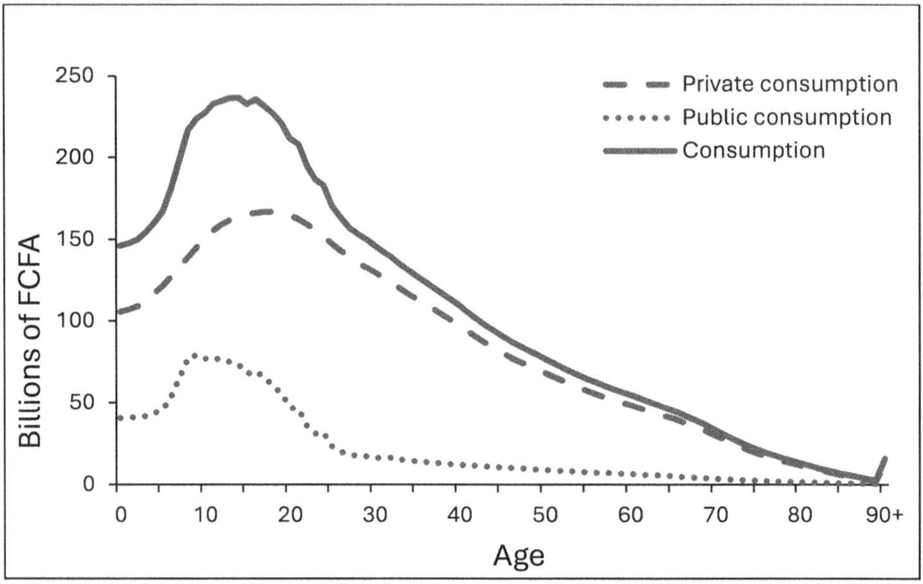

Source: National Team and CREG 2022 calculations

Average Total Labor Income Profile

The shape of the graph of total labor income almost mirrors that obtained previously between wage income and that of self-employment. It can be seen from the graph that from the age of 10 only, the income from work amounts to 6,145 CFA francs. Beyond that, it increases exponentially to reach its maximum level of 1,489,593 CFA francs at the age of 50. Considering the age group 31 to 56 years old, income from work is higher at this level with incomes varying between 1,054,863 FCFA and 1,608,709 FCFA held by individuals aged 47. As for individuals who are retired (60 years and over), they have an average working income equivalent to 741,682 CFA francs.

Graphic 3: Average Total Labor Income Profile

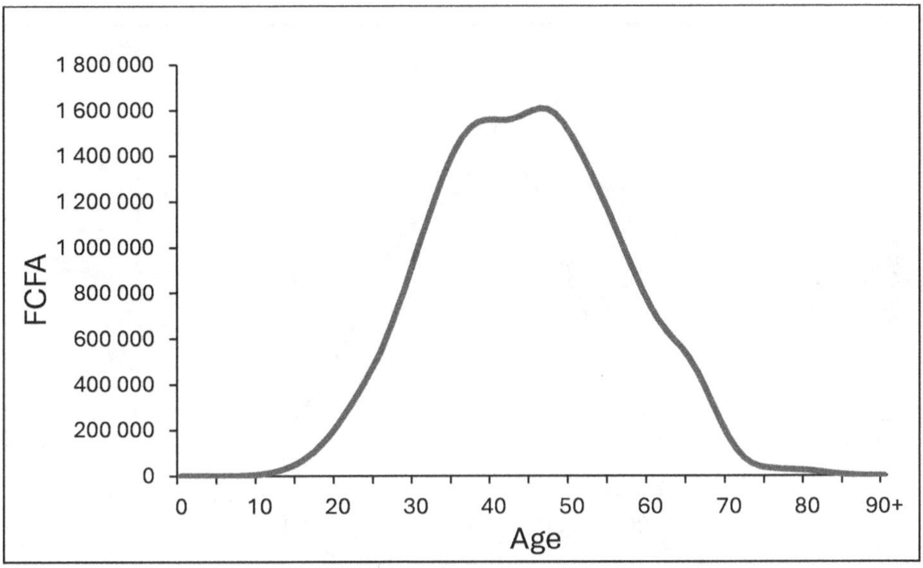

Source: national team and CREG, 2022

Aggregate Profiles of Total Labor Income

For the aggregate profile of income from salaried labor, it has an inverted U-shape. Indeed, the income from salaried work increases from 1 billion CFA francs at the age of 1 year to reach 108 billion CFA francs (maximum value) at 10 years. From this peak, the income from self-employment will gradually decrease to 1 billion for those aged 73 and over.

Compared to income from self-employment, income from salaried work remains relatively low from the age of 30 until the end of the life cycle. From birth to age 30, income from wage labor is slightly higher.

Graphic 4: Aggregate Profile of Total Labor Income

Source: national team and CREG, 2022

Average life cycle deficit

As for the average LCD, it is positive between the age groups 0-35 years and 60 years and older. In the first age group, the average LCD reached its peak at the age of 18 with more than 200,000 FCFA while in the last age group, the peak is noted between 79-82 years old with 400,000 FCFA. The average negative LCD concerns the 36-59 age group, and the peak is reached at 49 and 52 years old with about 200,000 FCFA.

Graphic 5: Average consumption and labor income profiles

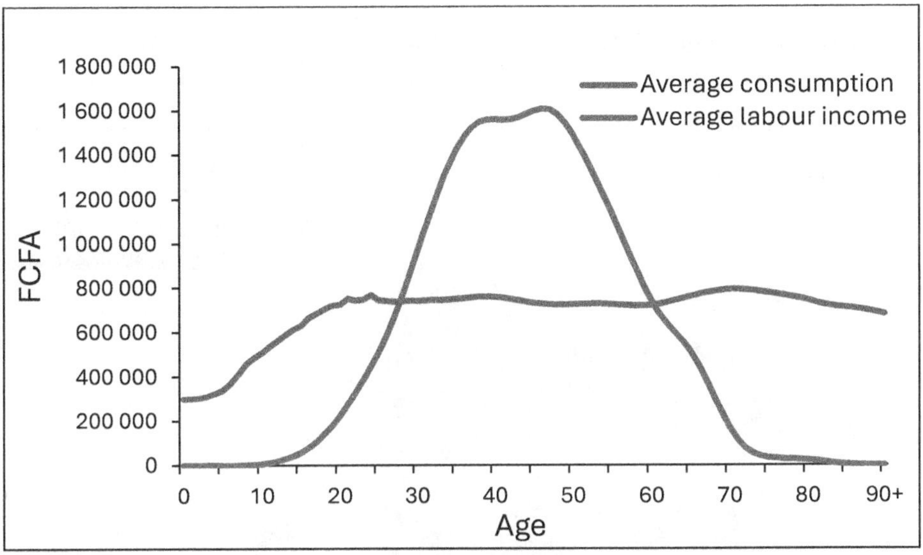

Source: national team and CREG, 2022

Graphic 6: Average Life Cycle Deficit Profile

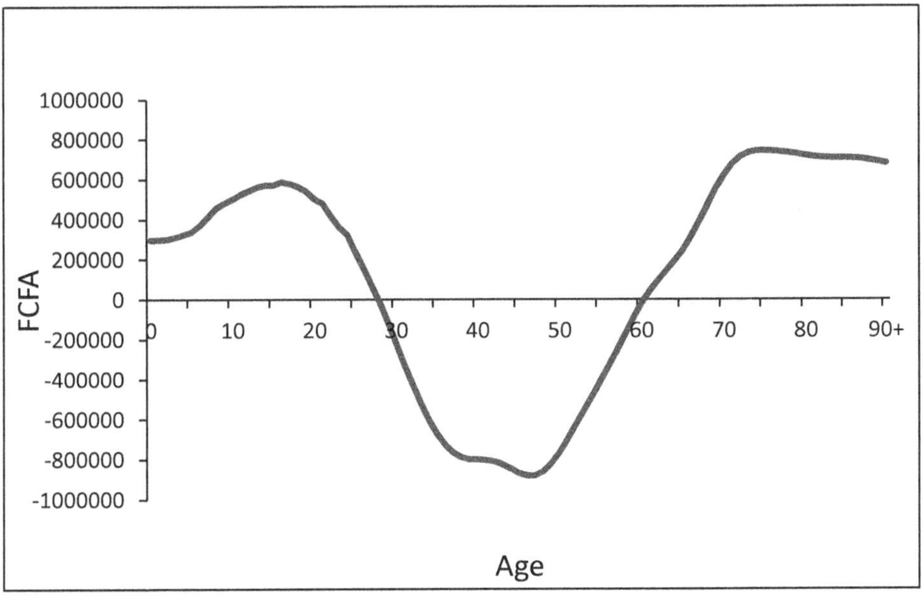

Source: national team and CREG, 2022

Aggregate life cycle deficit

Graphic 7: Aggregate Consumption and Income Profiles

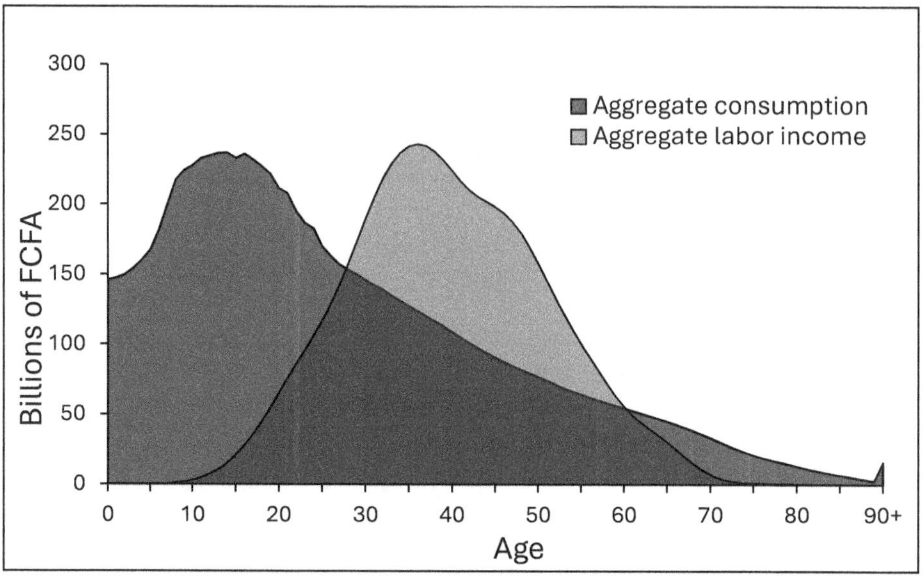

Source: national team and CREG, 2022

Graphic 8: Aggregate lifecycle deficit

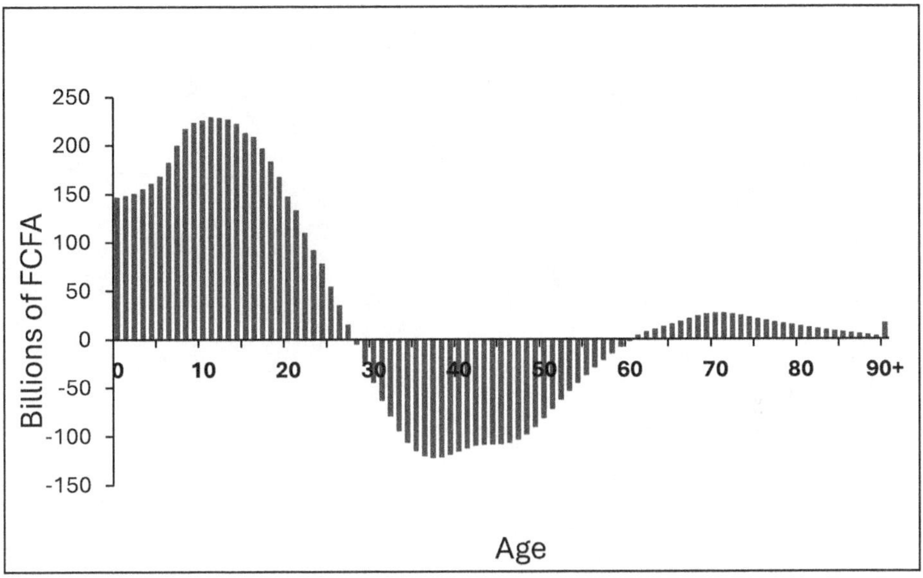

Source: national team and CREG, 2022

❖ **Factor analysis of countries' LCD-to-GDP ratio**

Figure 4: Multiple Correspondence Analysis (MCA)

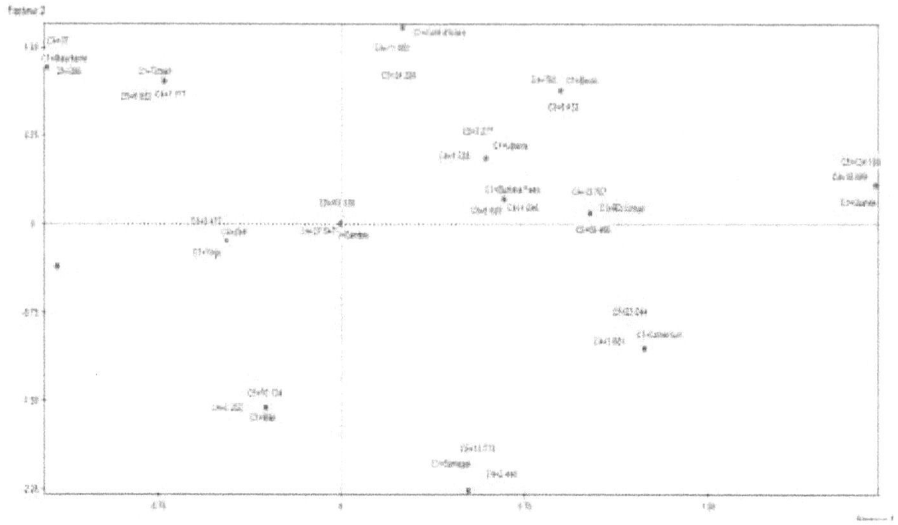

The factor analysis results provide a first insight into the positioning of countries in relation to the factors. The results first show that The Gambia is positioned in the center as a reference point with an LCD and a very high GDP. Then, countries like Ivory Coast, Benin, Liberia, Burkina Faso, Congo, and Guinea are closer and are on the same beach in the top right. Cameroon and Senegal are closer and are positioned on the lower right compared to Gambia. Finally, we notice that Mauritania and Chad are closer and are on the top left compared to Gambia. Togo and Mali are closer and are positioned at the bottom left of the country of The Gambia.

In short, the positioning of countries has been carried out in a general way in relation to GDP. The observation shows that the countries with the highest GDPs have grouped on the right and the countries with low GDPs on the left.

Section 5: Discussions

Consumption in the NTAs consists of public and private consumption. The counterpart of the System of National Accounts (SNA) aggregates is final consumption expenditure minus value-added and other consumption taxes.

Public consumption: public consumption distinguishes between three items of expenditure: health, education and other public goods and services. Public spending on health and education is affected by age, based mainly on administrative records. Budget data are used to estimate education per pupil as well as expenditure by level of education. These data are then combined with age and enrolment rate to estimate public education consumption per capita and age. The methods used to allocate public health spending are more varied and more prone to error. In some countries, for example, the age profiles of inpatients and outpatients are used and combined with cost estimates per inpatient or not. In others, very detailed estimates of public health spending by age are available from government agencies or polling institutes. The per capita and age profile of government consumption expenditure on other goods and services, such as military forces, roads and sewerage, is assumed to be constant by age (Lee and Mason 2011).

Private consumption: Symmetrically, private consumption is made up of three items, with expenditure related to education, expenditure on health, and finally other private expenditure apart from health and education. The allocation of private expenditure on education is based on the estimation of a regression model explaining household expenditure on education according to the number of children in school of each age. A similar procedure is used for health expenditure, which is estimated by a linear model based on the number of individuals of each age in the household. Other private consumption expenditure follows a discretionary allocation rule that sets exogenous weights for everyone in the household based on age (United Nations, 2013). The equivalence scale used assigns a value of 0.4 to children up to and including the age of 4, then this value increases proportionally with age until age 20 when it becomes equal to 1, and finally it remains constant beyond this age.

Labor income profiles

Labor income is the sum of wage income and self-employment income. Income from salaried work is made up of wages and social security contributions paid by employers. Self-employment income refers to the remuneration of the work of individuals who are self-employed.

The demographic dividend is the acceleration of economic growth that can result from a rapid decline in a country's fertility and subsequent changes in the structure of the population by age group. With fewer births each year, a country's working-age population is growing more relative to the young dependent population. With more people in the workforce and fewer young dependents, a country can tap into an opportunity for rapid economic growth with the right economic, social, and policy investments developed in health, education, governance, and the economy. While the benefits of a dividend can be significant, the gains are neither automatic nor guaranteed.

To realize a demographic dividend, countries need to make strategic investments in four key areas:

The evolution of the age structure of the population

As a first step, countries must go through a demographic transition with the decline of high birth and death rates. Although most countries have made significant progress in reducing mortality, countries that continue to experience sustained high levels of fertility are not ready to achieve a demographic dividend. As long as fertility rates and the resulting population growth rates remain high, the size of the child and adolescent population will be larger than that of the working-age adult population. Under these conditions, families and governments will generally not have the resources to invest in children's health and well-being and will not be able to make progress toward the dividend.

To achieve a demographic transition, countries must first focus on reducing fertility. A key strategy to achieve this goal is to provide women and men with information and services on voluntary family planning. In developing countries, one in four women does not want to get pregnant or wants to delay or space births but does not use any modern family planning methods.

These women account for nearly 80 per cent of unintended pregnancies.

Other factors, particularly education and child survival, contribute to the adoption of family planning and the decline in fertility.

When women can choose when and how far apart their pregnancies are, they are more likely to have fewer children and can more easily choose the size of the family they want to have. When women use modern contraception, the age structure of a country's population can begin to change, paving the way for the demographic dividend.

Investing in health programs for children and women

A demographic dividend depends on a healthy population. Investments in child survival play a key role in keeping fertility levels low. As child survival improves, the desire for a smaller family and the demand for family planning will increase. For children to make the most of educational opportunities, they need to be healthy and attentive at school. Health programs that vaccinate, prevent and treat the many common infections will help children excel in school and, in the long run, become better skilled workers. Good nutrition promotes cognitive development in infants and young children and promotes children's health.

When children become teenagers, their health needs change. They must have access to reproductive health information and services to prevent unwanted pregnancies, and to prevent HIV and sexually transmitted infections that can hinder educational opportunities, especially for girls. As young people develop behaviors that will shape the rest of their lives, health programs must address the issues related to tobacco use, excessive alcohol consumption, physical inactivity and obesity that place an increased burden on the health sector.

Appropriate care during pregnancy and childbirth plays a key role in reducing maternal and child mortality. For young women, family planning can help delay first pregnancy to an age when they are physically, psychologically, and socially prepared for motherhood. Delaying a first birth improves the health of both mother and child.

Education of children and youth

To fuel a country's economic growth, both boys and girls must have access to education. In the case of girls, education, especially at the secondary level, can delay the age at marriage and the first pregnancy. As countries enjoy a demographic dividend, they will need to adapt education policies in response to the changing needs of their labor markets. Training may be needed for the lowest-skilled and hardest-working jobs, as well as to improve the efficiency and added value of agricultural production. In addition, as the economy develops and diversifies, workers will need to acquire a variety of skills in business, technology and other types of trade.

Promoting good governance

In addition to health and education, an enabling environment for achieving a demographic dividend requires good governance, which helps attract domestic and foreign investment to local economies. Because the demographic transition is leading to a decline in the number of children to be cared for, households gradually have more income and savings that they can invest in their own businesses or in others. Similarly, good governance is essential to attract foreign investment that can create jobs and stimulate economic growth. Other aspects of good governance are equally important, such as reducing corruption and ensuring the operational effectiveness of governments.

Good governance also promotes gender equality. A gender-equitable environment promotes a demographic transition by enabling women to access and use family planning without the many barriers they currently face, particularly in developing countries. Women can therefore contribute more to the economic well-being of the family by working outside the home. In addition, more educated women are in higher-paying jobs and use their income to improve their children's human capital. Other policies that promote gender equality, such as access to credit and the right to inherit property and assets, reflect an environment that allows women to save and invest.

Conclusion

The demographic dividend is not automatic. It depends on both creating the opportunity and capitalizing on that opportunity for a specific set of policies and environments; This makes the demographic dividend a time-sensitive phenomenon.

All countries must empower, train and employ young people and people of working age to generate a demographic dividend. Similarly, public actions promoting a voluntary decline in fertility are a sine qua non condition for obtaining this dividend. Public action makes it possible to guarantee rights and freedoms, the services and information necessary for development, universal and quality coverage in education and health, and the political climate necessary for private investment. In addition, increasing the number of public jobs in health and education can have a multiplier effect on the demographic dividend, by promoting formal employment and providing the professionals needed for universal education and health coverage.

The private sector provides 90 per cent of jobs in developing countries and the best prospects for full and formal employment (one of the keys to increasing GDP per capita). Private sector partners can help anticipate labor needs, identify skills gaps, and provide the technical and vocational, initial and continuing training required to ensure that the education provided is in the context of economic growth. The private sector, in partnership with government and civil society, can better understand the current impediments to employment growth and help develop critical infrastructure and reform policies.

However, there is a need for countries to put in place policies with long-term impacts to reap the benefits of DD on the one hand through the creation of an environment conducive to growth through economic policies; the integration of new workers into the economy through a labor policy; increasing the supply of new skilled workers through education policies. And on the other hand, to prolong DD through economic policies, employment policies, health policies.

Bibliographical references

CREFAT, (2018), Training Manual on the Monitoring Dimensions and Indicators of the Demographic Dividend Observatory. 154 pages.

CREG, (2021), National Transfer Accounts Methodology, https://ordd.creg-center.org/wp-content/uploads/2021/05/Methodologie-NTA-CREG-CENTER-2021.pdf

DRAMANI L. and BIAO B (2017), Methodology for the Building of national transfer accounts, Training Manual-CREFAT, Thiès, Senegal, 210 p.

DRAMANI L, (2015), Generational Economy and Demographic Dividend: Diagnostic Elements in Senegal, L'Harmattan, Dakar, Senegal, Volume 1-210p.

POPULATION REFERENCE BUREAU, (2012), Achieving a Demographic Dividend vol. 67, no. 2, https://www.prb.org/wp-content/uploads/2013/10/Population-Bulletin-2013-67-2-achieving-demographic-dividend_fr.pdf

POPULATION REFERENCE BUREAU "Africa and the Demographic Dividend", 2013.

UNFPA: Capturing the Demographic Dividend: Empowering Women and Capitalizing on Youth, https://www.sweddafrica.org/sites/default/files/2022-10/Le-Magazine-de-lAfrique_dossier_unfpa_tire_a_part_16_pages.pdf

WORLD BANK, UNFPA, CREG (2016) Profile of Mauritania's Demographic Dividend, https://wcaro.unfpa.org/sites/default/files/pub-pdf/unfpa-dividende-fr-_0.pdf

CHAPTER 4

THE DDMI (DEMOGRAPHIC DIVIDEND MONITORING INDEX)

Introduction

The demographic dividend is the accelerated economic growth resulting from a change in the age structure of a population, because of a decline in fertility and mortality. It is a phenomenon that creates an opportunity for faster economic growth and human development for a country. Its capture becomes a major development challenge in the coming decades. It is in this dynamic that the African Union (AU), to take full advantage of the demographic dividend, has put in place a strategic framework (Agenda 2063) aimed at transforming Africa into a global power of the future. To achieve its objective of inclusive and sustainable development, the Heads of State and Government of the African Union, in the implementation of Agenda 2063, adopted a roadmap whose theme is "Harnessing the full benefits of the demographic dividend by investing in youth". This roadmap serves as a solid foundation to place African countries on the path to achieving this objective and is based on four (04) pillars which are:

- Employment and entrepreneurship.
- Education and skills development.
- Health and wellness.
- Youth Rights, Governance and Empowerment.

Thus, Africa is committed to transforming its huge youth population into an asset for its development. For example, Senegal, which, like other countries in sub-Saharan Africa characterized by rapid population growth, presents challenges in terms of meeting basic social needs and accelerating the demographic transition, has recently set up a National Observatory of the Demographic Dividend. The Observatory is a monitoring and analysis tool that informs decision-making on population and development issues by drawing on demographic, economic and social data. Its mission is to produce each year, a synthesis report and five other specific reports dealing with the five dimensions of the demographic dividend in relation to the four pillars of the African Union's roadmap.

Indeed, pillar 1 "Employment and entrepreneurship" which is related to the structure of the population, the subjective economy and the normative economy can be monitored through the indicators produced in the following dimensions:

- Coverage of Economic Dependency (dimension 1),
- Quality of the Living Environment (dimension 2),
- Dynamics of Poverty (dimension 3).

The second pillar "Education and skills development" and the third pillar "Health and well-being" which address health and education issues can be measured by the indicators of dimension 4 "Expanded Human Development Index". Finally, the last pillar, namely "Rights, governance and empowerment of youth", in relation to governance and institutions can be evaluated with dimension 5 "Networks and Territories".

Section 1: Economic Dependency Coverage Index (EDCI)

Dimension definition and description

Economic dependence is defined as a situation where an individual's income from work is lower than his consumption. In this case, the deficit is financed by the work of other individuals (transfers in particular, income from working people) or by dissaving. Numerous studies have focused on this (Bloom et al., 2006; Lee and Mason, 2011; Dramani, 2016; Dramani and Oga, 2017). EDCI estimates the share of deficits in economically dependent age groups covered by the surplus income generated by age groups with an economic surplus. It measures the capacity of a given country to satisfy social demand or to fill the consumption gap of economically dependent individuals solely on resources derived from work.

Fundamental equation of NTAs and the concept of the life cycle deficit

The NTAs are based on an accounting equation that states that, at each age, resources must be equal to the uses made of them (United Nations, 2013):

$$\underbrace{Y^l(a) + Y^a(a) + \tau^+(a)}_{\text{Inflows}} = \underbrace{C(a) + S(a) + \tau^-(a)}_{\text{Outflows}}$$

The left-hand side consists of all the current inputs of age group (a): labor income $Y^l(a)$, capital income $Y^k(a)$, wealth income $Y^p(a)$ and transfers received $\tau+(a)$. The right-hand side consists of all outflows of age group (a): consumption C(a), savings S(a) and transfers paid $\tau-(a)$. Thus, according to this equation, the sum of labor income, capital income, wealth income and transfers received must equal the sum of consumption, savings and transfers paid. This identity is obtained for both aggregate and per capita values at each age. The above equation shows all values indexed by age (a), but the identity is also valid for national aggregates, in other words, all age groups combined.

By rearranging the terms of inflows and outflows to match the conceptual foundations of NTAs, the equation helps to highlight the economic life cycle and the economic mechanisms used to reallocate resources across ages. The economic life cycle is represented on the left-hand side (of the equation below) by the life cycle deficit which corresponds, for a given age (a), to the difference between consumption and labor income ($LCD(a)=C(a)-Y^l(a)$).

This life-cycle deficit gives rise to reallocation of resources between ages in the form of either net public or private transfers ($\tau(a)=\tau+(a)+\tau-(a)$) or asset reallocations ($Y^k(a)+Y^p(a)-S(a)$). This has materialized on the right-hand side of the following equation:

$$C(a) - Y^l(a) = Y^a(a) - S(a) + \tau^+(a) - \tau^-(a)$$

Life Cycle Deficit (LCD)	Assets Based Reallocations	Net Transfer
	Age Reallocations	

Each stream in the equation is disaggregated to distinguish between public and private.

Building of consumption and labor income profiles

To determine which age groups, use more than income and which age groups are lower than income, it is necessary to determine the age profiles of consumption and income. This is done in several steps described as follows: the determination of an age profile at the individual level for a given flow, based on data from household surveys or administrative data. Data from the Harmonized Survey on Household Living Conditions (EHCVM-2018) are used for household consumption profiles. The data mobilized come from the State budget, education statistical yearbooks, and other administrative documents. These profiles from survey data can be a bit heckled because of the sample sizes. For this reason, they have been smoothed over the ages to make them more homogeneous; the use of demographic data to construct provisional aggregated (and no longer individual) profiles by age. Let x(a) be the value of a variable at the individual level for the age group (a), or N(a) the size of that age group, the aggregate profile X is $X = \Sigma x(a)*N(a)$; adjustment of the provisional profiles by the use of macroeconomic aggregates from the national accounts, so that the aggregate flow X coincides with the accounting control value at the corresponding aggregate level C. The age profiles are adjusted by the correction factor $c = C/X$. The adjusted profiles are $xaj = x*c$ at the individual level and $Xaj = X*c$ at the aggregate level. These adjusted profiles make it possible to eliminate possible sampling biases and to make the national transfer accounts compatible with public accounting.

Thus, two types of empirical work must be carried out. First, the required macroeconomic aggregates must be calculated, based on the national accounts. Secondly, it is necessary to estimate the individual (average) profiles by age that will make it possible to break down these macroeconomic variables.

Consumption profiles

Consumption in the NTAs consists of public and private consumption. The counterpart of the System of National Accounts (SNA) aggregates is final consumption expenditure minus value-added taxes and other consumption taxes.

Public consumption: public consumption distinguishes between three items of expenditure: health, education and other public goods and services. Public spending on health and education is affected by age, based mainly on administrative records. Budget data are used to estimate education per pupil as well as expenditure by level of education. These data are then combined with age and enrolment rate to estimate public education consumption per capita and age. The methods used to allocate public health spending are more varied and more prone to error. In some countries, for example, the age profiles of inpatients and outpatients are used and combined with cost estimates per inpatient or not. In others, very detailed estimates of public health spending by age are available from government agencies or polling institutes. The per capita and age profile of government consumption expenditure on other goods and services, such as military forces, roads and sewerage, is assumed to be constant by age (Lee and Mason 2011).

Private consumption: Symmetrically, private consumption is made up of three items, with expenditure on education, health, and other private expenditure apart from health and education. The allocation of private expenditure on education is based on the estimation of a regression model explaining household expenditure on education according to the number of children in school of each age. A similar procedure is used for health expenditure, which is estimated by a linear model based on the number of individuals of each age in the household. Other private consumption expenditure follows a discretionary allocation rule that sets exogenous weights for everyone in the household based on age (United Nations, 2013).

The equivalence scale used assigns a value of 0.4 to children up to and including the age of 4, then this value increases proportionally with age until age 20 or it becomes equal to 1, and finally it remains constant beyond this age. The age profile for each type of consumption (education, health, other) is obtained by averaging the consumption by age of all members for all households.

Labor income profiles

Labor income is the sum of wage income and self-employment income.

- Wage income: the age profile of wage income is calculated directly from survey data, taking the age average of wages and wage components.

- Self-employment income: The self-employment income profile is obtained from survey data by calculating the average age of the income of self-employed workers if the data allow it.

However, in the case only mixed income is available for the whole household, the approach advocated in the NTA is to treat two-thirds (2/3) of the reported mixed income as attributable to work and to distribute this family labor income to the household's self-employed (including unpaid family workers) in accordance with the proportion of the average labor income of employees of the same age.

Method of calculating the dimension indicator

- **Economic support ratio and demographic dividend**

Beyond the economic life cycle analysis, the NTAs make it possible to determine the Economic Support Ratio (ESR) and to measure the demographic dividend. ESR is an indicator designed to capture the weight that workers feel from the consumers to be taken care of (United

Nations, 2013). It is determined by dividing the number of actual employees (L) by the number of actual consumers (N):

$$\boldsymbol{ESR} = \frac{\boldsymbol{L}}{\boldsymbol{N}} = \frac{\sum_{\alpha} \boldsymbol{\varphi(\alpha)} * \boldsymbol{P(\alpha)}}{\sum_{\alpha} \boldsymbol{\rho(\alpha)} * \boldsymbol{P(\alpha)}}$$

The number of actual workers of a given age (a) is obtained by weighing the population of age a by φ(a)φ(a) which represents the productivity of labor at age (a). This labor productivity at age (a) is understood by labor income at age (a) in relation to the average income of individuals aged between 30 and 49. The numerator therefore considers actual participation in the labor market as well as the level of labor income by age and is not restricted to the labor force a priori.

Similarly, at a given age (a), the number of actual users is given by the size of the population of age (a) multiplied by the ratio between per capita consumption at age (a) and the average consumption of individuals aged between 30 and 49. The denominator considers the variation in consumption needs according to age.

The ESR is calculated on the entire population by measuring for each year of age (with reference to individuals aged between 30 and 49) what the level of work (through income) and the level of consumption of individuals at the age in question is worth. Thus, the ESR reflects both the effect of the age structure and the age profiles of consumption and income production. In terms of interpretation, the ESR therefore represents the number of effective workers per actual consumer. Thus, compared to 100, a support ratio of 45% means that there are 45 effective workers for every 100 effective consumers. When this ratio increases over time, it means that the actual worker bears fewer consumers, which frees up economic resources and corresponds to a capture of the demographic dividend. The demographic dividend is therefore apprehended by the growth rate of the economic support ratio.

- **Life Cycle Deficit Coverage Indicator**

The Economic Dependency Coverage Indicator (EDCI) is an extension of the Life Cycle Deficit (LCD). EDCI refers to the ratio of the surplus generated by economically independent age groups to the deficit of the economically dependent age groups. Mathematically, EDCI is determined as follows:

- $$\mathbf{EDCI} = -\frac{\sum_a \mathbf{LCD(a)D}_{[C(a)<YL(a)]}}{\sum_a \mathbf{LCD(a)D}_{[C(a)\geq YL(a)]}}$$

Where denotes the life-cycle deficit at age a; is an indicator function that takes the value 1 if the individual's consumption is less than his or her income from work and 0 otherwise, and an indicator function that takes the value 1 if the individual's consumption is greater than or equal to his or her income from work and 0 otherwise.

$$\mathrm{LCD(a)D}_{[C(a)<YL(a)]}\mathrm{D}_{[C(a)\geq YL(a)]}$$

The EDCI can also be written as:

- $$\mathbf{EDCI} = \frac{\textbf{Aggregate surplus}}{\textbf{Aggregate deficit}_{\textbf{Youth}} + \textbf{Aggregate deficit}_{\textbf{Ageing}}}$$

The EDCI estimates the share of deficits in economically dependent age groups covered by the surplus income generated by age groups with an economic surplus. It measures the capacity of a given country to satisfy social demand or to fill the consumption gap of economically dependent individuals solely on resources derived from work.

Interpretation of the results

Table 7: Economic Dependency Coverage Index (EDCI)

Country	Sex	EDCI
BENIN 2019	Man	100
	Woman	50,3
	Both	75,5
BURKINA FASO 2018	Man	80,2
	Woman	26,4
	Both	49,4
CAMEROON 2019	Man	100
	Woman	0
	Both	48,8
COTE D'IVOIRE 2019	Man	58,8
	Woman	0
	Both	14,2
GUINEA 2019	Man	100
	Woman	13,3
	Both	60,1
MAURITANIA 2019	Man	100

Country	Sex	EDCI
	Woman	0,1
	Both	58,8
SENEGAL 2019	Man	100
	Woman	8,5
	Both	50,5
CHAD 2018	Man	95,4
	Woman	0,1
	Both	41,6
TOGO 2018	Man	100
	Woman	28,8
	Both	50,5

Section 2: Quality of Living Environment Indicator (QLEI)

Dimension definition and description

The notion of living environment is very frequently used in territorial marketing and theories on the attractiveness of territories. In this sense, the quality of the living environment is on the one hand oriented towards access to "natural" environments or environments perceived as such, and sometimes to local services. In fact, it is all the facilities and services necessary for community life (e.g., school, health, recreational, commercial, cultural, etc.) and which are essential to ensure the existence, development and sometimes even the survival of several communities. On the other hand, it is a question of avoiding real or perceived nuisances such as pollution, insecurity, or congestion of transport networks. The living environment is fundamentally linked to the place of residence.

- **Housing conditions**

Housing is essential to meet basic needs, but it is not just about having four walls and a roof. Housing conditions are understood here by the number of rooms per person, access to sanitary facilities, mainly toilets, and the cost of housing (CREFAT, 2018).

- **Social Links**

Social ties are defined as the set of cultural, social, economic and political ties that link individuals in their daily lives within various groups and that ensure social integration both from the point of view of the individual and of society. The quality of the social network is the indicator that measures social ties. It is expressed by the proportion of individuals who have relatives or friends they can rely on in times of need. (CREFAT, 2018).

- **Environment**

The environment is defined as the set of biological, chemical and physical factors interacting with man and his activities (Stockholm, 1972). In the context of the quality of the living environment, the environment is characterized by two indicators: water quality and atmospheric pressure. The first indicator is defined as the percentage of individuals satisfied with the quality of their water and the second as the average annual concentration in micrograms per cubic meter of fine particles in residential neighborhoods (CREFAT, 2018).

- **Civic Engagement and Governance**

Civic engagement and good governance are key elements in achieving the SDGs. Stakeholder participation in regulation-making and electoral participation are indicators of civic engagement and governance. Stakeholder engagement measures the degree of government transparency in the regulatory development processes. As for the voter turnout indicator, it is the percentage of registered voters who voted in the most recent election.

- **Subjective well-being**

In the evaluation of the quality of the living environment, the measurement of feelings, although subjective, is an ideal complement to objective data to have a faithful picture of the real situation. Subjective data can provide a personal assessment of the health status, educational attainment, income, degree of well-being and social situation of the people concerned. Life satisfaction is the indicator that measures subjective well-being. This indicator is the overall judgment that individuals have about their lives, rather than their feelings at the time.

- **Security**

Security is a state in which hazards and conditions that may cause physical, psychological or material harm are controlled in a manner that safeguards the health and well-being of individuals and the community. The indicators of safety measures are people's sense of safety when walking alone at night and the homicide rate. The indicator of people's sense of safety when walking alone at night is the percentage of people who report feeling safe when walking alone at night. As for homicide rates, it is the annual number of intentional homicides per 100,000 individuals.

- **Work-life balance**

Time spent on leisure time and self-employment and long working hours are indicators for measuring work-life balance. Time spent on leisure and self is the average number of minutes per day spent on leisure and personal concerns such as sleeping and eating. Heavy work schedules are the percentage of employees working at least fifty (50) hours per week on average.

1- **A brief reminder of the theoretical basis**

The quality of the living environment is a complex and multi-dimensional concept that requires different definitions and approaches. In the early 1970s, in their paper "Is growth obsolete?", William Nordhaus and James Tobin proposed an indicator based on "adjusted GNP" by adding monetary equivalents of leisure and time spent on domestic activity.

According to Richard Easterlin (1974), in the United States between 1945 and 1970, the proportion of people who said they were happy had remained the same, while the average per capita income had increased by 60%. Similarly, the concept of quality of the living environment includes housing conditions, cleanliness, quality of outdoor spaces, proximity to services, improved sense of security, social ties, etc. It also aims to highlight the "blind spot" of GDP and national accounts (Stiglitz-Sen-Fitoussi, 2009) and completes the picture that can be had of national production.

Its measurement requires several data expressed in different units. According to the OECD (2013), the quality of the living environment is a: "set of elements surrounding a person's life; environment in which one lives, considered from the point of view of its influence on the quality of life". It defines eleven sub-dimensions considered essential in the quality of the living environment (the broadest). These sub-dimensions make it possible to directly or indirectly capture individual well-being (money alone cannot represent individual well-being). The living environment is thus divided into two main families: quality of life and material conditions.

Jeanneaux P. (2006) defines the living environment as a "mixed collective good under the influence of public authorities", and which is composed of 2 types of infrastructure: a material infrastructure and an informational infrastructure. Physical infrastructure consists of private economic goods, public goods provided by public authorities and natural assets. The information infrastructure, on the other hand, is a set of rules applicable to the media assets and governing their uses. For Colletis and Pecqueur (1995), the living environment is made up of "localized environmental goods" that can be assets or resources.

According to the OECD (2013), the living environment is defined as the set of elements surrounding a person's life. In other words, the living environment is the environment in which we live, considered from the point of view of its influence on the quality of life.

From a sustainable development perspective, a quality living environment has been defined as "an environment where one feels safe, which offers a healthy environment and in which the use of the car (at least solo driving) tries to be minimized. It is not a dormitory area, a place of uniformity and individualism. This environment must be plural, both in terms of functions and human resources, friendly and have character. It is also an environment in which it is possible to live and work, and which is part of a policy of parsimonious use of land and space.

To construct indicators of the quality of the living environment of the municipalities of Wallonia (SWITZERLAND) from a sustainable development perspective, the CAPRU of the Economics and Rural Development Unit (2014) reviewed the literature on the concept of "living environment" as well as its constituent dimensions. It appears that the living environment is a complex concept that does not admit to an unequivocal definition, but of many formulations through the problems it raises. The most frequent dimensions in the literature were safety, pollution and nuisances, places of services and consumption, social mix, heritage, residential space, green spaces, mobility and employment.

Method of calculating the dimension indicator

The quality of the living environment will be apprehended by a light survey in the regional/departmental capitals. This method is derived from the OECD's Better Life Index. QLEI is obtained by taking the weighted average of the normalized indices of the subdimensions.

- **The « Better Life Index »**

The Better Life Index is an economic indicator created by the OECD in 2011 to allow people to compare countries according to their own preferences using 11 themes (see figure below) that are considered essential for well-being.

Figure: OECD Framework for Assessing Well-being and Progress

Figure 5: Better Life Initiative

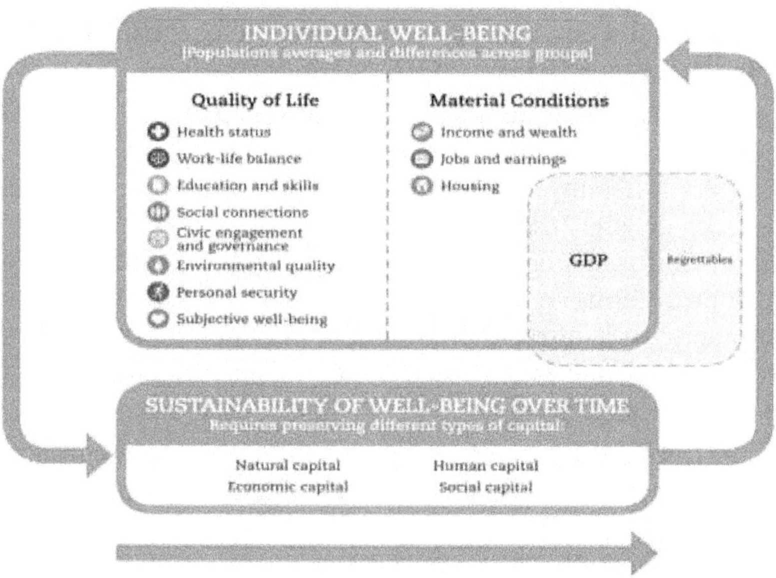

Source: OECD, 2013

The Better Life Index is part of the OECD's Better Life Initiative, launched in May 2011. This initiative is based on the report of the Stiglitz-Sen-Fitoussi Commission on the measurement of economic performance and social progress.

The eleven well-being criteria used in this indicator were selected based on both theory and practice, and after consultation on how best to measure well-being for comparison purposes.

Measuring well-being and progress is one of the main objectives of the OECD in the framework of the Better Life Initiative through various research axes and other ongoing studies (OECD). For measures of well-being to have a real impact on people's lives, they must be integrated into the policy-making process, according to the organization. Bridging the gap between measures of well-being and policy intervention is therefore a challenge. Based on the OECD's framework for assessing well-being and progress, the organization is advancing these issues through various analytical work.

The agenda on measuring well-being requires new and better statistical measures to fill the gap between traditional economic statistics, which are sometimes used as proxy indicators for measuring people's well-being, and indicators that relate more directly to people's lives. The OECD has developed several guidelines and conceptual frameworks to help those who want to develop better measures of well-being and are advancing the well-being measurement agenda with various works.

Weights are assigned by users who construct and adapt their own indicator. To do this, the user must rate each criterion from 0 ("not important") to 5 ("very important") and set the weight as a fraction of this criterion so that the sum of all weights equals 100%.

Each well-being criterion is measured using one to four indicators. Within each criterion, the average of the indicators used with the same weighting is calculated.

Normalization is done using a classic formula that converts the original values of the indicators into numbers between 0 (the worst possible outcome) and 1 (the best possible outcome).

- **The quality of the living environment in the case of the DD observatory**

The measure of the quality of life in our case is based on seven of the eleven themes that make up the OECD's Better Life Index. The other four not included are considered in other dimensions, including the NTA profiles (income and wealth, employment and wages) and the human capital index (health, education).

The indicator is thus designed around the following seven fields: (i) Housing conditions; (ii) Social Ties; (iii) Environment; (iv) Civic engagement and governance; (v) Subjective well-being; (vi) Security (vi) Work-life balance.

Each field is apprehended by one or more indicators allowing international, regional or departmental comparison. It will be a question of providing a score corresponding to the sub-dimensional indicator to understand the level of quality achieved in each sub-dimension. The synthetic indicator of the quality of life is obtained by aggregating the sub-dimensional indicators. These results are presented at the national level to understand the level of quality of the living environment; but are also presented at the regional level to identify spatial disparities in terms of the quality of the living environment.

Interpretation of the results

Table 8: Quality of Living Environment Index (QLEI)

		QLEI
BENIN 2019	Man	55,4
	Woman	56,1
	Both	55,4
BURKINA FASO 2018	Man	50,6
	Woman	55,6
	Both	52,8
CAMEROON 2019	Man	60,8
	Woman	62,8
	Both	61,8
COTE D'IVOIRE 2019	Man	53,8
	Woman	54,8
	Both	54,2
GUINEA 2019	Man	59,1
	Woman	61,8
	Both	59,9
MAURITANIA 2019	Man	57,9
	Woman	56,1
	Both	57,8
SENEGAL 2019	Man	57,2
	Woman	62,9
	Both	59,7
CHAD 2018	Man	47,1
	Woman	46,5
	Both	49,9
TOGO 2018	Man	49,5
	Woman	53
	Both	59,7

Source: CREG 2022

Section 3: Poverty Exit Synthetic Indicator (PESI)

Dimension definition and description

Poverty measurement and analysis are of particular importance in the process of monitoring and evaluating the effectiveness of public policies, but also in monitoring developments about the capture of the demographic dividend. Sen's poverty index (Amartya Sen, Nobel Prize 1998) indicates the complexity and multidimensional nature of the notion of poverty. Dramani et al., (2010) attempt to explain intergenerational poverty in Senegal.

Moreover, in view of the high inequalities in the distribution of wealth and the high vulnerability of households in developing countries, it seems even more important to better understand the phenomenon of poverty and to better target populations at risk. In this respect, studies of poverty dynamics aim to identify individuals who enter or exit poverty over time and to analyze the main factors that play an important role in poverty mobility.

It is in this sense that the Poverty Exit Synthetic Indicator (PESI) is designed to measure transitions into poverty to assess the greater or lesser risk of population well-being improving or deteriorating relative to the decrease in persistence in poverty.

A brief reminder of the theoretical basis

This section addresses the review of the literature that highlights the aspects related to poverty, whether monetary or not, paying particular attention to the multidimensional poverty index which integrates other dimensions such as education, health, living conditions, etc.

The Multidimensional Poverty Index (MPI) is a new composite statistical indicator developed in 2007 by the Oxford Poverty and Human Development Initiative (OPHI) and used by the United Nations Development Program (UNDP). This multidimensional poverty index aims to summarize several aspects of non-monetary poverty through a single number. Indeed, since the work of (Sen, 1998) placed the human development dimension at the center of poverty, the non-monetary aspect was very important. Since people's well-being encompasses access to a variety of services that their current monetary situation may not allow them to access, including health services, education, electricity, clean water, and other aspects of quality of life.

Thus, the MPI modifies the vision of poverty by broadening its field of analysis to highlight the fact that a single deprivation is not always synonymous with poverty. For (Alkire, 2011), there is no context for

the multidimensionality of poverty. Because poverty is a complex phenomenon that encompasses several dimensions. Thus, to be poor is to be deprived of those basic social services that are essential to a life considered socially acceptable and morally decent, and this multidimensional approach to poverty highlights an accumulation of deprivations. For (Seck, 2021) these non-monetary aspects provide information
on the effective ability of individuals to function better in society and to flourish in it.

Poverty is perceived as a situation characterized by multiple and simultaneous deprivations. This approach complements measures of income poverty and subjective poverty. The Multidimensional Poverty Index (MPI) reported by the United Nations Development Program (UNDP) is calculated for most countries in the world. Indeed, to determine the MPI, it is necessary to base ourselves on surveys carried out in most countries with a frequency of 5 to 10 years. It allows comparisons to be made between countries around the world and is calculated each year by the OPHI (Oxford Poverty & Human Development Initiative). However, it is possible that the choice of indicator is less relevant in some countries. It is estimated that about 1.75 billion people live in multidimensional poverty in 104 developing countries. This is higher than the 1.44 billion people living on less than $1.25 a day, but lower than the 2.6 billion people living on less than $2 a day. The Building of the MPI tries to capture all the non-monetary aspects of poverty and to indicate the extent of household deprivation. Thus, this index is calculated based on three main dimensions: health, education and living conditions, which are composed of 10 specific indicators. Each dimension and indicator have a weight allocated, as well as the poverty line. The dimensions represent the aspects of non-monetary poverty considered. OPHI and UNDP have chosen three main ones: education, health and living conditions. The selected indicators should highlight the corresponding deprivations for each dimension. When constructing an MPI at the national level, it is therefore necessary to first select the appropriate dimensions and indicators.

A detailed and relevant discussion on the choice of dimensions and indicators can be found in the report by Alkire and Santos. The authors noted that the potential dimensions that a measure of poverty could reflect are quite broad and include health, education, standard of living, empowerment, work, environment, safety from violence, social relations, and culture among others. Since poverty is a multidimensional phenomenon, it has been addressed using both the monetary and non-monetary approaches. The MPI was 0.288 for Senegal in 2019, indicating that about 53.2%, or 8.4 million Senegalese, are in a situation of multidimensional poverty.

Moreover, according to the World Bank (World Bank, 2000), poverty is a state of pronounced deprivation of well-being.

Thus, it is characterized by the inability of one or more people to achieve a minimum acceptable level of material well-being. This definition raises two questions: that of the identification of poor people and that of data aggregation. Identifying poor populations in a society involves assessing the well-being of individuals and determining a threshold at which a person is considered poor. However, the assessment of individual or family well-being is complex because utility is never directly observable. Therefore, it is important to find a counterpart to well-being that can be observed. In this context, the World Bank (1990) indicates that there is sufficient theoretical basis for considering expenditure to be a good assessment of welfare. This analytical approach, Lachaud (1994) points out, assumes two hypotheses: the hypothesis of maximizing the utility of individuals and that of the goods consumed as the main elements of analysis. Non-monetary poverty, on the other hand, is defined as the inability to satisfy the needs considered primary in the community.

In addition to the lack of financial resources to purchase the goods needed to meet basic needs, non-monetary poverty considers qualitative aspects such as the inability of an individual or community to adequate food, clothing or housing, to participate in community life and to benefit from basic social services. There is a disability, independent of monetary income, that prevents poor people from enjoying a minimum acceptable level of well-being.

The main assumption underlying the multidimensional analysis of poverty is that the analysis of the economic aspects of poverty is insufficient, with income and consumption being very unsatisfactory indicators for understanding poverty (Martinetti (2000). Health, longevity, education, social relationships, and a state of serenity are components that should not be ignored when we are interested in raising the level of well-being of individuals in society. Several social scientists have focused on the multidimensional aspect of poverty. The sociologists' approach has led to the design of several indicators.

In recent decades, the economic debate in this area has undergone significant revitalization thanks to the work of Sen (1987, 1992, 1993, 1994, 1997), which gave rise to the capability approach. This approach is closely linked to the socio-demographic characteristics of the individuals concerned, as well as to their environment and the process of transforming the resources and opportunities available into well-being. The multidimensional approach has the advantage of considering only the material conditions of individuals but also their general living conditions.

Method of calculating the dimension indicator

Regarding methodologies relating to poverty dynamics, the World Bank recommends approaches that seek to capture the movements in and out of poverty in terms of probability, duration or frequency. In this specific context, the analytical method used in this dimension 3 is inspired by the work of Dang and Lanjouw (2013) and Dang, Lanjouw, Luoto and McKenzie (2011). These authors explore an alternative statistical methodology for the analysis of mobility within poverty, based on two or more cross-sectional data. Unlike traditional, pseudo-panel methods that require multiple cross-sectional data sets to study the dynamics of poverty at the cohort level, the methodology proposed by Dang and Lanjouw (2013) and Dang et al (2011) can be applied to parameters with as few as two rounds of surveys and allows for a more disaggregated analysis at the household level. In short, these authors start from an income model that they estimate using data from a first survey, using a specification that includes only time-invariant variables. Parameter estimates from this model are then applied to the same atemporal explanatory variables from a second survey to obtain an estimate of the first survey income (unobserved) for respondents in that second survey. The transition analysis can then be based on the real income observed at the level of the second survey with this income estimated for the first survey. These observations constitute the pseudo panel or, in the authors' words, "the synthetic panel".

$$yi1 = b'1\ xi1 + \varepsilon i1 \quad (1)$$

Similarly, considering as the set of characteristics of household i in the round 2 survey that are observed in both round 1 and round 2, the linear projection of the income of round 2 (yi2) on xi2 is:

$$yi2 = b'1\ xi2 + \varepsilon i2 \quad (2)$$

Let Z1 and Z2 represent the poverty lines of period 1 (t1) and period 2 (t2) respectively. The objective is to estimate the joint distribution of poverty and non-poverty in t1 and t2. Like what:

P (yi1 < Z1 and yi2 > Z2) (3)

Which represents the probability of being poor at time t1 and of being non-poor at time t2.

Identifying the point estimate in (3) is not possible without imposing a structure on the data generating process. Since the probability in equation (3) depends on the joint distribution of the two error terms, the estimation of the bounds becomes simpler:

P (εi1 < z1 - β'1 xi1 et εi2 < z2 - β'2 xi2) (4)

The correlation between the two error terms captures the correlation of these parts of household income in the two periods that are explained by household characteristics xi1 and xi2. Intuitively, the more individuals cross the poverty line, the weaker the correlation between εi1 and εi2. An extreme case occurs when the two error terms are completely independent of each other. Another extreme case is obtained when these two error terms are perfectly correlated.

If the error terms εi1 and εi2 have a bivariate normal distribution with standard deviations σε1 and σε2 respectively and a known correlation coefficient ρ, then the estimation of relation (4) gives respectively and a known correlation coefficient ρ, then the estimation of equation (4) gives:

$$P(\varepsilon_{i1} < z_1 - \beta'_1 x_{i1} \; and \; (5) \varepsilon_{i2} > z_2 - \beta'_2 x_{i2}) = \Phi_2(\frac{z_1 - \beta'_1 x_{i1}}{\sigma_{\varepsilon 1}}, -\frac{z_2 - \beta'_2 x_{i2}}{\sigma_{\varepsilon 2}}, -\rho)$$

Where Φ2(.) represents the bivariate function of cumulative normal distribution (Φ2(.) being the density function of the bivariate normal distribution). However, the correlation coefficient ρ is not generally known.

In this case, Dang and Lanjouw (2013) suggest considering the approximation of the correlation coefficient ρyi1yi2 between the household consumption of the household in the two rounds, and then estimating ρ by the formula:

$$\rho = \frac{\rho_{y_{i1} y_{i2}} \sqrt{var(y_{i1}) var(y_{i2})} - \beta'_1 var(x_i) - \beta_2}{\sigma_{\varepsilon 1} \, \sigma_{\varepsilon 2}} \quad (6)$$

It should be noted that there are a few important assumptions to be made about this methodology. The first assumption requires that the population from which the sample comes is the same for the first and second rounds of surveys. This assumption will not be satisfied if, for example, the population changes through births, deaths or migrations.

The second hypothesis constrains the correlation between the error terms $\varepsilon i1$ and $\varepsilon i2$ to be non-negative. This assumption is taken into account in most methods using household survey data for at least three reasons: (i) if the error term contains a household fixed effect, then households that have higher income than predicted from the x variables in round 1 will also have higher income than what is predicted based on the x variables in round 2; (ii) if income shocks have some persistence, and if incomes respond to these shocks, then income errors will also exhibit a positive autocorrelation, and (iii) the type of factors that can lead to a negative correlation between incomes over time are unlikely to apply to an entire population at the same time.

In view of these assumptions, estimates of the upper bound of the transition from poverty are given by the probability in relation (5) when the two error terms are completely independent of each other, while estimates of the lower bound of the transition from poverty are given by the probability of expression (5) when the two terms of error are identical. Thus, equation (5) provides a framework for analyzing two-by-two movements in poverty (poor and non-poor) using the transition matrix. Indeed, it makes it possible to determine the following indicators:

– **PP** refers to individuals (or households) who were poor in period t1 who have always remained poor in period t2. So, they have not changed their state of poverty. Thus, PP stands for chronic poverty or poverty traps.

– **NPP** refers to those who were non-poor in the t1 period but fell into poverty in the t2 period.

– **PNP** refers to those who were poor at the start (i.e. in year t1) but who emerged from poverty in year t2.

– **NPNP** includes individuals (or households) who experienced a prolonged state of non-poverty over the two years t1 and t2. The NPNP indicator therefore refers to pure non-poverty. Without any indication to the contrary, this nomenclature is adopted throughout the rest of the document.

Poverty Exit Synthetic Index (PESI)

At the level of dimension 3, the composite indicator used is the poverty exit synthetic index (PESI). The aim of this program is to capture those who are emerging from poverty among the populations in a transitional situation or in a static state. Mathematically, the PESI is presented as a geometric mean of two sub-indices: the transition index and the stability index. These are obtained from the formulas below:

$$Transition\ Index = \frac{PNP}{PNP + NPP}$$

And

$$Stability\ Index = \frac{NPNP}{NPNP + PP}$$

The transition index captures the degree of transition from poverty to non-poverty among the vulnerable or transitory poor. As for the stability index, it measures the weight of pure non-poor households among households that remain in a stable state over the two periods. Thus, PESI translates the potential for emergence in terms of improving the level of well-being in each area.

Interpretation of the results

Table 9 : Poverty Exit Synthetic Index (PESI)

		PESI
BENIN 2019	Man	60,4
	Woman	62,9
	Both	61,3
BURKINA FASO 2018	Man	55,2
	Woman	61,6
	Both	55,3
CAMEROON 2019	Man	59
	Woman	61,7
	Both	59,7
COTE D'IVOIRE 2019	Man	60,4
	Woman	63,6
	Both	61,6
GUINEA 2019	Man	56,5
	Woman	56
	Both	56,8
MAURITANIA 2019	Man	62,5
	Woman	72,8
	Both	65,6
SENEGAL 2019	Man	60,9
	Woman	79,1
	Both	61,7
CHAD 2018	Man	57,5
	Woman	58,8
	Both	57,6
TOGO 2018	Man	52,3
	Woman	54,3
	Both	61,7

Source: CREG 2022

Section 4: Expanded Human Development Index (EHDI)

Dimension definition and description

The Expanded Human Development Index (EHDI) measures the level of human development of a locality, while considering sustainability and the optimality of human resources. Its methodology derives from that of the Human Development Index, developed by the UNDP. It considers three essential dimensions: education, health and living standards.

The major innovation is the introduction of the total fertility rate to consider the optimality of the population necessary to trigger sustained economic growth on the one hand, and on the other hand, per capita consumption instead of GDP/capita, which makes it possible to better understand their well-being in addition to the standard of living of the population.

A brief reminder of the theoretical basis

In his famous work Investigations into the Nature and Wealth of Nations, published in 1776, Smith said: "A man who has expended much time and labor to make himself fit for an occupation which requires extraordinary skill and experience, may be compared to one of those expensive machines. It is to be hoped that the position for which he is preparing will give him, in addition to the wages of simple work, enough to compensate him for all the expenses of his education." Through these words, Smith (1776) alluded to human capital to emphasize the importance of investing in the education and training of individuals. In the same vein, Mill (1873), in recounting the role of human capital in the development process of countries, considers the need to promote education because of its role as a driving force in economic and social progress.

The concept of human capital has given rise to a proliferation of debates and contributions with Becker's seminal work on the theory of human capital. This is understood by productive capacities, the accumulation of general or specific knowledge or know-how, the accumulated skills and the investment of companies. Becker (1957) argues that human capital represents the stock of productive resources incorporated into individuals themselves, consisting of elements as diverse as the level of education, training and work experience, the state of health or knowledge of the economic system. Other definitions from the work of Schultz (1961) and Becker (1964) denote the role of the quality of the labor factor in the development process.

In more recent times, other currents of research have revived interest in human capital. The endogenous growth theory developed by Romer (1986) and Lucas (1988) is based on the idea of endogenous growth. The "self-sustaining" nature of growth is possible thanks to human capital. Technical progress and innovation are the work of researchers or engineers, who are themselves the result of an investment in human capital. They also say that savings invested in the training of citizens are a powerful accelerator of growth.

The OECD (1998) considers that human capital is constituted by the knowledge, skills, competencies and other qualities possessed by an individual and relevant to economic activity.

The theory of human capital has undergone several innovative developments and deepening's. Sen's (2000) approach, with the theory of capabilities, proposes an extension of the theory of human capital. He conceives of education from the power of the individual over his own life. He explores a new path by which he/she values the well-being and benefits that a person can derive from his/her ability to perform certain acts that he/she values and allow him/her to become the person he/she wants to be. According to him, it is the combination of what a person can do (ability to act) and what he/she can be (the different types of functioning that he or she is able to achieve). The capability approach is primarily based on individual benefits. These benefits are assessed by the ability to perform a variety of functions deemed important over the course of a lifetime.

Method of calculating the dimension indicator

The EHDI is a geometric mean of the sub dimensional composite indices; the latter being themselves determined from the geometric mean of the indicators that make up each sub-dimension. Since the indicators are not expressed in the same unit, they are normalized between the values 0 (worst) and 1 (excellent).

- **The Health sub-dimension**

Health is measured by life expectancy at birth and the total fertility rate.

– Life expectancy, a fundamental element in the assessment of the general state of health of a population, is defined as the average age at which a generation would die which, from birth to death, would suffer the mortality conditions of the year of observation.

– The total fertility rate (TFR) gives the average number of children a woman would have throughout her life, under current fertility conditions, i.e. if the fertility rates observed in the year in question at each age remained unchanged. It allows us to assess the demographic vitality of a country.

- **The Education sub-dimension**

It gives an idea of the efforts made or to be made in terms of education. It includes two indicators:

– The mean year of schooling (MYS), which gives an adult the number of years he or she spends on average in education. This indicator reflects, among other things, the quality of a country's workforce.

– School life expectancy (SLE) shows the overall level of development of an education system in terms of average duration. It is defined as the average time (number of years of schooling) that a school-age child expects to receive in the future of the education system.

- **The standard of living sub-dimension**

It refers to the number of goods and services that an individual, a household or a social group can have, depending on its resources. In the context of the EHDI measurement, the standard of living is approximated by per capita consumption instead of GNI per capita.

Table: sub-dimensions, indicators, data sources and methods of calculation of the EHDI

Figure 6 : EHDI Indicators

Dimension	Indicators	Data sources	Standardization Method	Minimum value	Maximum value
Health (HI)	**Life expectancy at birth (LEB)**	Census	**Life Expectancy at Birth Index** $ILEB = \frac{\text{Value Used} - \text{Minimum value}}{\text{Maximum value} - \text{Minimum value}}$	20	85
	The total fertility rate (TFR)	DHS/MICS/Census	**Standardized total fertility rate** $ISTFR(x) = \frac{x}{3} \times 1_{[0,3]}(x) + \frac{(8-x)}{(8-3)} \times 1_{]3,8]}(x)$ with $x=TFR$		
	The Health Index (HI) $HI = \sqrt{ILEB \times ISTFR}$ This index is obtained by taking the geometric mean of the index of life expectancy at birth and the standardized total fertility rate				
Education (EI)	**Mean Year of schooling** (MYS)	Census, Household Surveys, Education Statistics, UNESCO	**Mean year of schooling index** $IMYS = \frac{\text{Value Used} - \text{Minimum value}}{\text{Maximum value} - \text{Minimum value}}$	0	15
	School Life Expectancy (SLE)	Census, Household Surveys, Education Statistical Yearbooks, UNESCO	**School Life expectancy Index** $ISLE = \frac{\text{Value Used} - \text{Minimum value}}{\text{Maximum value} - \text{Minimum value}}$	0	18
	Education index or combined index or educational attainment index (EI) $EI = \frac{\sqrt{IMYS \times ISLE}}{0.978}$ This index is obtained by normalizing the geometric mean of the indices of the Average Duration of Schooling and the Expected Duration of Schooling between the values 0 and 0.978.			0	0.978
Standard of living (IPCC)	**Per capita consumption**	Household Surveys and National Accounts	**Per capita consumption Index** $IPCC = \frac{\ln(\text{Value Used}) - \ln(\text{Minimum value})}{\ln(\text{Maximum value}) - \ln(\text{Minimum value})}$	$67	CAS 20,723
The Extended Human Development Index (EHDI) **EHDI**=$\sqrt[3]{HI \times EI \times IPCC}$ This index is obtained by making the geometric average of the three indices of health, education and consumption					

Interpretation of the results

Table 10 : Expanded Human Development Index (EHDI)

		EHDI
BENIN 2019	Man	50,1
	Woman	44,5
	Both	47,4
BURKINA FASO 2018	Man	45,7
	Woman	42,4
	Both	43,9
CAMEROON 2019	Man	59,9
	Woman	56
	Both	58,4
COTE D'IVOIRE 2019	Man	64
	Woman	55,2
	Both	60,7
GUINEA 2019	Man	54,3
	Woman	44,1
	Both	49,9
MAURITANIA 2019	Man	57,2
	Woman	54,7
	Both	56,2
SENEGAL 2019	Man	56,8
	Woman	49
	Both	53,5
CHAD 2018	Man	41,1
	Woman	32
	Both	37,2
TOGO 2018	Man	58,8
	Woman	51,1
	Both	53,5

Source: CREG 2022

Section 5 : Network and Territory Synthetic Index of (NTSI)

Dimension definition and description

Etymologically, the term comes from the Latin "retiolus" designating a set of threads, strings regularly intertwined to capture certain animals. By analogy, the network designates a permanent or accidental set of intertwined or intertwined elements that are regular to achieve the same objective. Thus, different types of networks are distinguished: hydraulic network, fortress network, road network, railway network, radio network, telecommunications network, social network, etc.

Antonelli (2003) writes that "a network is an organized set of partially separable production units, characterized by high levels of diversity, complementarity and interdependence, both with regard to existing and potential technologies".

As part of this work, the network will be considered as the existing interconnectivity system between territories and understood through the development of the road and transport sector, the development of the cash transfer services sector as well as the development of productive and/or commercial activities.

Territory

From the Latin "territorium" with the root "terra", a territory means an area of the earth's surface on which a human group lives. The word will evolve in meaning to specify the surface on which an authority is exercised. For Bailly (1994), the territory is "a specific space that cannot be separated from its content. It is characterized by location and a group, a process of appropriation, a management process, a heritage and a project." It therefore integrates space, legal and institutional character, political, sociological and cultural aspects.

From this point of view, territory refers to the legally delimited administrative unit. Possessing the attributes of a territorially divided and circumscribed space, it most often contains a seat, a capital or a capital which constitutes the main center of decision-making and governance of general development affairs. It therefore has an administrative function to define the contours of the scope and to facilitate coordination.

In addition, the development of a territory is carried out first according to knowledge and practices, and then according to the systems of ideas, values and projects to which it gives substance. These corpora fall under all registers of spatial dynamics and integrate the cultural, religious and political references that underlie the cognitive processes of territorial "Building" (Diakhaté, 2011).

A brief reminder of the theoretical basis

The existence of economic poles in contemporary economies refers to the notion of polarization. Boudeville (1966) defines polarization as "a complex phenomenon, decomposable into a series of blocks of events, which unfold over time. It describes how the poles of development are born and how the impulses that emanate from them propagate in time and space. In other words, it is a dynamic process of expansion and sequential evolution, both technical and social."

In the literature, there are two approaches to the concept of spatial polarization depending on whether it is in the French-speaking or Anglo-Saxon context. Among French-speakers, spatial polarization basically covers two aspects, namely attraction and diffusion, while Anglo-Saxons emphasize concentration. The first aspect is the most classic and refers to the attraction exerted by a place, called a center or pole, on an extensive and heterogeneous space that is in a situation of dependence on this center (Elissalde, 2011). Space can be likened to a field of economic forces in which there are one or more localities (municipality, department, region, etc.) which exert an attraction proportional to its level of development on the other surrounding localities. The second aspect covered by polarization concerns the diffusion or entrainment effect that the cluster exerts on the development of the surrounding localities. This approach is mainly attributable to the work of two economists, Perroux (1950) and Boudeville (1966). Perroux approaches an approach to development that considers the existence of a center, made up of developed countries, and a periphery, made up of poor countries, so that the development of the periphery depends mainly on the influence of the center. Given these inherent characteristics of spatial polarization, it is often equated with the result of the effects of geographical spillovers.

According to the Anglo-Saxon approach, a phenomenon is said to be spatially polarized when it tends to be more concentrated in particular localities. According to Lajugie et al. (1985), Anglo-Saxon authors refer to "polarization" as the attraction exerted by poles on the surrounding space, with the result not of the diffusion of development but its concentration in a limited space and, consequently, not the attenuation but the aggravation of development inequalities.

Today, the term is used by other human sciences such as sociology, which use it to account for a worsening of social contrasts within an entity. Sassen (1996) thus speaks of "social polarization" to describe the social dynamics in the "global city". Thus, the concept of spatial polarization refers to the relations of attraction and diffusion that one or more poles exert on the surrounding localities.

The economic development of territories as initially conceived, based on the production system, favors metropolitan territories to the detriment of peripheral territories. Indeed, territorial economic development depends almost exclusively on its production system, whether it is based on generic or specific resources (territorial resources, know-how, localized production systems). The only challenge for economic development would therefore be the attractiveness of the territory to companies and their competitiveness in the context of globalization of trade. This phenomenon was observed in the 80s with a concentration of activities in urban areas and their immediate peripheries. Talandier (2008), who is interested in the economic development of non-metropolitan territories, concludes that the development of a territory depends not only on its attractiveness but also on its ability to capture income streams, as well as to create wealth. The author concludes that development becomes a production issue but also a population issue that captures these external revenues.

By analyzing the link between the local development of territories and the forces of urban polarization, Aubert, Lepicier and Perrier-Cornet (2006) highlight the relationship that the peripheries establish with urban centers, where most of the markets are located and where the forces of agglomeration give rise to the dynamics of economic growth. For them, regional growth is mainly driven by urban growth, thanks to the effects of agglomeration, which are favorable to economies of scale and externalities. In this way, metropolises increase their power of attraction for consumers thanks to a wide variety of products available. Activities and populations thus benefit from grouping together, cumulatively, in the centers.

Method of calculating the dimension indicator

Each sub-dimension of the Networks and Territories is apprehended by a certain number of indicators.

Table 11: NTSI Indicators

Indicators	Definitions
Sub-dimension: Urbanization	
Population density of the area	Number of inhabitants per km^2
Average household size	Average number of people per dwelling
Urbanization rate	Share of the urban population in the total population of the area
Tenant-to-landlord ratio	Ratio of the number of tenants to the number of owners
Sub-dimension: Basic infrastructure	
Rate of access to basic social services (water, electricity, health, etc.)	Proportion of population accessing services
Quality indicator of basic social services (education, electricity, water, etc.)	Proportion of the population satisfied with the quality of services
Rate of births attended by skilled health care personnel	Proportion of births attended by skilled personnel
Rate of Satisfied Demand for Modern Contraception	Proportion of demand for contraception met by modern means
Sub-dimension: Migration	
Index of entry into a zone	Ratio of entrants to an area to the total population of the area
Zone Exit Index	Ratio of the leavers of an area to the total population of the area
Sub-dimension: Financial flows and capacity	
Remittance Index in the Zone	Weight of total transfers received and paid in the zone's GDP
Rate of access to formal transfer services	Proportion of individuals with access to formal transfer services
Per capita consumption in the area	Average level of consumption per capita in the area
Cost of the housewife's basket	Cost of the most consumed products in the area (operationalized by food expenditure)

Source *: CREG-CREFAT 2019.*

Step 2: Normalization

Normalization is done using a classic formula that converts the original values of the indicators into numbers between 0 and 1.

Step 3: Calculation of the sub-dimensional indicators

For each subdimension, the indicator is obtained by making a geometric mean of the indicators that compose it. The geometric mean method is preferred to the arithmetic mean in the sense that the latter does not consider the weight of the values of each variable in the overall indicator (the compensating effects between values do not exist with the geometric mean method).

$$\boldsymbol{I_k = \left(\prod_{d=1}^{n} ind_d\right)^{\frac{1}{n}}}$$

$k = 1, \ldots, 4$ and where n is the number of indicators monitored in the relevant sub-dimension.$d = 1, \ldots, n$

Step 4: Calculation of the Synthetic Networks and Territories Index

Collect all the under dimensional clues (4 in total).

Apply a geometric mean to these indicators to obtain the Networks and Territories Synthetic Index (NTSI):

$$\boldsymbol{NTSI = \left(\prod_{k=1}^{m} I_k\right)^{\frac{1}{m}}}$$

With the number of sub-dimensions of the global dimension networks and territories (here), is the indicator calculated for each dimension $mm = 4I_k k,\ k = 1, \ldots, 4$.

Interpretation of the results

Table 12: Networks and territories Synthetic index (NTSI)

		NTSI
BENIN 2019	Man	23
	Woman	21,6
	Both	21,8
BURKINA FASO 2018	Man	17,2
	Woman	16,2
	Both	17,2
CAMEROON 2019	Man	22,5
	Woman	21,6
	Both	22,2
COTE D'IVOIRE 2019	Man	33,9
	Woman	34,2
	Both	34,6
GUINEA 2019	Man	23,3
	Woman	19,8
	Both	21,8
MAURITANIA 2019	Man	24,7
	Woman	19,9
	Both	22,5
SENEGAL 2019	Man	30,7
	Woman	27,1
	Both	29,1
CHAD 2018	Man	11,2
	Woman	8,1
	Both	9,2
TOGO 2018	Man	21,1
	Woman	18,1
	Both	29,1

Source: CREG 2022

Section 6 : Demographic dividend monitoring index (DDMI)

Definition

The Demographic Dividend Monitoring Index (DDMI) is an indicator used to monitor the demographic dividend in synergy with sustainable development. It allows a country or territory to assess its progress in capturing the demographic dividend. The DDMI covers five (05) dimensions:

- Economic dependence,
- The quality of the living environment,
- Transitions in poverty,
- Expanded human capital and
- Networks and territories.

Theoretical basis

The methodology used in the first dimension is the National Transfer Accounts (NTA) approach. The purpose of this method is to produce a measure, both individual and aggregate, of the acquisition and distribution of economic resources at different ages. This consists of introducing age into National Accounts. These accounts are intended to understand how economic flows flow between different age groups of a population for a given country and for a given year. They indicate at each age the different sources of income and the different uses of this income in terms of consumption, whether private or public, and savings. They thus make it possible to study the economic consequences of changing the age structure of the population (United Nations, 2013).

Dimension 2 (Quality of the living environment) is inspired by the Better Life Index methodology developed by the OECD (2011). In its standard formulation, the living environment covers eleven (11) sub-dimensions considered essential to well-being. But in the context of DD monitoring, only seven (Civic Engagement, Social Ties, Environment; Work-life balance and Safety) of the eleven are retained, the other four (04) being considered by the other dimensions.

Each sub-dimension of the living environment is measured using one to four indicators. Within each subdimension, the basic indicators that make up the sub-dimension are averaged with the same weighting, with the latter being normalized beforehand.

The Quality of Living Environment Indicator (QLEI) is a weighted average of the sub-dimensional composite indicators. The analysis of poverty dynamics carried out at the level of dimension 3 is based on a new approach to measuring transitions in poverty by Dang and Lanjouw (2013). The latter have developed a method for constructing pseudo-panels and estimating the transition matrix on two or more poverty surveys. The idea is to follow cohort of individuals (or households) over time.

Dimensions 4 and 5 are inspired by the HDI and Clusters method respectively. Based on the three classic sub-dimensions of the HDI, dimension 4 introduces fertility into the Building of the indicator to consider aspects relating to demography and the sustainability of development. As for dimension 5, it covers four (04) sub-dimensions: urbanization, migration, infrastructure and financial flows. Each sub-dimension has several indicators to quantify it. The indicators are normalized so that the values are between 0 (the worst score) and 1 (the best score). The sub dimensional index is obtained by the geometric mean of the indicators that make up the subdimension. The Networks and Territories Synthetic Index (NTSI) also represent the geometric mean of the sub dimensional index.

Method of calculating the dimension indicator

By Building, the DDMI is devoid of units, and its value varies between 0 which indicates a terrible situation and 1 which indicates an excellent situation. It is obtained by the geometric mean of the synthetic indicators resulting from the five (05) dimensions mentioned above. Its formula is as follows:

$$\boldsymbol{DDMI} = \sqrt[5]{\boldsymbol{EDCI} \times \boldsymbol{QLEI} \times \boldsymbol{PESI} \times \boldsymbol{EHDI} \times \boldsymbol{NTSI}}$$

Where:

- EDCI is the indicator of coverage of economic dependency,
- QLEI is the indicator of the quality of the living environment,
- PESI is the synthetic indicator of exit from poverty,
- EHDI is the Broader Human Development Index, and
- NTSI is the indicator for networks and territories.

The demographic dividend is the economic contribution that results from a decline in fertility followed by a change in the age structure of the population. The consequences of such a phenomenon go beyond the purely demographic or economic aspect and concern other sectors. While the demographic transition is its starting point, achieving the demographic dividend is accompanied by change in several sectors that interact with it. These include the living environment, transitions in poverty, human capital, territorial mobility, among others. The DDMI makes it possible to understand the positive or negative developments in these sectors that make it possible to create favorable conditions for the optimization of the demographic dividend.

The dimensions or components of the DDMI are degraded or low when their value is less than 50% (red area in the graph below). Between 50% and 79%, the component is moderately satisfactory (yellow part). For values greater than or equal to 80%, the component is at a high level and therefore very satisfactory (green part).

Figure 7: Porter's diagram on the dimensions of the DDMI

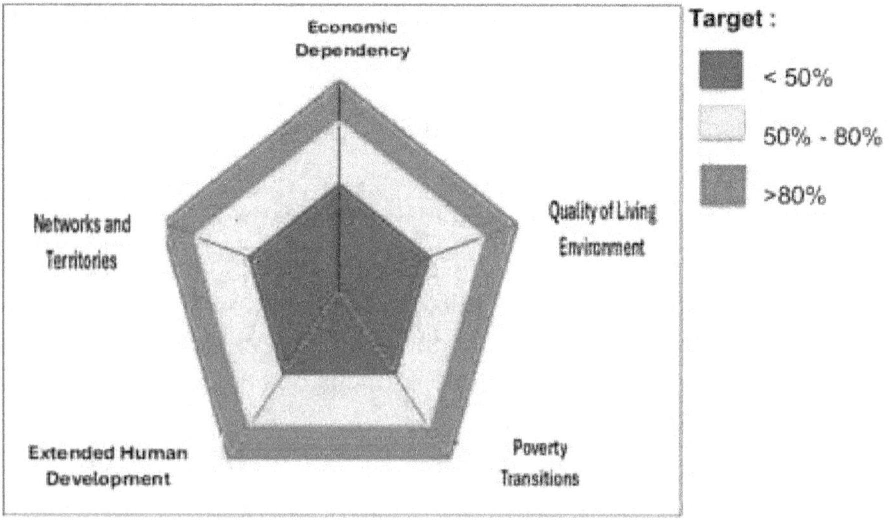

The DDMI is interpreted differently depending on its value. Indeed, the DDMI is considered low if its value is less than 50%. This implies that the country (or the zone) does not exploit the demographic dividend. A value between 50% and 79% reflects a low dividend exploitation. On the other hand, the demographic dividend is best exploited when the DDMI is greater than or equal to 80%.

DDMI is a geometric mean aggregation of the synthetic indicators of the five dimensions. Its interpretation is made through a given grid. In this grid, countries or territories are divided into three categories according to the value of the indicator. Thus, when the indicator has a value below 0.50, the situation of the country or territory is qualified as weak. On the other hand, the situation is qualified as average when the indicator has a value between 0.5 and 0.8. Finally, when the value of the indicator is greater than or equal to 0.8, the situation of the country or territory will be described as good (or high or better).

Interpretation of the results

Table 13: DDMI of West and Central African countries

		DDMI
BENIN 2019	Man	52,1
	Woman	44,3
	Both	48,4
BURKINA FASO 2018	Man	44,6
	Woman	36,2
	Both	40,5
CAMEROON 2019	Man	54,6
	Woman	21,6
	Both	47,2
COTE D'IVOIRE 2019	Man	52,9
	Woman	23,1
	Both	39,8
GUINEA 2019	Man	53,1
	Woman	33,2
	Both	46,7
MAURITANIA 2019	Man	55,2
	Woman	13,5
	Both	49
SENEGAL 2019	Man	57,1
	Woman	35,4
	Both	49,2
CHAD 2018	Man	41,2
	Woman	8,5
	Both	33,2
TOGO 2018	Man	50,3
	Woman	37,8
	Both	49,2

Source: CREG 2022

Graphic 9: GDDI 2019 of West and Central African countries

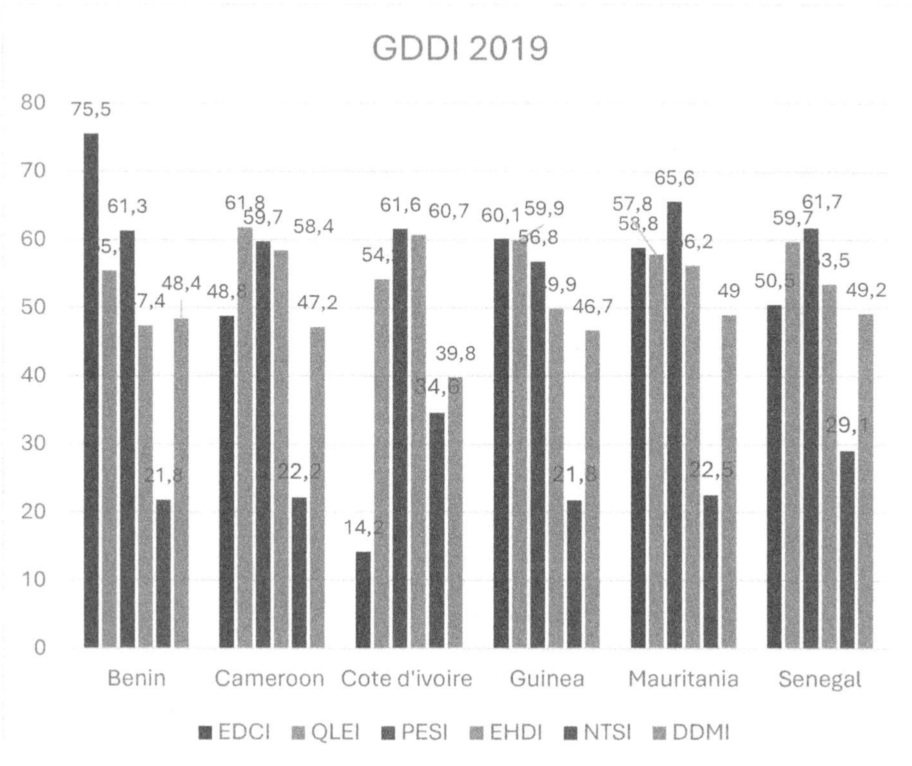

Source: CREG 2024

Graphic 10: GDDI 2018 of West and Central African countries

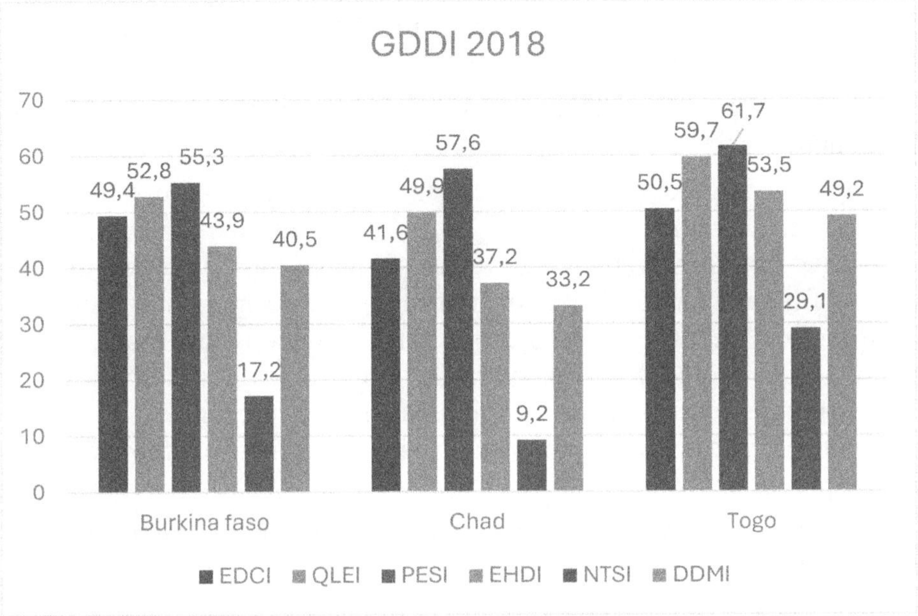

***Source*: CREG 2024**

Conclusion

The level of interaction and networks are poorly developed in most countries. These include human and financial mobility and the state of the structure (availability and quality of infrastructure and basic social services) necessary for optimal exploitation of the demographic dividend. In addition, there are huge regional disparities, which, despite the efforts of governments in the quest for territorial equity, persist.

Thus, to mitigate this phenomenon and achieve balanced and sustainable development, much remains to be done, particularly in:

– The periodic elaboration, political adoption and effective implementation of land use master plans with a view to defining the specific vocations of each sub-area, considering the priorities of harmonious development and thus anticipating harmful forms of spatial occupation. Constituting the basis for a better prospective structuring of territories, these spatial planning tools promote the optimal location of activities, socio-economic investments and therefore the rational settlement of the population.

– The more adequate networking of basic infrastructure throughout the national space through an efficient territorialization of public policies, so that the population has easy and equitable access to fundamental services. In the absence of such a network, it is almost impossible to ensure a balance in terms of basic social infrastructure between the different geographical areas of the country.

– The adoption of land use and urban development plans as political references for a significant reduction in development disparities.

– The strengthening of the legal framework for land use planning through establishment, adoption and, above all, the application of legislative instruments enforceable against third parties. These instruments seek to fill gaps related to the inadequacy of the normative frameworks of reference necessary for the ordering of occupation, both at the national and regional levels, of major socio-economic activities and infrastructures. This situation, which has not yet been resolved, is one of the main causes of the major inadequacies of the regional development policy.

– The synergy of local authorities sharing the same experience, the same infrastructure network and natural potential in a dynamic of rural-urban integration.

– The creation of statistical databases to better monitor the dynamics of networks and territories and to better position the demographic dividend in the national development process.

Bibliographical references

Colletis, G., & Pecqueur, B. (1995). Politiques technologiques locales et création de ressources spécifiques. Économie industrielle et économie spatiale, 445-463.

CREG (2021) Demographic Dividend Monitoring Index, approche méthodologique, https://ordd.creg-center.org/methodologie-ddmi/ministère de l'Économie du plan et de la coopération (2021) : rapport de l'observatoire national du dividende démographique, https://www.economie.gouv.sn/sites/default/files/2021-08/Senegal_a_lheure_du_bonus_demographique_compressed.pdf

Dang, H. A., & Lanjouw, P. F. (2013). Measuring poverty dynamics with synthetic panels based on cross-sections. World Bank Policy Research Working Paper, (6504).

Dramani, L. (2016). Impact du dividende démographique sur la croissance économique au Sénégal. African Population Studies, 30(2).

Dramani, L., & Oga, I. J. B. (2017). Understanding demographic dividends in Africa: The NTA approach. Journal of Demographic Economics, 83(1), 85-101.

Jeanneaux, P. (2006). Économie de la décision publique et conflits d'usages pour un cadre de vie dans les espaces ruraux et périurbains. Développement durable et territoires. Économie, géographie, politique, droit, sociologie, (Dossier 7).

Lee, R. D., & Mason, A. (Eds.). (2011). Population aging and the generational economy: A global perspective. Edward Elgar Publishing.

Martinetti, E. C. (2000). A multidimensional assessment of well-being based on Sen's functioning approach. Rivista internazionale di scienze sociali, 207-239.

Stiglitz, J. E., Sen, A., & Fitoussi, J. P. (2009). Commission sur la mesure des performances économiques et du progrès social. Rapport au président de la République. France. http://www. stiglitz-sen-fitoussi. fr/fr.

CHAPTER 5

THE DDMI RETROPOLATION

Introduction

The demographic transition offers a window of opportunity for accelerated economic growth. Indeed, once the youth dependency ratio decreases and frees up resources for government and families, a demographic dividend can be realized if the resources released are invested in strengthening the accumulation of physical and human capital. The size of the dividend depends largely on the ability of the economies concerned to create enough jobs for the large masses of young people (girls as well as boys) entering the labor market. The demographic dividend is the economic gain that results from changing the age structure of a population. However, its impact goes beyond the economy to many other sectors. These include the living environment, poverty eradication, territorial mobility, to name but a few.

In synergy with the UNFPA Office for West and Central Africa and as part of the implementation of the recommendations of the Heads of State of the African Union, the Regional Consortium for Research in Generational Economics (CREG) has set up two indicators to monitor the demographic dividend. The Demographic Dividend Monitoring Index (DDMI), a composite index based on generational economics theories that assesses and tracks the progress of countries (or regions) in capturing and exploiting the demographic dividend. The DDMI covers five (05) dimensions: economic dependence, quality of the living environment, poverty dynamics, human development and finally, networks and territories. The DDMI makes it possible to understand the positive or negative developments in these dimensions and identifies the sectors requiring greater investment to create conditions favorable to the optimization of the demographic dividend and the achievement of the Sustainable Development Goals.

Indeed, the national budget is the main tool for allocating resources to the various economic and social sectors of a country. Its evolution and composition have significant consequences for the results of the public policies implemented in the country. This instrument, if it is brought into line with the components of the DDMI, can accelerate the achievement of the conditions for sustainable, inclusive growth that are conducive to the capture of the demographic dividend and sustainable development. Thus, after active participation in several capacity building and advocacy sessions, the national actors involved in the mechanisms of strategic planning, budgeting and coherence of public policies, are considered, through the Directorates General in charge of Budget and Planning and other Directorates involved, to be trained on Budgeting Sensitive to the Demographic Dividend (BSDD). The BSDD is a process for evaluating the consideration of the Demographic Dividend (DD) in budget allocations. It is an approach to integrate DD and gender capture concerns into the design, implementation, monitoring and evaluation of policies and programs. The BSDD is of paramount importance in assessing the fiscal structure and directing public spending. Also, the BSDD contributes to accelerating the achievement of the Sustainable Development Goals, and more specifically those related to the capture of the demographic dividend and Agenda 2063. Its process includes four main steps, namely: the transformation of the classic budget into a functional budget over the last 15 to 20 years, the retropolation of the DDMI over the last 15 to 20 years; the alignment of the DDMI with the functional budget and the analysis of budgetary elasticities. These results can be used in national budgeting and advocacy processes for a more optimal allocation of public resources to the pillars of the demographic dividend.

In addition, back-casting is a process that consists of estimating or reconstructing old data. The process of moving from the DDMI to the budget functions consists of combing through all the series of the budget and the previously calculated DDMI, the objective being to check the overall consistency of the quantities, to control the quality of the series and to construct the DDMI accounts corresponding to the budgetary functions before the descriptive analysis and estimation phase. As for the linkage, it consists of assigning the sub-dimensions of the DDMI to the eight (08) budgetary functions defined in the functional budget.

To this end, several countries have initiated training on the back-casting and connection of DDMI over the last 15 years. These training courses benefited from the technical support of the Regional Consortium for Research in Generational Economics (CREG) and the support of financial partners. Thus, these workshops are the continuation of the implementation of the BSDD to support these countries, including Benin, Burkina Faso, Cameroon, Ivory Cost, Mali, Guinea, Niger, and Chad.

Section 1: Back-casting methodology

The exercise of back-casting and linking the countries' DDMI consisted of the one hand of calibrating the DDMI of the remote points for which survey data are available, and on the other hand, of coupling or estimating the DDMI of other years between two consecutive surveys, i.e. in the case of Benin over the periods 2004-2010, 2012-2018.

This allows us to have a continuous series over the period 2003-2020. It should be noted that most countries in this exercise had at least two points of DDMI.

Step 1: Calibration of DDMI of remote points

The DDMI for the years in which survey data are available are calculated in accordance with the methodology developed in the Manual of Indicators and Dimensions of the Demographic Dividend Observatories and summarized in the following paragraph.

a) DDMI: concept and methodological overview

The DDMI is a composite indicator that allows us to understand the economy as a whole and to monitor achievements in terms of capturing the demographic dividend. In its Building, the DDMI encompasses economic and social life by covering five distinct dimensions: (i) economic dependence; (ii) the quality of the living environment; (iii) poverty dynamics; (iv) extended human development, and (v) networks and territories. Each of the five dimensions has its own method of analysis.

The first dimension is based on the National Transfer Accounts (NTA) method. The purpose of this method is to produce a measure, both individual and aggregate, of the acquisition and distribution of economic resources at different ages. This consists of introducing age into National Accounts. These accounts are intended to understand how economic flows flow between different age groups of a population for a given country and for a given year. They indicate at each age the different sources of income and the different uses of this income in terms of consumption, whether private or public, and savings. They thus make it possible to study the economic consequences of changing the age structure of the population (United Nations, 2013).

Dimension 2 (or Quality of the living environment) is inspired by the *Better Life Index* methodology developed by the OECD (2011). In its standard formulation, the living environment covers eleven (11) sub-dimensions considered essential to well-being. But in the context of DD monitoring, only seven (Civic Engagement, Social Ties, Environment; Work-life balance and Security) of the eleven are retained in the analysis of the living environment, the other four (04) being considered by the other dimensions. Each sub-dimension of the living environment is measured using one to four indicators. Within each subdimension, the basic indicators that make up the sub-dimension are averaged with the same weighting, with the latter being normalized beforehand. The Quality of Living Environment Indicator (QLEI) is a weighted average of the sub-dimensional composite indicators.

The analysis of poverty dynamics carried out at the level of dimension 3 is based on a new approach to measuring transitions in poverty by Dang and Lanjouw (2013). The latter have developed a method for constructing pseudo-panels and estimating the transition matrix on two or more poverty surveys. The idea is to follow cohort of individuals (or households) over time.

Dimensions 4 and 5 are inspired by the HDI and Clusters method respectively. Based on the three classic sub-dimensions of the HDI, dimension 4 introduces fertility into the Building of the indicator to consider aspects relating to demography and the sustainability of development. As for dimension 5, it covers four (04) sub-dimensions: urbanization, migration, infrastructure and financial flows. Each sub-dimension has several indicators to quantify it. The indicators are normalized so that the values are between 0 (the worst score) and 1 (the best score). The sub dimensional index is obtained by the geometric mean of the indicators that make up the subdimension. The Synthetic Indicator of Networks and Territories (NTSI) also represent the geometric mean of the sub dimensional indices.

DDMI is a geometric mean aggregation of the synthetic indicators of the five dimensions. Its interpretation is made through a given grid. In this grid, countries or territories are divided into three categories according to the value of the indicator. Thus, when the indicator has a value below 0.50, the situation of the country (or region) is considered unsatisfactory, and it does not exploit DD. However, the country or region uses DD when the indicator has a value between 0.5 and 0.79. But the profits in this case are still average or low. Finally, when the indicator value is greater than or equal to 0.8, the country or region is making optimal use of the DD system.

b) **Data Sources for Remote Point DDMI Calibration**

The tables below reflect the different indicators and data sources that were used in the calibration of countries' DDMIs.

Table 14: Dimension 1 Indicators and Data Sources

Sub-dimensions	Indicators	Profile data sources where survey data exists
Consumption	Public health consumption	- Health Programs Budget (Department) - National Accounts (INS[1]) - Population Projections (INS)
	Public consumption of education	- Health Education Budget (Ministry) - National Accounts (INS) - Population Projections (INS)
	Public consumption other than education and health	- National Accounts (INS) - Population Projections (INS)
	Private health consumption	- National Investigations [2] - National Accounts (INS) - Population Projections (INS)
	Private consumption of education	
	Private consumption other than education and health	
Income from work	Compensation of employees	- National Investigations - National Accounts (INS) - Population Projections (INS)
	Self-employment income	

Source: CREG 2023

[1] The acronym INS refers to the National Statistics Office (NSO). The name differs from country to country. In Benin, it is the National Institute of Statistics and Economic Analysis (INSTAD); the National Institute of Statistics and Demography (INSD) in Burkina Faso; the National Institute of Statistics (INS) in Côte d'Ivoire and Guinea. In Chad, the National Institute of Statistics and Economic and Demographic Studies (INSEED).

[2] National surveys refer to all the surveys on living conditions, perceptions and poverty carried out regularly by countries among households.

Table 15: Dimension 2 indicators and data sources

Sub-dimensions	Indicators	Years of investigations[3]	
		Variables proxy	Data sources
Civic Engagement & Governance	Voter turnout		Electoral Commission
	Stakeholder participation in regulatory development	Voice and Accountability	WGI 2022
Social Links	Quality of the social network	National surveys (if data do not exist, considered or carried over from the nearest survey year)	
Environment	Air concentration of PM2.5 particles		WDI 2022
	Proportion of population satisfied with water quality	National surveys (if data do not exist, considered or carried over from the nearest survey year)	
Housing	Number of rooms per person		National Investigations
	Rate of access to basic sanitation facilities		National Investigations
	Housing budget coefficient		National Investigations
Subjective well-being	Overall Life Satisfaction	Happiness Index	World Happiness Report
Work-Life Balance	Proportion of employees working	National surveys (if data do not exist, considered or carried over from the nearest survey year)	

[3] The years of the surveys differ from one country to another. As part of the retropolation exercise, the following years of investigations were considered:
Benin, EMICOV (2015)
Burkina : EHCVM (2019)
Côte d'Ivoire : EHCVM (2019)
Guinée :
Niger : EHCVM (2019)
Tchad : ECOSIT2 (2003), ECOSIT3 (2011) et ECOSIT4 (2019)

Sub-dimensions	Indicators	Years of investigations[3]	
		Variables proxy	Data sources
	more than 50 hours per week		
	Number of hours per day devoted to self and leisure	National surveys (if data do not exist, considered or carried over from the nearest survey year)	
Security	Feeling safe walking alone at night		Gallup Institute (global law and order)
	Homicide rate		UNODC

Source: CREG 2023

Table 16: Dimension 3 indicators and data sources

Sub-dimensions	Indicators	Data sources	
		Previous survey year	Survey year
Transition	Getting out of poverty		National Investigations
	Falling into poverty		
Stability	Chronic poverty		
	Pure non-poverty		

Source: CREG 2023

Table 17: Dimension 4 Indicators and Data Sources

Sub-dimensions	Indicators	Data sources
		Years of investigations
'Health	Life expectancy at birth	UN/DESA/PD
	Total fertility rate	UN/DESA/PD
Education	Average length of schooling	UNDP & UNESCO
	Expected duration of schooling	UNDP & UNESCO
Standard of living	Per capita consumption	National Accounts (NIS)

Source: CREG 2023

Table 18: Dimension 5 Indicators and Data Sources

Sub-dimensions	Indicators	Years of investigations	
		Variables proxy	Data sources
Urbanization	Population density		National Investigations
	Household size		National Investigations
	Urbanization rate		National Investigations
	Tenant-to-Owner Ratio		National Investigations
Migration	Number of in-migrants (including internal migration)		UN/DESA/PD
	Number of out-migrants (including internal migration)		UN/DESA/PD
	Total population		NSO
Infrastructure	Rate of access to basic social infrastructure and services (water, electricity,		National Investigations

Sub-dimensions	Indicators	Years of investigations	
		Variables proxy	Data sources
	health, primary school, public transport, market)		
	Proportion of households are satisfied with the quality of basic social infrastructure and services (water, electricity, health, primary school, public transport, market)		National Investigations
Financial flows and capacities	Transfers of Funds Received		Balance of Payments, Central Bank, World Bank
	Transfers of funds paid		
	GDP		National Accounts (NSO)
	GNI per capita		National Accounts (NSO)
	Rate of access to formal transfer services	Rate of banking	National Investigations
	Per capita food consumption		National Accounts (NSO)

Source: CREG 2023

Step 2: Connection of the DDMI between 2004 and 2019

The second step of the back-casting is linkage, which consists of estimating the missing values of the years in which there is no survey. Data for some indicators are available on a continuous basis over all years (in time series). The latter are therefore not subject to estimates. In contrast, several other indicators are calculated from the survey data. For this last category of indicators, different techniques (calibration, linear extrapolation, etc.) are used to estimate the missing data. The principle of calibration consists in applying to a given indicator the trend of a variable (called a standard) available in a time series and theoretically correlated with it. Therefore, the annual growth rates of the benchmarked indicator are consistent with those of the benchmark.

- **Dimension 1: NTA Profile Update Method**

The general approach of the NTAs is to disaggregate aggregates from the national accounts by age (e.g. consumption and labor income), using individual profiles estimated from survey data carried out at a reference year *k* and statistics from administrative sources (e.g. sectoral ministries and education and health). Thus, the Building of new profiles is conditioned by the availability of new survey data. However, NTA profiles may be updated annually when national accounts aggregates are available for years after reference year *k*.

Let be the $x_r(a)$ average NTA age profile a $(a = 0,1,...,90)$ developed at a given reference year r.

If k refers to a year subsequent to the base year r, the average profile is updated to the year k by an adjustment coefficient θ_k calculated as follows:

$$\theta_k = \frac{M_k}{\sum_{a=0}^{90} x_r(a) N_k(a)}$$

where M_k corresponds to the aggregate of national accounts (also called macro-control) of the Year k and $N_k(a)$ the number of individuals of age a year-round k.

The average profile updated to the year k, noted $x_k(a)$, is obtained by multiplying the average profile for the reference year and the adjustment coefficient for the year k:

$$x_k(a) = \theta_k \cdot x_r(a)$$

Thus, the principle of updating an NTA profile for a year k is to apply the structure of a profile from a previous year r to the macroeconomic aggregate for the year k. For most countries, national accounts aggregates are available for all years, so the NTA profiles of the non-survey years were updated using the method described above.

- **Dimension 2: Connecting sub-dimensions**

As far as dimension 2 is concerned, the connection operation was carried out directly on the sub-dimensions of the Living Environment. The table below shows the standards and/or methods used to estimate the missing points of the sub-dimensions

Table 19: Calibration variables and methods applied for dimension 2

Sub-dimensions	Calibration Variables	Data sources	Connection method
Civic Engagement & Governance	Voice and accountability	WGI 2022	Growth rate of the benchmark applied to the indicator
Social Links			Available data from the nearest survey
Environment	Air concentration of PM2.5 particles	WDI 2022	Growth rate of the benchmark applied to the indicator
Housing	Growth rate of the Building sub-branch	National Accounts (INS)	- Growth rate of the benchmark applied to the indicator
Subjective well-being			Available data from the nearest survey
Work-Life Balance			- Carry over the data from the nearest survey or proceed with linear interpolation if the distant points are not very far apart
Security	Political Stability and Absence of Violence	WGI 2022	- Growth rate of the benchmark applied to the indicator

Source: CREG 2023

- **Dimension 3: Connecting Poverty Transitions**

The linking of poverty transitions between two surveys consisted of using a learning model. Where appropriate, given the sensitivity of the poverty data, it is recommended that the dynamics of the first survey be carried out over to the years preceding the second survey. Thus, the indicators of poverty dynamics do not change until the new survey.

- **Dimension 4: Calibration of the EHDI**

Since all the basic indicators of dimension 4 are available for all years, the EHDI of countries was calculated annually between 2004 and 2019 using data from the sources mentioned above (see Part 1).

- **Dimension 5: Estimation and Connection**

For dimension 5, the connection technique is applied to the sub-dimensions "Urbanization" and "Infrastructure". In contrast, the other two sub-dimensions "Migration" and "Financial flows and capacities" are calculated for all years because their basic indicators are available in time series, except for remittances and the rate of access to formal remittance services. For the latter indicators, linear interpolation was applied between two surveys to arrange the series continuously between 2004 and 2019.

Table 20: Calibration Variables and Methods Applied for Dimension 5

Sub-dimensions / Indicators	Calibration Variables	Data sources	Connection method
Urbanization	Urbanization rate	WDI	Growth rate of the benchmark applied to the indicator
Infrastructure			Apply the growth rate of the standard to the indicator or perform linear interpolation if the distant points are not very far apart

Sub-dimensions / Indicators	Calibration Variables	Data sources	Connection method
Transfers of funds received and paid			Apply the growth rate of the standard to the indicator or perform linear interpolation if the distant points are not very far apart
Rate of access to formal transfer services			Apply the growth rate of the standard to the indicator or perform linear interpolation if the distant points are not very far apart

Source: CREG 2023

Section 2: Back-casting of DDMI series

In this section, a presentation of the DDMIs back-cast from the different countries is made. Thus, we have:

Evolution of the DDMI retropolated from Benin

Chart 11 below shows the evolution of Benin's back-cast DDMI over the period from 2001 to 2020. We can see an upward evolution of the trend of this DDMI. Chart 11 shows that Benin's DDMI is above its component indices. Indeed, all 5 dimensions, namely the quality of the living environment, the coverage of economic dependence, the exit from poverty, extended human development and the networks and territories, contribute to improving the DDMI and therefore to the capture of the demographic dividend over the period 2000 to 2020. To better capture DD, we should invest above all in networks and territories, the living environment and human development.

Graphic 11: Evolution of Benin's DDMI retropolated between 2000-2020

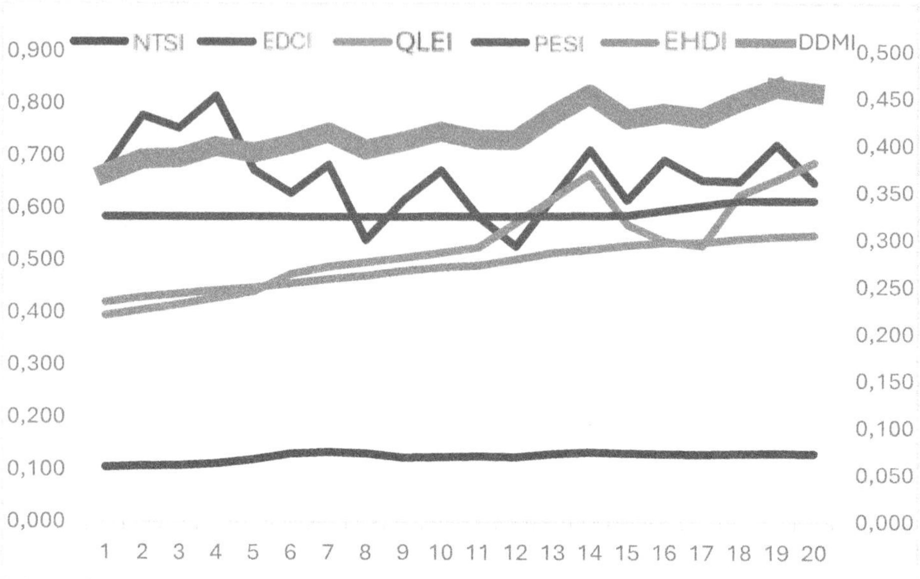

Source: CREG, 2024

Evolution of Cameroon's DDMI

This part analyzes the evolution of Cameroon's DDMI retropolated over the period 2001 to 2017. Chart 12 shows this evolution. The curve of the DDMI is below those of the Total Poverty Exit Index, the Quality of Living Environment Index and the Extended Human Development Index. Thus, it can be said that the DDMI is lower than the PESI, the QLEI and the EHDI in Cameroon. In addition, during this period, the DDMI is above the NTSI and the EDCI. This graph shows that the DDMI is pulled down by the index of economic dependency coverage and that of the Network and territory. Indeed, the weakness and unattractiveness of the territories in Cameroon tends to delay the capture of the demographic dividend. In addition, the life cycle deficit is very significant in Cameroon. All these factors are contributing to the downward trend in the DDMI. This is not the case for the indices of exit from poverty, extended human development and the living environment. On average, Cameroon is a country with a very low DDMI and therefore does not capture the demographic dividend (DD).

Graphic 12: Evolution of Cameroon's DDMI retropolated over the period 2001-2017

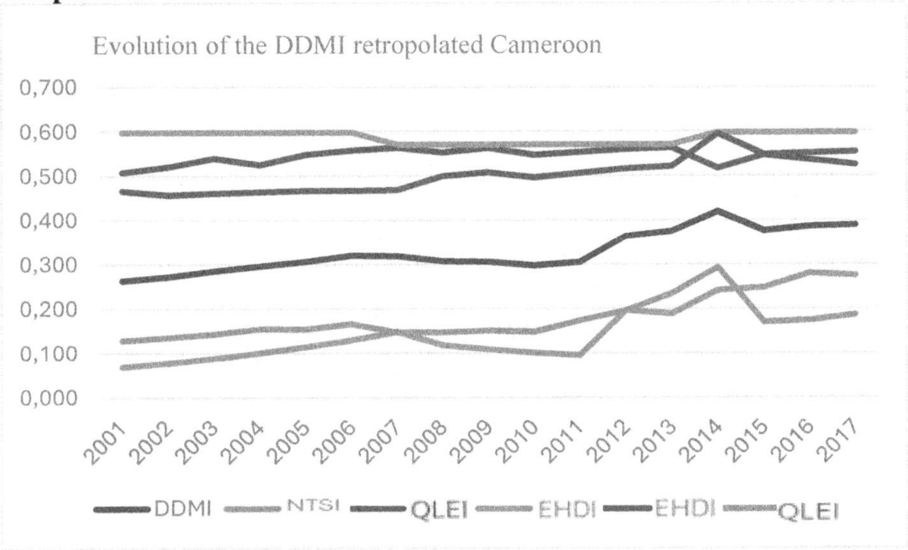

Source: CREG, 2024

3-1- Evolution of Guinea's DDMI

This subsection presents the evolution of Guinea's back-cast DDMI over the period 2002 to 2019. Indeed, in graph 13 below, we can see that the DDMI is lower than the EDCI, PESI, QLEI and EHDI. This means that these indicators are driving the DDMI upwards. This is not the case for the NTSI, which is below the DDMI over the period 2002 to 2019. The capture of DD is very low in Guinea. Indeed, the Networks and territories are not developed and attractive. There is no interconnection of territories in Guinea because of the lack of attractiveness. In addition, for a better capture of DD, Guinea should improve especially the networks and territories, and extensive human development by improving its human capital.

Graphic 13: Evolution of Guinea's DDMI retropolated over the period 2002-2019

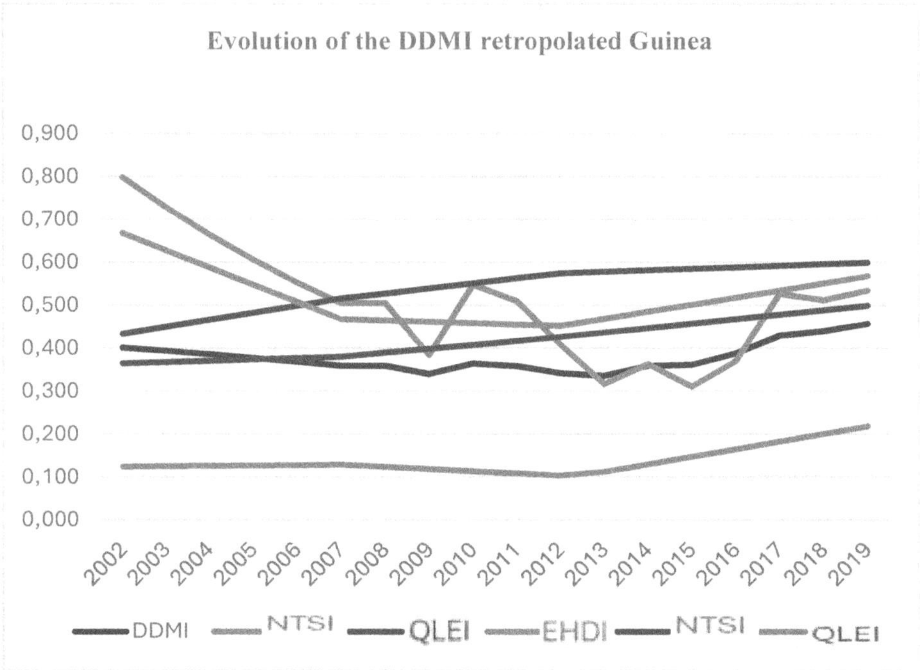

Source: CREG, 2024

Evolution of the DDMI retropolated from Chad

This subsection presents the series back-cast from Chad's DDMI over the period 2003 to 2018. Figure 4 below shows this evolution. Indeed, we can see that the DDMI is below the PESI, QLEI, EDCI and EHDI indices. In addition, the DDMI is higher than that of the NTSI. Of all the indices that make up the DDMI, we can see that the NTSI pulls down the DDMI over the period 2003-2018.

Graphic 14: Evolution of Chad's DDMI retropolated over the period 2003-2018

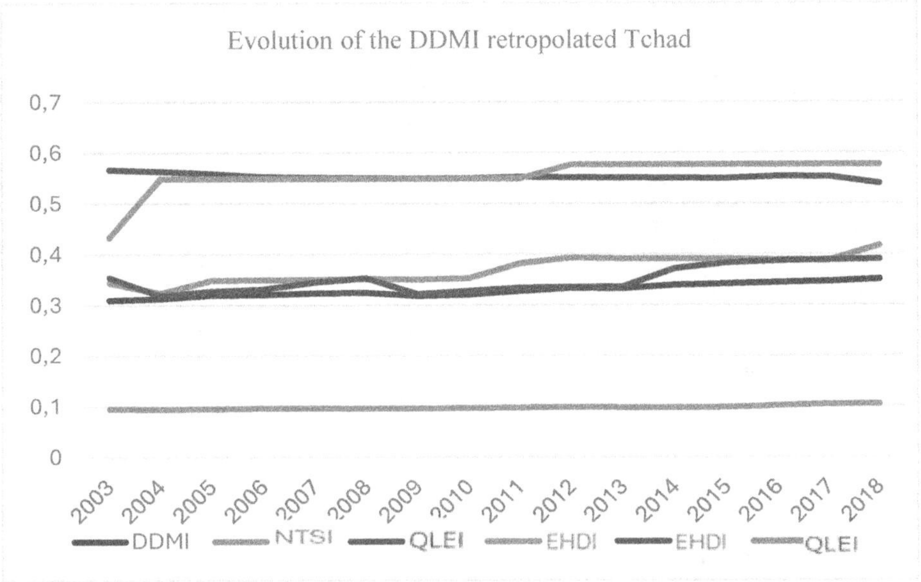

Source: CREG, 2024

Evolution of Niger's DDMI retropolated over the period 2001-2020

This subsection presents the results of Niger's DDMI back-cast over the period 2001 to 2020. Chart 15 below shows the evolution of the DDMI back-cast over this period. The QLEI and PESI curves lead to an increase in the DDMI, implying that an improvement in the living environment and the exit from poverty leads to an increase in the DDMI. Since their curves are higher than that of the DDMI. In addition, the PESI and EHDI curves are lower than those of the DDMI.

Graphic 15: Evolution of Niger's DDMI retropolated over the period 2001-2020

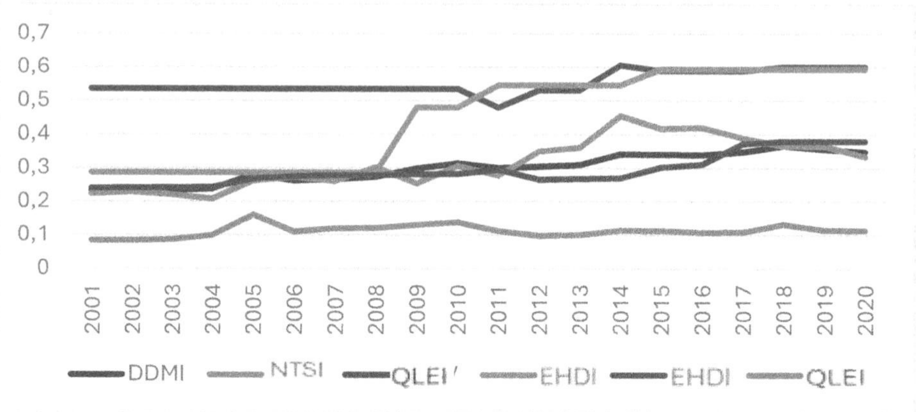

Source: CREG, 2024

Evolution of the DDMI retropolated from Mali

Chart 16 below shows the evolution of Mali's DDMI over the period 2001 to 2022. We can see that an upward trend in Mali's DDMI from 2001 to 2014 when it coincides with the EHDI curve. This was followed by a steady decline before resuming with a peak in 2019. In 2020, the DDMI experienced a sharp drop before increasing in 2022. Also, we note that the DDMI curve is lower than those of the EDCI, the PESI and the QLEI. This means that these indices have a significant value and are higher than that of the DDMI. In other words, these indices lift the DDMI and contribute strongly to the capture of the demographic dividend in Mali. By indices such as the NTSI and the EHDI are below the DDMI. This contributes to dragging down DDMI. To improve Mali's DDMI, more emphasis should be placed on networks and territories that have a low contribution to DDMI, as well as human development, which is low in Mali.

Graphic 16: Evolution of Mali's DDMI retropolated over the period 2001-2022

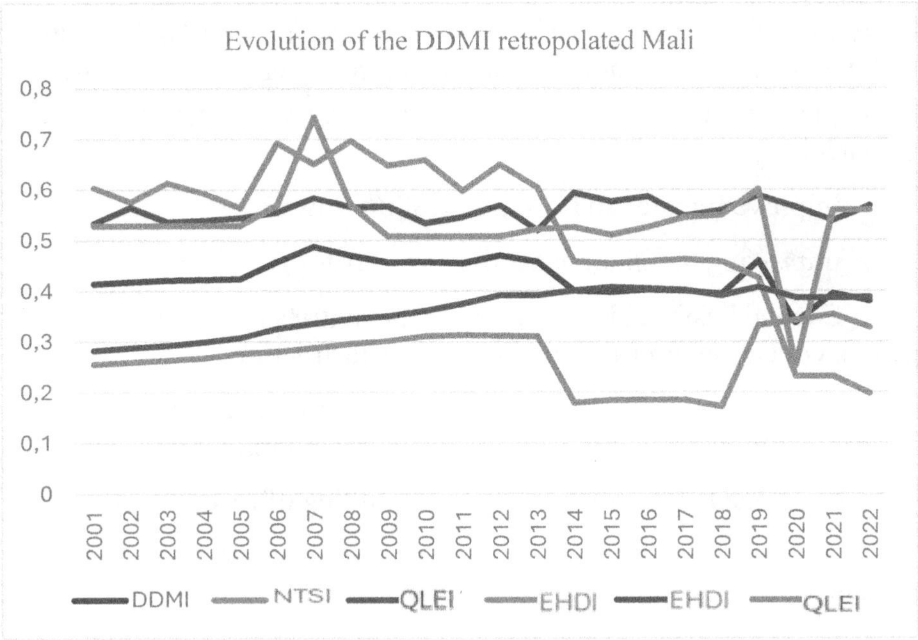

Source: CREG, 2024

Conclusion

The analysis of the back-casting of the countries made it possible to highlight the evolution of the different DDMI profiles of the countries in the study. Indeed, the DDMI has experienced a rise for its countries. However, the network and territory index is the sub-dimension that pulls the DDMI down in all the countries studied. In West and Central Africa, networks and territories are not interconnected and developed. As for Benin, apart from the NTSI, the quality of the living environment is low, as is human development. These sub-indicators are deteriorating the capture of the demographic dividend in Benin. Secondly, human development is very low in Mali and has little impact on the capture of the demographic dividend. This is not the case for the PESI, the EDCI and the QLEI, whose curves are higher than those of the DDMI. To better capture the demographic dividend in Mali, the quality of the living environment should be improved, economic dependence and poverty dynamics should be reduced. Moreover, in Niger, Chad and Guinea, in addition to the NTSI, the EHDI is very low. This implies that these countries have low human capital. Improving the quality of the living environment and exiting poverty improves the DDMI in these countries. In addition, in Cameroon, the NTSI and the EDCI are dragging down the DDMI. This is not the case for the EHDI, the PESI and the QLEI, which contribute to the improvement of the DDMI.

In view of the above, some public policy recommendations can be made:

– Improve transfer and communication flows.

– Improving the interconnectivity of territories.

– Expand basic social services in all countries to improve access to health, education, transport and market infrastructure.

– Strengthen good governance measures to open to foreign direct investment to improve financial flow and inward migration flows.

– Continue the efforts noted in the Building of road infrastructure.

– Promote incentives to boost the urban planning and housing sectors.

– Creating industrialized free zones in regions with weak infrastructure and urbanization

– Create employment centers to make the territories more attractive (factories, agri-food processing industries in areas with low attractiveness).

– Create easy access to formal transfers by reducing transaction costs

– Regulate external migration through responsibility and controlled migration.

– Reduce informality by reducing taxation through attractive tax rates to improve the formal employment rate and contribute to the national GDP.

– To improve the level of human capital of men and women in countries with low EHDI.

Bibliographical references

Dang, H. A., & Lanjouw, P. F. (2013). Measuring poverty dynamics with synthetic panels based on cross-sections. World Bank Policy Research Working Paper, (6504).

OECD, http://www.oecdbetterlifeindex.org/wpsystem/wpcontent/uploads/2011/05/YourBetterLifeIndex_ExecutiveSummary2.pdf

OECD, http://www.oecdbetterlifeindex.org/wpsystem/wpcontent/uploads/2011/06/BetterLifeIndex_Data_2011V6.xls

United Nations. (2013). National transfer accounts manual: Measuring and analyzing the generational economy. UN.

CHAPTER 6

FUNCTIONAL TRANSFORMATION OF THE BUDGET

Introduction

The interrelationship between population and development has become a topic of interest in countries with high prospects for population growth. It is estimated that in 2019, about 230 million young people (aged 15-24) lived in Africa, accounting for about 19% of the global youth population. Projections indicate that by 2030, the number of young people living in Africa will increase by up to 42% Ibrahim M. (2019). Aware of this challenge, African countries have adopted the African Union's roadmap, the main objective of which is to transform the potential of the population into economic opportunity. However, given funding constraints and scarce resources, optimal budget allocation becomes an imperative for capturing the demographic dividend. There is therefore a need to better understand the structure of public spending to redirect it towards investments sensitive to the demographic dividend.

The national budget is the main tool for allocating resources to the various economic and social sectors of a country. Its evolution and composition have significant consequences for the results of the public policies implemented in the country. This instrument, if it is brought into line with the components of the DDMI (Demographic Dividend Monitoring Index), could accelerate the achievement of the conditions for sustainable, inclusive growth that is conducive to the capture of the demographic dividend and sustainable development in Africa.

The general objective of this chapter is to transform the classic budget into a functional budget according to the eight (8) functions associated with the demographic dividend, namely: Health, Education, Institution, Security, Economy, Building-Energy, Social Network and Professional Network.

Section 1: Literature Review

The management tool studied is budgetary control, which presupposes, on the one hand, the existence of a numerical forecast in an accounting language covering the entire activity of the company, and on the other hand, the production of comparative statements between forecasts and realizations. If we do not wish to go further into the characteristics of the implementation of this budgetary control, it is precisely because its history is also that of the debates on the “good ways” of using it (Berland, I999a and b; Burchell and al., 1980).

For France, we can identify three historical phases in the Building of budgetary control. The first one roughly overlaps with the 1930s. It began with the International Conference on Budgetary Control, which was held in Geneva within the framework of the International Institute for the Scientific Organization of Work in 1930. His conception of budgetary control tinged with the rationalist ideas of the engineers who promoted it. The second phase takes us to the end of the 1950s. Budgetary control was then part of the reformist context of the post-war period and the Building of the Fordian compromise (Aglietta, 1976; Boyer, Mistral, 1978). While its rational nature has not disappeared, budgetary control has been entrusted with other missions such as humanizing the economy, contributing to growth and social progress by facilitating an equitable sharing of added value, and promoting the decentralization of information within companies and the professionalization of managers. The third phase covers the 1960s and sees the entry into force of reflections on motivation at work. The emphasis is then placed on the use of the budget as a target to be achieved and budgetary control as a means of motivating and evaluating performance.

De Crombrugghe and Lipton (1994) analyzed the evolution of the Polish budget between 1989 and 1991, a period of major economic transformation following the fall of the communist regime. They use fiscal and macroeconomic data to examine the structural and macro-economic forces that influenced the budget. The authors note that in 1989, a large deficit appeared due to the collapse of the communist tax system. In 1990, a budget surplus was achieved thanks to economic stabilization and liberalization. However, the fiscal correction has eroded over time due to the negative impact of the economic transformation on fiscal management. Changes in the tax base and spending priorities also played an important role. The budget has been constrained by financial problems and pressures to improve public services and social safety nets.

Chugunov and Makogon (2016) used abstraction, analysis, and synthesis methods to examine Ukraine's fiscal indicators and public debt for the year 2016. They show that Ukraine's budget deficit is identified as one of the factors of inflation, affecting financial and economic stability. The authors stress the need to improve fiscal policy, by using the budget deficit as a tool for financial and economic regulation.

In the complex landscape of economic governance, fiscal transformation is a key pillar. It is the process by which a country's tax policies, structures and practices evolve to adapt to changing economic, social and political contexts. Understanding the importance of fiscal trans-formation requires examining its many facets, considering the views of economists, policymakers, and citizens.

Fiscal transformation is essential to maintain economic resilience. A strong fiscal framework ensures stability in the event of economic shocks, such as recessions or global crises. Countries that have successfully transformed their tax systems are better equipped to weather financial storms.

For example, after the 2008 global financial crisis, several European countries undertook fiscal reforms to strengthen stability. The constitutional amendment of Germany's "debt brake" has limited deficits, thus contributing to its strong recovery.

Budget transformation involves optimizing the allocation of resources. Governments must prioritize spending in critical sectors (e.g., health, education, infrastructure) while minimizing waste.

Case in point: New Zealand's fiscal transformation in the 1980s shifted the focus from input-based budgeting to results-based approaches. This has led to improved efficiency and better results.

Figure 8: The functions of the state according to Musgrave

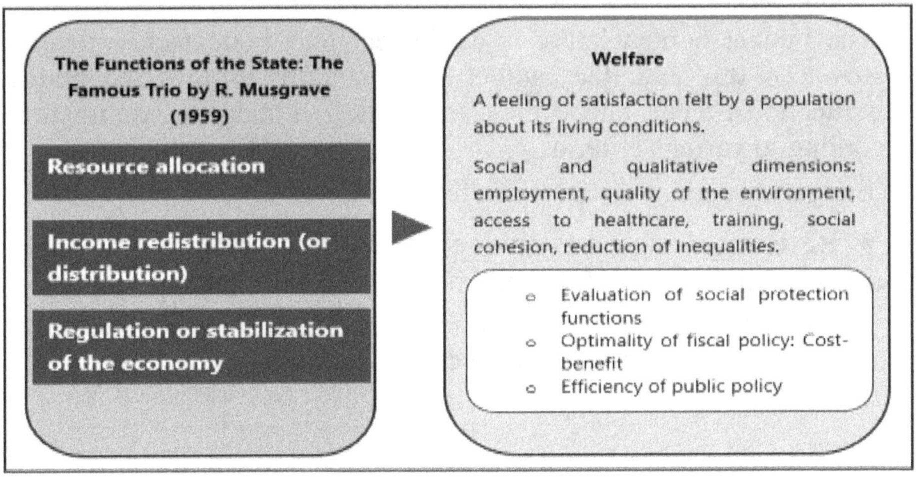

Source: Musgrave (1959)

Section 2: Methodology

Clarification des concepts

- **State budget**

It is an "Act by which the annual revenues and expenditures of the State are provided for and authorized". Also, the State budget is the "set of accounts that describe for a calendar year all the resources and expenses of the State".

- **General Budget**

It is a document that traces all budget revenues and all State expenditure (except for revenues allocated to annexed budgets and special accounts).

- **Program Budget (PB)**

It is the nomenclature of the State budget that makes it possible to relate the use of budgetary appropriations to the public policies implemented. The credits are grouped within the program.

- **Functional Classification**

The classification of expenditure transactions according to the purposes for which these transactions are carried out. A functional classification does not depend on the units that carry out the activities concerned.

This calls for a nomenclature to be used because of the existence of different headings in the budget.

The budget nomenclature is equivalent to a budget classification system. To this end, the budget nomenclature follows the budget classification system. This is the classification of budgetary transactions according to various criteria.

Budgetary operations are classified into:

- Revenue: budget revenue classified according to its nature corresponding to the tax base, and possibly according to its source.
- Expenditures: Budget expenditures are presented by administrative, program, functional and economic classifications.

The budget nomenclature is a mandatory reference framework.

Framed 1: Concept of public goods and services

General equilibrium theory studies the production and exchange of private goods. Private goods are both rival and excludable. The principle of rivalry implies that the quantity consumed by one consumer reduces the quantity available to other consumers by the same amount. As for the criterion of excludability, it is the possibility of excluding or preventing any individual from using goods. Thus, as opposed to private property, public property is neither exclusionary nor rival (Mankiw and Taylor, 2013). The two above-mentioned criteria are valid for characterizing all goods and services produced in an economy and allow them to be classified into four main families, namely: private goods, communal goods, public goods and club goods. The table below summarizes the typology of properties classified according to the criteria of rivalry and excludability.

Table 21: Typology of properties

	With exclusion of use	**Without exclusion of use**
Rival	Private property e.g. apple	Communal property e.g. pasture
Non rival	Club Properties e.g. encrypted TV	Public goods e.g. National Defense

According to Mankiw and Taylor (2013), the three most important public goods are national defense, basic research and the fight against poverty. For Bozio et al., 2010, public action is not limited to the sovereign functions of the State but is now expanding to the provision of goods and services in education, health, social protection and the reduction of inequalities.

Classification Type

- Administrative classification: this involves (i) presenting budgetary expenditure according to the services or groups of services responsible for managing it and (ii) identifying the hierarchy of the service responsible for implementing the expenditure.

- Classification by program: here, budget appropriations are broken down into program (or allocations) at the level of the country's institutions and ministries. The program aggregates the credits of a directorate (or set of branches) or a service (or set of services).
- Functional classification: classify budgetary expenditures according to their socio-economic objectives.
- Economic classification: this is to be consistent with the State's chart of accounts with a codification that makes it possible to identify expenditure by nature.
- Other types of classifications: there is the classification by sources of financing where the means of financing budgetary expenditure are identified and monitored. Finally, the classification by beneficiaries, where the link between budgetary expenditure and final beneficiary is established.

Budgetary functioning and convergence

To meet the functions of resource allocation, income redistribution, and economic stabilization, the different budgeting methods appear to be converging.

From this, there are four (04) budgetary components and eight (08) budgetary functions. The functional budget is therefore a key focus in the demographic dividend-sensitive budgeting process. To this end, it distinguishes the functions relating to human capital (Education and health), governance (Security and institutions), the structure of the economy (Building-Energy and economic affairs) and professional and social networks (communication, leisure).

Transformation from traditional to functional budget

This step consists of making an exhaustive survey of the classic budget to classify each of the budget lines with the budget function that corresponds to it. This transformation process is carried out in three stages:

- Classification according to Principal Functions.
- The classification according to Secondary Functions.
- Classification according to the Budgetary Nature.

Classification according to Main Functions:

The Classic Budget with all its structural components is being remodeled considering the eight main functions. To do this, it was necessary to group the various ministerial departments and Republican Institutions considering their respective missions in these eight functions of the Functional Budget, namely:

- Education
- Health
- Security
- Institutions
- Professional Network
- Social Network
- Building and Energy
- Economic affairs

Classification according to Secondary Functions

This exercise consists of matching the expenditure made within the departments and institutions to the eight functions, this time taking into account the spending services, the purpose of the expenditure and, above all, the actual impact of the expenditure

Classification according to the Budgetary Nature

The latter consists of reclassifying the expenditure during the first two treatments according to the budgetary natures, namely

- Operation
- Transfer
- Investment

The result of these different exercises is then presented in two Pivot Tables:

- Pivot Table 1 by taking:
  - Online: the main function and the budget function
  - In column: the year and nature of the expenditure
- Pivot Table 2 by taking:
  - Online: The Budget Function
  - In column: the year and nature of the expenditure

Types of analysis

- Economic analysis of the budget.
- Determination of sectoral budgetary optimums.
- Analysis of the effectiveness and efficiency of budget allocation.
- Determination of sectoral budget thresholds.

In the following, we will discuss the economic analysis of the budget

Figure 9: Functional transformation of the budget

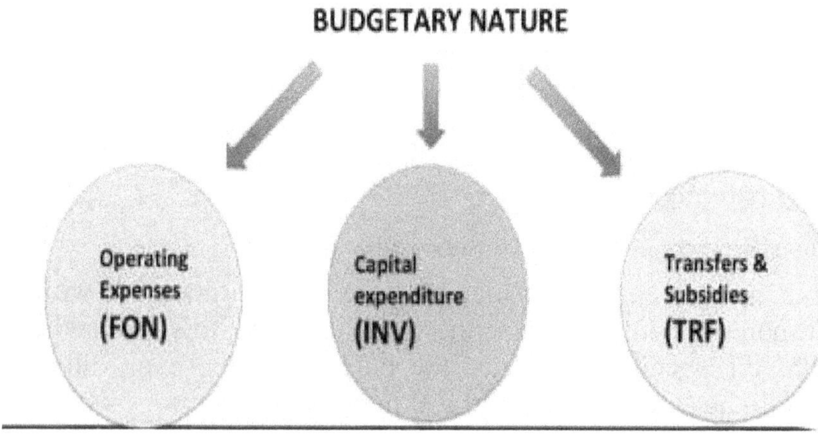

Source: CREG 2023

Figure 10: Linking Budget Functions and the DDMI Index

Development Components	Budget Functions	Sub-dimensions of DDMI	Characteristics
Human Capital	Education	Education	Non-composite
	Health	Health	Non-composite
Governance	Institutions	Civic Engagement	Non-composite
	Security	PESI + Security	Composite
Professional and social network	Social network	Social network	Non-composite
	Professional network	Work-life balance + Subjective Well-being	Composite
Structure of the economy	Construction-Energy	Urbanization + Infrastructure + Housing	Composite
	Economic affairs	EDCI + PESI + Standard of living + Urbanization +Infrastructure + Environment	Composite

Source: CREG 2023

Principle of Functional Budget Transformation

This principle consisted of identifying for each institution (budget section) and sub-institution of the State its main mission/function, then assigning the DDMI function (a structure defined in advance by the BSDD) to a budgetary expenditure of these institutions and finally identifying the nature of this expenditure. It is indeed a table for the transition from the classic budget to the functional budget of the State.

In accordance with the dimensions of the demographic dividend, eight (08) major budgetary convergence functions have been defined to ensure the alignment of the traditional budget with the DDMI. These are:

Table 22: The 08 DDMI functions defined by the BSDD structure

Number	DDMI Function	Definition
01	**Education**	Total expenditure on the production of goods and services for skills building
02	**Health**	All expenses that serve people's health
03	**Institution**	Expenditure on the production of goods and services determining the legal and institutional environment in which the individual is attached
04	**Security**	Expenditure on the production of goods and services to ensure the peace of mind of the individual and the people
05	**Economic Affair**	Budgetary expenditure contributing to the production of market goods and services
06	**Building & Energy**	Expenditure related to the production of market and non-market goods and services
07	**Social network**	Expenses related to the production of any good and service aimed at cementing social relations
08	**Professional network**	Spending on behavior change interaction

Source: CREG 2023

According to the functional approach of the budget, three (03) categories of nature of expenditure have been defined:

1. **Capital expenditure (INV):** Capital expenditure is the value of the amounts of a producer's fixed asset acquisitions during the accounting period, plus some specific expenses spent on services that add value to non-produced assets. In the case of DDMI, debt charges are counted as capital expenditures.

2. **Operating Expenditures (FON):** Operating expenditures are measured by the value of goods and services and the value of compensation paid to employees in the process of a good or service.

3. **Transfers & Subsidies (TRF):** A transfer or subsidy is an operation in which one institutional unit provides goods, services, or assets to another unit, without receiving goods, services, or assets from the latter in direct consideration.

Table 23: Table for the transition from budgetary nature (classical) to functional nature (DDMI)

Code	Budgetary nature	Nature DDMI
01	Financial Expenses	Investments
05	Investments	
02	Personnel	Operation
03	Goods and Services	
04	Transfers and subsidies	Transfers

Source: CREG 2023

Section 3: Analysis of the budget structure

Analysis of the structure of the budget by function over the last 5 years in Africa

Table 24: Structure of the budget according to functions over the last 5 years

Development Components	Human Capital		Economy		Governance		Professional & Social Networks	
Budget Functions	Education	Health	Economic Affairs	Construction & Energy	Institution	Security	Professional network	Social network
BENIN	21%	5%	24%	9%	22%	7%	3%	9%
BURKINA FASO	21%	9%	24%	14%	16%	9%	2%	5%
MALI	18%	5%	30%	11%	13%	17%	1%	5%
MAURITANIA	10%	17%	9%	8%	10%	16%	14%	15%
NIGER	12%	5%	47%	17%	3%	9%	1%	7%
SENEGAL	15%	7%	27%	25%	12%	7%	2%	4%
CHAD	5%	6%	43%	14%	15%	14%	1%	3%
TOGO	17%	4%	30%	15%	15%	10%	2%	1%
TOGETHER	18%	6%	32%	13%	14%	10%	2%	5%

Source: CREG, 2024

The table above shows the evolution of budgetary functions over the period from 2017 to 2021. These functions, which are eight (08) in number, represent the four (04) economic and social dimensions inherent in the capture of the demographic dividend. Each of these dimensions includes two (02) budgetary functions as follows: Human Capital (Education and Health); structure of the economy (Building-Energy and Economic affairs), Governance (Institution and Security) and Networks (Professional and Social).

The analysis of the table shows that the economic functions occupy the largest share of the budget, with 45%. They are followed by Governance (24%), Human Capital (24%) and Professional Networks (7%).

The functions of the "Human Capital" component

Regarding the budget component of human capital, it is observed that for the above 8 countries, the budget allocated to this component is much more oriented towards education with 18% of the total budget than on health with only 6% of the total budget.

In terms of education, Benin and Burkina Faso lead the way with 21% of their budgets each. Chad comes in last place in terms of its budget allocated to education with only 5%. In terms of health, Mauritania leads the way, allocating 17% of its budget to health, compared to less than 10% for all the other countries in the sample.

The functions of the "Economic affairs" component

Regarding the budgetary component of the economy, for the above 8 countries, the budget allocated to this component is much more oriented towards economic affairs, representing 32% of the total budget compared to Building - Energy, which represents about 13% of the total budget. In terms of economic affairs, Niger and Chad lead with 47% and 43% of their total budgets, respectively. Mauritania comes in last place in terms of its budget allocated to economic affairs with only 9%. As for Building and energy, Senegal comes out on top, allocating 25% of its budget to Building and energy, compared to less than 20% for all the other countries in the sample.

The functions of the "Governance" component

Regarding the budgetary component of governance, it is noted that for the above 8 countries, the budget allocated to this component is 14% for Institutions and 10% for Security. As for the Institutions, Benin comes in first place by allocating 22% of its total budget and Niger comes in last place with only 3% of its total budget. As for security, Mali and Mauritania come out on top, allocating 17% and 16% of their total budgets, respectively. Senegal and Benin come in last place with 7% of their total budget each.

The functions of the "Network" component

Regarding the budget component of Network, it is observed that for the above 8 countries the budget allocated to this component is 5% for the social network and 2% for the Professional network. As for the social network, Mauritania comes in first place by allocating 15% of its total budget and Togo comes in last place with only 1% of its total budget. As for the Professional network, Mauritania still comes out on top, allocating 14% of its total budget. Thus, only Mauritania allocates a budget of more than 10% in the Network component. All other countries in the sample allocate less than 10%.

Analysis of structures by budgetary nature

Table 25: Structure of the budget according to the nature of expenditure over the last 05 years

	Operation	Investment	Transfers
BENIN	44%	21%	35%
BURKINA FASO	44%	36%	20%
MALI	42%	40%	18%
MAURITANIA	64%	35%	1%
NIGER	24%	62%	14%
SENEGAL	42%	19%	39%
CHAD	47%	23%	30%
TOGO	48%	34%	18%
TOGETHER	**44%**	**29%**	**27%**

Source: CREG, 2024

With a view to comparison, a benchmarking analysis of the structure by budgetary nature was carried out on some African countries. The results of this analysis are presented in the table above. It appears from this table that over the period 2017-2021, recurrent expenditure in the budgets of the countries concerned is the most dominant, i.e. 44% of the total budget on average, except for Niger, whose investment expenditure is the most dominant (62%). The investment and transfer expenditure of these countries represents over the same period, 29% and 27% on average of their total budget.

Mauritania is the country that stands out as a leader with the highest share in operating expenditure, i.e. 64% of the overall budget. Niger for this nature is the last with 24% of the overall budget. It is also noted that Senegal is the country that allocates the least in investment expenditure (19%) of the overall budget.

Finally, on the other hand, about transfer expenditure, Senegal is the country that allocates the most with 39% of the overall budget, followed by Benin (35%) of the overall budget. The last country for this nature is Mauritania with 1% of the overall budget.

Analysis of budget structures by nature and functions

Table 26: Structure of the budget by nature and functions over the last 05 years for all countries combined

Components	Duties	Operation	Investment	Transfers	TOTAL
Human Capital	Education	11%	3%	4%	**18%**
	Health	2%	1%	2%	**6%**
Economy	Economic Affairs	10%	13%	9%	**32%**
	Energy, Building	3%	6%	4%	**13%**
Governance	Institutions	8%	2%	4%	**14%**
	Security	7%	2%	1%	**10%**
Professional and social networks	Professional network	1%	0,4%	1%	**1%**
	Social network	2%	1%	2%	**5%**
TOTAL		**44%**	**29%**	**27%**	**100%**

Source: CREG, 2024

Conclusion

The results of the Functional Transformation of the State Budget show that at the national level, the average structure of the State Budget allocates a significant share to the national economy. Indeed, it is observed that for the above 8 countries, the budget allocated to this component is much more oriented towards economic affairs with 32% of the total budget. Secondly, the Analysis of Structures by Budgetary Nature indicates that recurrent expenditure in the budgets of the countries concerned is the most dominant, i.e. 44% of the total budget on average.

In terms of recommendations, in view of the results of the functional transformation of the budget, it is desirable to:

– give pride of place not only in the structure of the economy but also to the basic social sectors (health, education, standard of living).

– also giving pride of place in investments, a guarantee of the structural transformation of an economy.

– accelerate the transition from the traditional budget to the program budget.

– promote the use of the BSDD tool in budget conferences.

– increase investments related to human capital (health, education, etc.) in the State budget.

Bibliographical references

Berland N. (1999a), L'Histoire du contrôle fiscale en France. The Functions of Budgetary Control, Influences of Ideology, the Environment and Strategic Management, doctoral thesis in management sciences, University of Paris Dauphine.

Berland N. (1999b), "What is the purpose of budgetary control? The Roles of the Budget", Finance-Contrôle Stratégie, September, Vol. 2, No. 3, p. 5-24

Burchell S., Clubb C., Hopwood A, Hughes, Nahapiet J. (1980), The Roles of Accounting in Organizations and Society, Accounting, Organizations and Society vol. 5, n° l, p. 5-27

Chugunov, I., & Makogon, V. (2016). Budget policy under economic transformation. *Економічний часопис-XXI*, (158), 66-70.

De Crombrugghe, A., & Lipton, D. (1994). The government budget and the economic transformation of Poland. In *The Transition in Eastern Europe, Volume 2, Restructuring* (pp. 111-136). University of Chicago Press.

Faster Capital 2024: Budget Transformation Analysis: How to Achieve and Sustain Budget Transformation

Mo Ibrahim Foundation. 2019. 2019 Ibrahim Forum Report: African Youth: Migration for Lack of Jobs? Demography, economic prospects and mobility.

CHAPTER 7

OPTIMAL BUDGET CONTROL

Introduction

Monetary and fiscal policy are two instruments in the organization of economic policies in countries. These tools participate, among other things, in the control of inflation and public deficits, the revival of economic growth, the reduction of unemployment, etc. On the other hand, the implementation of these tools in an economic and monetary union poses enormous challenges because of the coordination of a policy mix in which monetary policy is managed by an autonomous central bank and fiscal policy is implemented by each sovereign country. This situation, which is dangerous for economic efficiency, if not controlled, is at the origin of many controversies in the implementation of economic policies, on the one hand, between public deficit and interest rates, and on the other hand, between monetary policy and fiscal policy (Creel, 2001; Creel and Sterdyniak, 1998).

Senegal and the other countries of the West African Economic and Monetary Union (WAEMU) are perfectly in the situation described above. As the management of monetary policy in the union is the prerogative of the BCEAO (Central Bank of West African States), whose main objective is to control inflation, countries are practically reduced to the use of fiscal policy for the implementation of economic policies and the production of collective well-being.

The countercyclical fiscal policy advocated by Keynesians allows countries to navigate between an increase in public spending in times of recession and an increase in taxes in times of economic growth (Llorca, 2016; French-Davis, 2010). The use of an expansionary fiscal policy, particularly through increased public investment, has the disadvantage of increasing debt, undermining countries' solvency. This policy may even be ineffective at times in WAEMU countries because of procyclical biases induced by factors such as high debt levels, rising oil prices, and rigid public spending (Kane, 2018).

The failure to implement the Washington Consensus under the initiative of the International Monetary Fund (IMF) has resulted in a reduction in public spending and has not been conducive to an increase in tax revenues (Llorca, 2016; Adli and Akacem, 2012). According to BCEAO data, Senegal's pressure rate is the highest in the region but remains below the community standard of 20% of GDP. The tax burden has risen from an average level of 14.91% over the period 2002-2014 to 15.75% over the period 2014-2019, an increase of 0.84 percentage points between the two periods (Trinnou, 2021).

Faced with the difficulty of maneuvering fiscal policy instruments, it is important for countries like Senegal to go back to basics by focusing on the optimal allocation of available public resources to ensure economic effectiveness and efficiency. Most of the empirical work on the optimal allocation of fiscal resources has focused more on the determinants of public expenditure efficiency. Thus, weak institutional quality, corruption and the political regime are the main factors in the inefficiency of public spending in countries in the Middle East, North Africa and Sub-Saharan Africa region (Guèye, 2021; Rota-Graziosi, et al., 2021; Mtiraoui, 2015). In addition to the determinants, it is important to look at the functional structure of the budget because it has been proven that the optimal allocation of public spending has the advantage of promoting the structural transformation of the sectors of the economy (Aguey, 2020; Kuate Fotue, 2015). To this end, it is therefore possible to envisage a functional allocation of resources that optimizes collective well-being by minimizing the cost of the budget.

The objective of this paper is to determine the structures of the functional allocation of the budget that optimizes the function of producing well-being under budgetary constraints in Senegal. In the following, we present in section 1 the general information on the structure of the budget and its operation. Section 2 is devoted to the literature review on optimal control theories. The research methodology is presented in Section 3. Section 4 discusses the interpretation, analysis and discussion of the results, before concluding.

Section 1: The budget structure, how does it work?

The optimal allocation of the State budget, like the sound management of public resources, is the keystone of the efficiency of public spending. Indeed, the allocation of public resources is closely linked to the structure of the budget. Before making any decisions on the allocation of the budget, it is important to take a close look at the typology of the budget in question, how it works and the principles surrounding the analysis of budget structures.

1.1. **Classification Type**

The State budget can take several forms. These include:

o Administrative classification: this involves (i) presenting budgetary expenditure according to the services or groups of services responsible for managing it and (ii) identifying the hierarchy of the service responsible for implementing the expenditure.

o Classification by program: here, budget appropriations are broken down into program (or allocations) at the level of the country's institutions and ministries. The program aggregates the credits of a directorate (or set of branches) or a service (or set of services).

o Functional classification: classify budgetary expenditures according to their socio-economic objectives.

o Economic classification: this is to be consistent with the State's chart of accounts with a codification that makes it possible to identify expenditure by nature.

o Other types of classifications: there is the classification by sources of financing where the means of financing budgetary expenditure are identified and monitored. Finally, the classification by beneficiaries, where the link between budgetary expenditure and final beneficiary is established.

1.2 **Budgetary functioning and convergence**

To meet the functions of resource allocation, income redistribution, and economic stabilization, the different budgeting methods appear to be converging.

From this, there are four (04) budgetary components and eight (08) budgetary functions. The functional budget is therefore a key focus in the demographic dividend-sensitive budgeting process. To this end, it distinguishes between functions relating to human capital (education and health), governance (security and institutions), the structure of the economy (Building-energy and economic affairs) and professional and social networks (communication-leisure).

1.3 **Transformation from traditional to functional budget**

This step consists of making an exhaustive survey of the classic budget to classify each of the budget lines with the budget function that corresponds to it. This transformation process is carried out in three stages:

- Classification according to Principal Functions.
- Classification according to Secondary Functions.
- Classification according to the Budgetary Nature.

Classification according to Main Functions:

The Classic Budget, with all its structural components, is being remodeled considering the eight main functions. To do this, it was necessary to bring together the various ministerial departments and Republican Institutions considering their respective missions in these eight functions of the functional budget, namely:

- Education
- Health
- Security
- Institutions
- Professional Network
- Social Network
- Building-Energy
- Economic affairs.

Classification according to Secondary Functions

This exercise consists of matching the expenditure made within the departments and institutions to the eight functions, this time considering the spending services, the purpose of the expenditure and above all the actual impact of the latter.

Classification according to the Budgetary Nature:

The latter consists of reclassifying the expenditure during the first two processing operations according to the budgetary nature, namely:

- Operation
- Transfer
- Investment.

The result of these different exercises is then presented in two Pivot Tables:

- Pivot Table 1 by taking:
- Online: the main function and the budget function

- In column: the year and nature of the expenditure.

- Pivot Table 2 by taking:
- Online: The Budget Function
- In column: the year and nature of the expenditure.

1.4 **Types of analysis**

- Economic analysis of the budget.
- Determination of sectoral budgetary optimums.
- Analysis of the effectiveness and efficiency of budget allocation.
- Determination of sectoral budget thresholds.

In the following, we will discuss the economic analysis of the budget.

Section 2: Theoretical and Empirical Literature Review

2.1. **Origin of Optimal Control**

In mathematics, the theory of optimal control is a continuation of the calculus of variations. It appeared after the Second World War and makes it possible to meet practical guidance needs, particularly in the field of aeronautics and flight dynamics. Historically, the theory of optimal control is closely linked to classical mechanics, particularly to the variational principles of mechanics (Fermat principle, Huygens principle, Euler-Lagrange equations). The key point of this theory is the principle of the Pontryagin maximum, formulated by L. S. Pontryagin in 1956, which gives a necessary condition of optimality and thus allows calculating optimal trajectories (Pontryagin, 1959).

The strengths of the theory have included the discovery of the dynamic programming method, the introduction of functional analysis into the theory of optimal systems, the discovery of the links between the solutions of an optimal control problem and the results of Lyapunov stability theory (Lyapunov, 1992). Later, the foundations of the theory of stochastic control and filtering of dynamical systems, game theory, and the control of partial differential equations appeared.

The modern theory of optimal control is considered to have begun in the 1950s, with the formulation of Pontryagin's maximum principle, which generalizes the Euler-Lagrange equations of the calculus of variations. Since then, the theory has experienced spectacular growth, as well as many applications. Nowadays, automated systems are completely part of our daily lives (we are often unaware of them), with the aim of improving our quality of life and facilitating certain tasks: ABS braking system, driving assistance, servomotors, thermostats, humidity regulation, refrigeration circuits, control of road, rail, air, stock market, river flows, EDF dams, digital photography, etc. image filtering and reBuilding, CD and DVD players, computer networks, internet search engines, electrical circuits, electronics, telecommunications in general, chemical process control, oil refining, industrial assembly lines, peacemakers and other automated medical systems, laser operations, robotics, satellites, aerospace guidance, bioreactors, distillation, etc. The list is endless, the applications concern any system on which one can have an action, with a notion of optimal efficiency.

Note that the pace of the optimal trajectories depends strongly on the optimization criterion. For example, to make a slot and park your car, it is obvious that the trajectory followed differs if you carry out the operation in a minimum time (which presents a risk) or by minimizing the amount of petrol spent. The shortest path between two points is therefore not necessarily the straight line. In 1638, Galileo Galilei studied the following problem: to determine the curve on which a ball rolls, without initial velocity, from point A to point B, with a minimum travel time, under the action of gravity (optimal slide).

This is the famous problem of the brachistochrone emanating from the Greek words brakhistos, which means "the shortest", and chronos, which refers to "time"). Galileo thought that the curve he was looking for was the arc of a circle, but he had already noticed that the straight line was not the shortest way in time. In 1696, Jean Bernoulli posed this problem as a challenge to the mathematicians of his time. He found the solution himself, as well as his brother Jacques Bernoulli, Newton, Leibniz and the Marquis de l'Hôpital. The solution is an arc of a cycloid starting with a vertical tangent. This result motivated the development of the theory of calculus variations, which later became the theory of optimal control (for more details on the history of the brachistochrone problem).

2.2 Principle of Optimal Control

Control theory analyzes the properties of controlled systems, i.e. dynamical systems that can be acted upon by means of a command (or control). The goal is then to bring the system from a given initial state to a certain final state, possibly respecting certain criteria. The systems covered are multiple: differential systems, discrete systems, systems with noise, with delay, etc. Their origins are very diverse: mechanics, electricity, electronics, biology, chemistry, economics, etc. The objective may be to stabilize the system to make it insensitive to certain disturbances (stabilization), or to determine optimal solutions for a certain optimization criterion (optimal control).

The problem of optimal control is to guide the evolution in time of a given system towards a desired final configuration, while minimizing a certain criterion. The salient point of this theory, which generalizes the calculus of variations, is the Pontryagin maximum principle, which gives necessary conditions for first-order optimality. From a numerical point of view, this principle reduces the initial problem to a problem at both ends that can be solved by a firing method. In practice, it is very difficult to digitally converge a firing method, and it must be combined with other approaches. Here we will discuss examples motivated by aerospace, numerical continuation methods, geometric control, and then elements of dynamical systems theory that, properly used, make it possible to plan interplanetary space missions.

In modern industries where the notion of efficiency is predominant, the role of automation engineers is to design, implement and optimize, or at least to improve existing methods. Thus, the fields of application are multiple: aerospace, automotive, robotics, aeronautics, internet and communications in general, but also the medical, chemical, process engineering, etc.

From a mathematical point of view, a control system is a dynamic system dependent on a dynamic parameter called control. To model it, we can use differential, integral, functional, finite difference, partial and stochastic equations, etc. For this reason, control theory is at the interconnection of many mathematical fields. Controls are functions or parameters, usually subject to constraints.

Pontryagin's maximum principle is a necessary condition of optimality, while dynamic programming provides sufficient condition. On the other hand, the maximum principle gives as a solution an open-loop control (a function of time) while dynamic programming leads to a closed-loop control (a function of the state of the system).

However, the solution control of the maximum principle can, in favorable cases, be put in the form of a closed-loop control. One of the great advantages of the maximum principle over dynamic programming is that it is easier to implement, the latter when applied to continuous-time systems, involving the solution of a partial differential equation (the Hamilton-Jacobi-Bellman equation), while the former is reduced to the solution of ordinary differential equations (a resolution that is seriously complicated by the fact that the problem is "at both ends").

Dynamic programming applies to both deterministic and stochastic systems, while the principle of the maximum applies practically only to deterministic systems.

Nevertheless, a common step in these approaches is the maximization of the pseudo-Hamiltonian on the set of admissible controls. As Pontryagin and his collaborators themselves revealed, the maximum principle can be deduced from Bellman's theorem, the proof of which is very simple, if we make sufficient regularity assumptions about the "Bellman function". However, these hypotheses are not verified in cases where the maximum principle is of great interest, and for which it was designed, for example in the case of the "Bang-Bang control".

2.3 The problem of Controllability, linear and nonlinear cases

A control system is said to be controllable if it can be brought (in finite time) from an arbitrary initial state to a prescribed final state. For finite-dimensional linear control systems, there is a very simple characterization of controllability, due to Kalman (Kalman, 1960; Kalman, 1959). For nonlinear systems, the mathematical problem of controllability is much more difficult.

Definition

The controlled system,

$$\mathbf{x'(t) = A(t)x(t) + B(t)u(t) + r(t)},$$

is said to be *controllable in time* T if **Acc(x0, T) = IRn** , *i.e.* , for all x0, x1 ∈ IRn , there exists a control u such that the associated trajectory connects x0 to x1 in time T.

Controllability of autonomous linear systems

In the linear case, we can distinguish two situations: the case without constraint on the control and the case with constraint on the control.

In the first case, we speak of **the Kalman condition**. Formally, the following theorem gives us a necessary and sufficient condition of controllability in case where the matrices A and B do not depend on t.

Theorem : It is assumed that Ω = mIR (no constraint on the control).

The system

$$\mathbf{x'(t) = Ax(t) + Bu(t) + r(t)}$$

is controllable in time T (any) if and only if the matrix

$C = (B, AB, \ldots, A^{n-1B)}$ is of rank **n**.

The matrix C is called the Kalman matrix, and the condition **rg C = n** is called **the Kalman condition**.

It will be noted that the Kalman condition does not depend on T or x0. This means that if an autonomous linear system is controllable at time T since x0, then it is controllable at any time from any point.

In the presence of constraints on the control, under the previous Kalman condition, if **r = 0 and if 0 ∈ Ω**, then the accessible set **Acc(x0, t)** in time **t** contains a neighborhood of the point **exp(tA)x0.**

The properties of global controllability are related to the stability properties of matrix A. For example, if Kalman's condition is met, **r = 0 and 0 ∈ Ω**, and all eigenvalues of matrix A are of strictly negative real part (i.e. matrix A is stable), then any point of **IRn** can be led to the origin in finite (possibly large) time.

Controllability of unsteady linear systems

A necessary and sufficient condition of controllability in the unsteady case is given by the following two theorems:

Theorem 1 :

The system x'(t) = A(t)x(t) + B(t)u(t) + r(t) is controllable in time T if and only if the matrix

$C(T) = M(t)^{-1B(t)B(t)\,TM(t)\,-1T}$ dt,

The so-called controllability matrix is invertible.

Note that this condition depends on T, but does not depend on the initial point x0. In other words, if an unsteady linear system is controllable in time T since x0, then it is controllable in time T from any point. We also notice that we have C(T) =∫To C(T) ^{T} , and x $^{TC(T)}$ x > 0 for all x ∈ IRn , i.e. C(T) is a positive symmetric real square matrix.

Theorem 2 :

Consider the system,

x'(t) = A(t)x(t) + B(t)u(t) + r(t)

where the applications A, B are of class C^{∞} on [0, T]. Let's define by recurrence

$B0(t) = B(t), Bi+1(t) = A(t)Bi(t) - dB_i(t)/dt$.

✓ If there exists $t \in [0, T]$ such that Vect $\{B_i(t)v \mid v \in MRI, i \in IN\} = IR^n$, then the system is controllable in time T.

✓ If in addition the applications A, B are analytical on [0, T], then the system is controllable in time T if and only if $\forall t \in [0, T]$ Vect $\{B_i(t)v \mid v \in IRm, i \in IN\} = IRn$.

This theorem is easily shown in optimal control theory, by the application of the maximum principle (see below).

Optimal control in non-linear cases

Now, in addition to a control problem, we give ourselves a minimization problem: among all the solutions of the system linking x0 to x1, find a trajectory that minimizes a certain cost function C(T, u). Such a trajectory, if it exists, is said to be optimal for this cost. The existence of optimal trajectories depends on the regularity of the system and the cost. It may also be that an optimal control does not exist in the class of controls considered, but exists in a larger space: this is the Lavrentiev phenomenon. In particular, it is in your interest to work in a complete control area that has good compact properties.

Existence of optimal trajectories

Consider the control system,

$$\mathbf{x'(t) = f(t, x(t), u(t)),}$$

where f is C^1 of IR1+n+m in IR^n, the controls u are valued in a compact $\Omega \subset Rm$. Let M_0 and M1 be two compacts of IR^n such that M1 is accessible from M0.

Let U be the set of checks with values in Ω joining M0 to M1. Let f0 be a function of class C1 on IR1+n+m, and g a continuous function on IR^n. Consider the cost:

$$\mathbf{C(u) = \int t(u)_o\ f0\ (t, x(t), u(t))dt + g(t(u), x(t(u))),}$$

where $t(u) > 0$ is such that $x(t(u)) \in M1$. It is assumed that:

✓ there exists a positive real b such that any trajectory associated with a control $u \in U$ is uniformly bounded by b on [0, t(u)], as well as the time t(u),

✓ for all $(t, x) \in IR1+^n$, the set

$$\mathbf{\tilde{V}\ (t, x) = \{(f(t, x, u), f^0\ (t, x, u) + \gamma) \mid u \in \Omega, \gamma > 0\}}$$

is convex.

Then, there is an optimal control u over [0, t(u)] such that the associated trajectory joins M0 to M1 in time t(u) and in minimum cost.

We can show a more general result where the starting set M0 and the target M1 depend on the time t, as well as the domain of the constraints Ω on the control.

Optimal control of dynamic systems

Dynamic programming involves solving a problem by breaking it down into subproblems, and then solving the subproblems, from smallest to largest, by storing the intermediate results. It was a great success from the outset, as many of the industry's economic functions were of this type, such as the operation and optimization of chemical processes or inventory management.

We are interested here in optimal control and the stochastic **Pontryagin** principle, in other words, the necessary conditions of optimality by studying dynamical systems whose evolution is random.

In deterministic control problems, the dynamics of the system are modeled by an ordinary differential equation (ODE); in contrast, in the stochastic case, evolution is described by a diffusion process solution of a stochastic differential equation (SDE) defined in the following form:

$$dxt = b(x_t ; u_t)dt + \sigma (x_t, u_t)dw_t \text{ et } x(0) = x_0:$$

The associated cost is given by:

$$J(t, x, u) = E(\int^T_0 l(x_t , u_t)dt + h(x_T));$$

where $b (x, u) : Rn \times Rd \rightarrow Rn :$

$$\sigma (x; u) : R^n \times R^d \rightarrow L(Rd \times R^n)$$

The function l is assumed to be continuous in (x,u) continuously differentiable in x; h is continuously differentiable in x.

From a mathematical point of view, there are two approaches to solving the control problem: The first approach is known as dynamic programming or Bellman's principle. It was introduced by **Bellman (1953)** and is based on the notion of the **optimal policy**, which consists of solving a second-order, nonlinear partial differential equation. The second method is **the Pontryagin maximum principle**, known as the necessary conditions of optimality which was introduced by Pontryagin. It is based on the following idea: if an optimal control exists using the Lagrange approach by calculating variations on the functional J(u) with respect to some perturbation parameter θ must be positive.

Section 3: Research Methodology

3.1. Modeling the production function of well-being

Let DEPj represent the budget of the sector or function j.

j represents the eight budget functions. More specifically, these are the following functions:

D=1- Education; d=2- Health; in the Human Capital component

D=3 - Institutions; j=4 – Security; in the Governance component

D=5 - Building & Energy; j=6 – Economic Affairs; in the Economy component

D=7 - Professional networks; j=8 – Social network; in the Networks component.

For each sector we have the following accounting identity:

For each budget year t: DEPj = Budgetj = Fonj + Invj + Trj (1)

Fonj represents **operating expenses**[4]

Incj represents **capital expenditure**[5]

Trj represents **Transfer expenses**[6]

It is assumed that in *public economics*[7], the main role of the state is to use public resources to generate public goods and services. In the economic literature, the economic agent "state" is the only one whose function-objective is to generate collective well-being.

It is known that public goods and services meet very strict criteria on their allocation. Indeed, they are non-excludable and non-rivals.

---

[4] Explain the concept of operating expenses in the economic sense or make a box
[5] Explain the concept of investment expenditure in the economic sense or make a box
[6] Explain the concept of transfer expenditure in the economic sense or make a box
[7] Define the principles of public economy in a box

Box 1: Concept of public goods and services

General equilibrium theory studies the production and exchange of private goods. Private goods are both rivals and excludable. The principle of rivalry implies that the quantity consumed by one consumer reduces the quantity available to other consumers by the same amount. As for the criterion of excludability, it is the possibility of excluding or preventing any individual from using goods. Thus, as opposed to private property, public property is neither exclusionary nor rival (Mankiw & Taylor, 2013). The two above-mentioned criteria are valid for characterizing all goods and services produced in an economy and allow them to be classified into four main families, namely: private goods, communal goods, public goods and club goods. The table below summarizes the typology of properties classified according to the criteria of rivalry and excludability.

Table: Typology of properties

	With exclusion of use	**Without exclusion of use**
Rival	Private property e.g. apple	Communal property e.g. pasture
Non rival	Club Properties e.g. encrypted TV	Public goods e.g. National Defense

According to Mankiw and Taylor (2013), the three most important public goods are national defense, basic research and the fight against poverty. For Bozio et al., 2010, public action is not limited to the sovereign functions of the State but is now expanding to the provision of goods and services in education, health, social protection and the reduction of inequalities.

Moreover, producing public goods and services implies priori supply and demand functions, but above all production and cost functions.

In sector j, the public services use the budget allocated to their sector to produce the public goods and services of sector j.

By denoting the output of sector j in public goods and services such as Prodj, the following *Cobb-Douglas*[8] production function is specified:

$$(PROD_{jt}) = A_j(Fon_{jt})^{\alpha_j}(Inv_t)^{\beta_j}\ (Tr_{jt})^{\gamma_j} \quad (2)$$

α_j = elasticity of the "factor" Functioning in the production of public goods and services in sector j.

β_j = elasticity of the "factor" Investment in the production of public goods and services in sector j.

γ_j = elasticity of the "factor" Transfer in the production of public goods and services in sector j.

Log linearizing equation (2), we obtain:

$$log(Prod_{jt}) = \log(A_t) + \alpha_j log(Fon_{jt}) + \beta_j log(Inv_{jt}) + \gamma_j log(Tr_{jt}) \ (3)$$

Given the budgetary constraint of the state and the principle that there is no carry-over again in terms of public accounting, it is estimated that the use of resources is completely saturated. In other words, this implies that:

$$\log(A_t) = 0 \quad (4)$$

Thus, equation (3) becomes:

$$log(Prod_{jt}) = \alpha_j log(Fon_{jt}) + \beta_j log(Inv_{jt}) + \gamma_j log(Tr_{jt}) \ (5)$$

With $\alpha_j \geq 0$; $\beta_j \geq 0$; $\gamma_j \geq 0$

DD = 1 (6)$\alpha_j + \beta_j + \gamma_j$

Musgrave (1959) in his theory of public economics presented the basis of the role of the state and its three sovereign functions: i) *the function of allocating resources*, ii) *the function of redistributing income*, iii) *the function of regulation and stabilization.*

We assume that the production function defined in equation (2) is in fact a production function of well-being.

Indeed, Equation 2 highlights the exclusive allocation of public resources and technology to produce purely public goods and services.

---

[8] Encadré sur la fonction de production Cobb-Douglas et ses caractéristiques.

Based on the work of Dramani et al (2022), this function of producing well-being is apprehended by the Demographic Dividend Monitoring Index (DDMI).

So, we have (7).$(Prod_{jt}) \equiv (DDMI_{jt})$

Thus, from the above at the level of equivalence in the identity obtained at the level of equation (7), equation (5) becomes:

(8) $log(DDMI_{jt}) = \alpha_j log(Fon_{jt}) + \beta_j log(Inv_{jt}) + \gamma_j log(Tr_{jt})$

Constraints on parameters

The estimate of equation (8) gives the following estimated model:

$log(DDMI_{jt}) = \widehat{\alpha_j} log(Fon_{jt}) + \widehat{\beta_j} log(Inv_{jt}) + \widehat{\gamma_j} log(Tr_{jt})$ (9)

At the level of equation (9) we have the following parameters:

$$\widehat{\alpha_j};\ \widehat{\beta_j};\ \widehat{\gamma_j}$$

In the context of the search for optimality, the above parameters constitute control functions that must be optimized to improve budget allocation.

3.2 **The question of the definition of the standard**

The following standard is defined:

$Norme1\text{:}\ \left[log(DDMI_{jt}) - log(\widehat{DDMI_{jt}})\right]^2$ (10)

Positivity constraints

There are 24 parameters, i.e. 8 sectors X 3 natures. All 2' parameters must be positive.

Constraints on the Line Profile

The structure of the weight according to the eight sectors implies eight constraints. Each line in terms of structure has 100%.

Whatever j we have: = 1 (11)$\frac{\alpha_j}{\alpha_j + \beta_j + \gamma_j} + \frac{\beta_j}{\alpha_j + \beta_j + \gamma_j} + \frac{\gamma_j}{\alpha_j + \beta_j + \gamma_j}$

Constraints on Columns

There are three types of operations, investment, and transfers

For each sector j, we have

$$\sum_{j=1}^{8} \frac{\beta_j}{\alpha_j + \beta_j + \gamma_j} = A_j \text{ pour le fonctionnement } (12)$$

Constraint Optimization

The overall structure gives 100%, this implies a constraint.

In total

$$\sum_{j=1}^{8} \left(\frac{\alpha_j}{\alpha_j + \beta_j + \gamma_j} + \frac{\beta_j}{\alpha_j + \beta_j + \gamma_j} + \frac{\gamma_j}{\alpha_j + \beta_j + \gamma_j} \right) = 1 \quad (13)$$

3.3 **Optimization program with optimal control**

The Matrix of Weighting Controls Parameters for each sector is written as follows:

Table 27: Parameters Structure

	Operation	Investment	Transfer	Total
Education	α_1	β_1	γ_1	$\alpha_1 + \beta_1 + \boldsymbol{\gamma}_1$
Health	α_2	β_2	γ_2	$\alpha_2 + \beta_2 + \boldsymbol{\gamma}_3$
Economy	α_3	β_3	γ_3	$\alpha_3 + \beta_3 + \boldsymbol{\gamma}_3$
Building & Energy	α_4	β_4	$\boldsymbol{\gamma}_4$	$\alpha_4 + \beta_4 + \boldsymbol{\gamma}_4$
Institutions	α_5	β_5	$\boldsymbol{\gamma}_5$	$\alpha_5 + \beta_5 + \boldsymbol{\gamma}_5$
Security	α_6	β_6	$\boldsymbol{\gamma}_6$	$\alpha_6 + \beta_6 + \boldsymbol{\gamma}_6$
Professional network	α_7	β_7	$\boldsymbol{\gamma}_7$	$\alpha_7 + \beta_7 + \boldsymbol{\gamma}_7$
Social network	α_8	β_8	$\boldsymbol{\gamma}_8$	$\alpha_8 + \beta_8 + \boldsymbol{\gamma}_8$
Total	$\sum_{j=1}^{8} \alpha_j$	$\sum_{j=1}^{8} \beta_j$	$\sum_{j=1}^{8} \gamma_j$	$\sum_{j=1}^{8} (\alpha_j + \beta_j + \gamma_j)$

Transforming Table 27 to have a unit structure, we obtain the following Table 28:

Table 28: Unitary structure of parameters

	Operation	Investment	Transfer	Total
Education	α'_1	b'_1	γ'_1	$\alpha'_1 + b'_1 + c'_1$
Health	α'_2	B'_2	γ'_2	$\alpha'_2 + b'_2 + c'_3$
Economy	α'_3	b'_3	γ'_3	$\alpha'_3 + b'_3 + c'_3$
Building & Energy	α'_4	B'_4	γ'_4	$\alpha'_4 + b'_4 + c'_4$
Institutions	α'_5	b'_5	γ'_5	$\alpha'_5 + B'_5 + C'_5$
Security	α'_6	b'_6	γ'_6	$\alpha'_6 + b'_6 + c'_6$
Professional network	α'_7	B'_7	γ'_7	$\alpha'_7 + B'_7 + C'_7$
Social network	α'_8	b'_8	γ_8	$\alpha'_8 + B'_8 + C'_8$
	$\sum_{j=1}^{8} \alpha'_j$	$\sum_{j=1}^{8} \beta'_j$	$\sum_{j=1}^{8} \gamma'_j$	$\sum_{j=1}^{8} (\alpha'_j + \beta'_j + \gamma'_j) = 1$

With; and $\alpha'_j = {}^{\alpha_j}\!/_{\sum_{j=1}^{8}(\alpha'_j + \beta'_j + \gamma'_j)}$ $\beta'_j = {}^{\beta_j}\!/_{\sum_{j=1}^{8}(\alpha'_j + \beta'_j + \gamma'_j)}$ $\gamma'_j = {}^{\gamma_j}\!/_{\sum_{j=1}^{8}(\alpha'_j + \beta'_j + \gamma'_j)}$

$$Minimum_{j,t}\left(\sum_{t=1}^{20}\sum_{j=1}^{8}\left[log(DDMI_{jt}) - log(\widehat{DDMI}_{jt})\right]^2\right) Sous\ Contraintes$$

$$log(DDMI_{jt}) = \alpha_j log(Fon_{jt}) + \beta_j log(Inv_{jt}) + \gamma_j log(Tr_{jt})$$

$$\sum_{j=1}^{8} \frac{\beta_j}{\alpha_j + \beta_j + \gamma_j} = A$$

Continuation of constraints:

$$Suite\begin{cases} \sum_{j=1}^{8}\left(\frac{\alpha_j}{\alpha_j+\beta_j+\gamma_j}+\frac{\beta_j}{\alpha_j+\beta_j+\gamma_j}+\frac{\gamma_j}{\alpha_j+\beta_j+\gamma_j}\right)=1 \\ \alpha_j+\beta_j+\gamma_j=1 \\ \forall j, \quad \frac{\alpha_j}{\alpha_j+\beta_j+\gamma_j}+\frac{\beta_j}{\alpha_j+\beta_j+\gamma_j}+\frac{\gamma_j}{\alpha_j+\beta_j+\gamma_j}=1 \end{cases}$$

3.4 Generalized Reduced Gradient (GRG) Method

Framed 2: General information on GRG (Generalized Reduced Gradient)

The Microsoft Excel solver uses the nonlinear generalized Reduced Gradient (GRG) optimization code developed in 1978 in the United States by Leon Lasdon of the University of Texas (Austin) and Allen Waren of Cleveland State University.

The Generalized Reduced Gradient (GRG) is a mathematical algorithm for solving optimization problems. This technique is used in several fields, particularly in finance, to solve linear programming and portfolio allocation problems.

This method, one of the most popular for solving nonlinear optimization problems, requires that the objective function be differentiable. The main idea of this method is to solve the nonlinear problem dealing with active inequalities. Variables are separated into a set of basic (dependent) variables and non-basic (independent) variables. Then, the reduced gradient is calculated to find the minimum in the direction of the research objective. This process is repeated until convergence
is achieved.

- **Gradient-free optimization**

There are problems for which the objective function is not differentiable. Such problems are called non-smooth problems. Their objective functions are also referred to as non-smooth (as opposed to smooth functions).

A function *f*: is said to be non-smooth if it is not differentiable everywhere.$\mathbb{R}^d \rightarrow \mathbb{R}$

Since non-smooth functions are not differentiable everywhere, it is not possible to solve non-smooth problems via gradient-based methods.

However, there are several possible approaches to dealing with these problems.

One technique is for example to find a smooth formulation equivalent to that of the non-smooth problem. The minimize problem is, for example, equivalent to:$w \in \mathbb{R}$ $|\omega|$

$\underset{w,t^+,t^- \in \mathbb{R}}{\text{minimiser}} t^+ + t^-$ s. c. $w = t^+ - t^-, t^+ \geq 0, t^- \geq 0.$

This reformulation is a linear program, which is part of the classical classes of problems, for which very efficient algorithms and code exist.

When the function is non-smooth but Lipschitzian (which we will denote, by analogy with), we can try to apply a gradient method, because of the following property:$C_L^{0,0}$ $C_L^{1,1}$

Let f be a Lipschitzian function. Then, $\mathbb{R}^d \to \mathbb{R}$ f is differentiable at almost any point of $\mathbb{R}^d$.

On the other hand, there are Lipschitzian functions such as neural networks that are not differentiable at all points. On the other hand, it is possible to treat these problems as derivable almost everywhere; This remains a problem in certifying that a point is local minimum, because it is common for non-smooth functions to be non-differentiable at their extreme points. Thus, the notion of generalized gradient is used for this purpose.

➢ **Optimization with the generalized reduced gradient**

Let f be a convex function. A vector is called a sub gradient or reduced gradient from $\mathbb{R}^d \to \mathbb{R}$ $g \in \mathbb{R}^d$ f to if:$w \in \mathbb{R}^d$

$\forall z \in \mathbb{R}^n, .f(z) \geq f(w) + g^T(z - w)$

The set of sub gradients of f in is called the subdifferential of w f in; it is denoted. $w\theta f(w)$

When the function f is differentiable in, we have, which shows that the notion of subdifferential generalizes well that of the gradient.$w\theta f(w) = \{\nabla f(w)\}$

Subdifferentials allow us to characterize the (global) optimality for convex functions, as shown in the result below:

Let f: a convex function, and $\mathbb{R}^d \to \mathbb{R}$ $w \in \mathbb{R}^d$

$$0 \in \theta f(w) \Leftrightarrow w \; minimum \; de \; f$$

References

- Chapra, S., Canale, R., 2009. Numerical Methods for Engineers, sixth ed. McGraw-Hill, New York, NY.

- Lasdon, L.S., Waren, A.D., Jain, A., Ratner, M., 1978. Design and testing of a generalized reduced gradient code for nonlinear programming. ACM Trans. Math. Softw. (TOMS) 4 (1), 34–50.

- Maia, A., Ferreira, E., Oliveira, M. C., Menezes, L. F., & Andrade-Campos, A. (2017). Numerical optimization strategies for springback compensation in sheet metal forming. Computational Methods and Production Engineering, 51–82. doi:10.1016/b978-0-857094810.00003-3.

- Royer, C. W. (2024), Optimization Tools for Data and Decision Sciences, Paris Dauphine University.

- Venkataraman, P., 2009. Applied Optimization with MATLAB Programming. John Wiley & Sons, New York, NY.

Section 4: Results and Discussions

This section presents the results of the analyses of the evolution of the different dimensions of the DDMI and that of the five-year average shares of budgetary functions.

4.1. Evolution of the dimensions of the DDMI

- **The Economic Dependency Coverage Index (EDCI)**

The economic dependency coverage index (EDCI)[9] has undergone a dichotomous evolution over the period 2001-2020. The 1st phase is marked by a continuous decline in the EDCI from 18.7% in 2001 to 5.7% in 2010, showing a loss of the country's capacity in terms of covering social demand. This period of underperformance in meeting the needs of economically dependent individuals coincides with the successive drought seasons recorded over the period and the economic and financial crisis of 2008-2009.

From 2011 onwards, there was a continuous growth of the EDCI until 2020, reaching 46%. This renewed dynamism in the coverage of social demand can be explained, in part, by the strengthening of social protection and social transfer programs implemented under the Emerging Senegal Plan (Sesame Plan for the Elderly, Family Security Grants, Universal Health Coverage, Equal Opportunity Cards for People Living with Disabilities).

[9] EDCI = ratio between the surplus generated by economically independent age groups and the deficit generated by economically dependent age groups.

Graphic 17: Evolution of the EDCI between 2001 and 2020

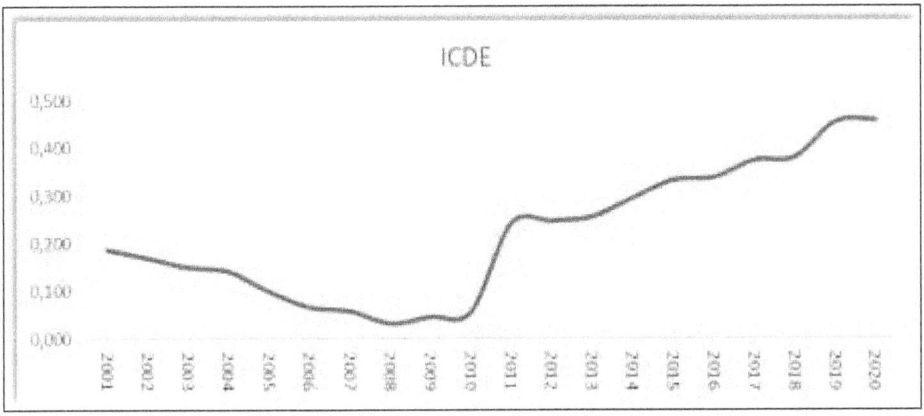

Source: CREG, ECA and Country Team calculations, 2023

- **The Quality of Living Environment Index (QLEI)**

The Quality of the Living Environment Index (QLEI) is marked by a rollercoaster trend over the period 2001-2020. One of the main causes of this erratic evolution is the disruptions recorded throughout the period in the sub-dimension related to governance, democracy and citizens' civic engagement. The political regimes that succeed one another in power seem to operate according to their own vision, thus weakening the country's institutional and good governance achievements. It is also found that the stakeholder participation component in the development of regulations and the participation rate component in elections fluctuate intensely and remain at relatively low levels.

Graphic 18: Evolution of the QLEI from 2001 to 2020

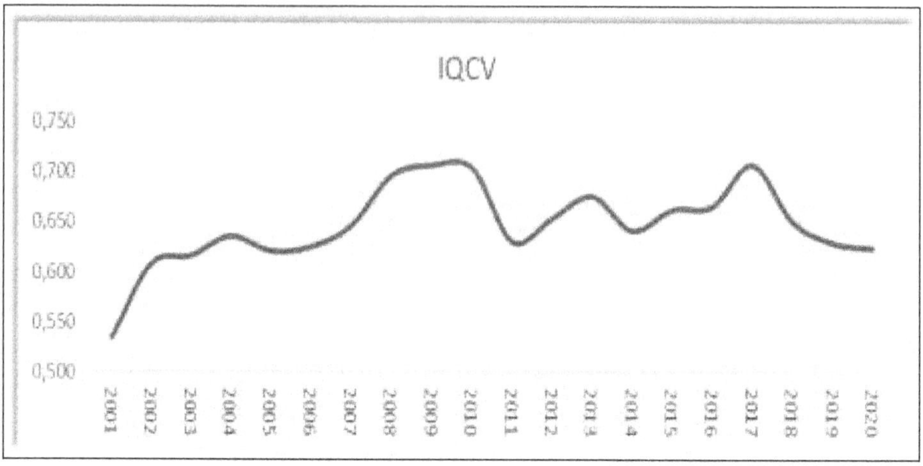

Source: CREG, ECA and Country Team calculations, 2023

- **Poverty Exit Synthetic Index (PESI)**

The analysis of the dynamics of the poverty exit synthetic index (PESI) shows the evolution of the proportion of households that have been able to maintain non-poverty. This evolution is marked by three main phases. A 1st phase (2001-2004) where the PESI remained around 63.6%. A 2nd phase (2005-2010) marked a break from 2005 with a drop in the PESI reaching a low level of 50.7% until 2010. The 3rd phase is marked by a renewed growth of the PESI over the period 2011-2020.

On the other hand, the proportion of households that remained poor during the three phases of the transition has decreased significantly, as has the share of the population in vulnerable situations. Thus, this improvement in the living conditions of the population constitutes the positive impact of the poverty reduction policies undertaken by the State for more than two decades.

Graphic 19: Evolution of the PESI from 2001 to 2020

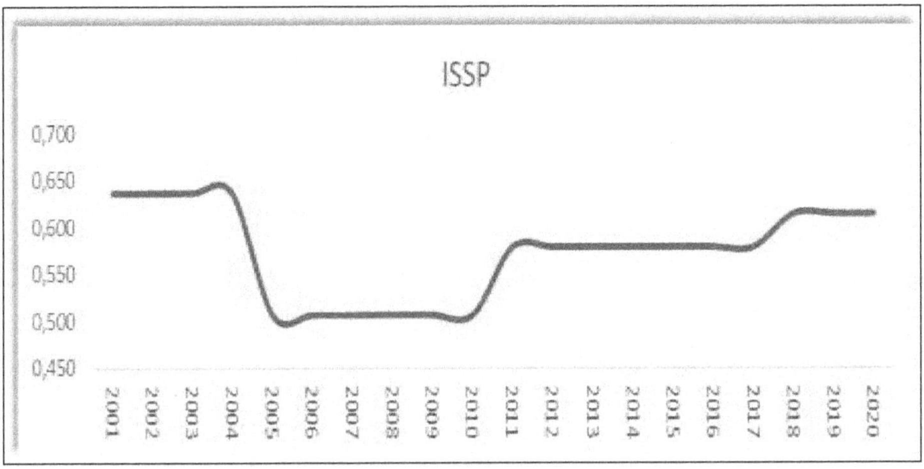

Source: CREG, ECA and Country Team calculations, 2023

- **The Extended Human Development Index (EHDI)**

The Extended Human Development Index (EHDI) follows a three-phase evolution over the period 2001-2020. The first period, from 2001 to 2008, was marked by an erratic evolution of the EHDI with a fluctuating value between 0.063 and 0.067. From 2008 to 2017, corresponding to the second phase, there was meteoric growth of the EHDI, reaching its peak in 2017 with a value of 0.106. This strong and sustained growth of the EHDI is the result of the implementation of health and education development plans and programs (PNDS, PDEF, PAQUET, PES, etc.)[10]. The third phase, between 2017 and 2020, is marked by a resumption of the rollercoaster evolution of the EHDI and corresponding to the intense period of the COVID-19 pandemic with all its harmful consequences on the economic and social levels.

[10] PNDS: National Health Development Plan (2009-2018) ; PDEF : Ten-Year Education and Training Program ; PAQUET-EF : Program to improve quality, equity and transparency in education and training ; PSE : Emerging Senegal Plan.

Graphic 20: Evolution of the EHDI from 2001 to 2020

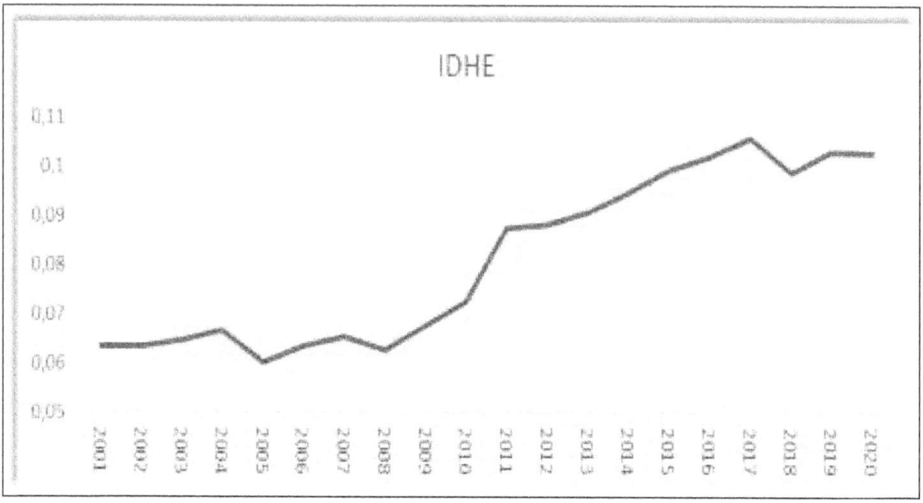

Source: CREG, ECA and Country Team calculations, 2023

- **Networks and Territories Synthetic Index (NTSI)**

Regarding the evolution of the networks and territories synthetic index (NTSI), there is an overall upward trend over the period under review, from 0.0185 to 0.0627 between 2001 and 2020. However, the evolution of the NTSI can be divided into two phases of growth with different rates. The 1st phase of growth (2001-2007) saw a slight increase in the NTSI of 0.0035 points, from a value of 0.0185 in 2001 to 0.0220 in 2007. The second phase (2008-2020) is marked by a remarkable growth in the NTSI, reaching its peak in 2020 with an estimated value of 0.0628.

Graphic 21: Evolution of the NTSI between 2001 and 2020

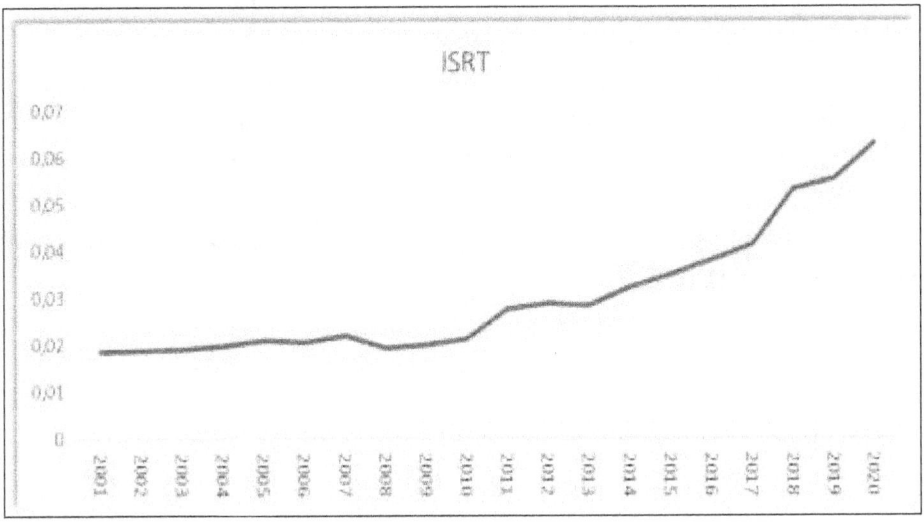

Source: CREG, ECA and Country Team calculations, 2023

4.2 Five-Year Contributions to the DDMI

Regarding the evolution of the five-year average shares or contributions of the different dimensions of the DDMI, the QLEI occupies the 1st place since its contribution to the DDMI is preponderant, starting from 9.7% over the period 2001-2005, it reaches 12.4% over the period 2016-2020.

The 2nd place is occupied by the PESI with an average contribution to the DDMI estimated at 9.9% over the period 2001-2005, reaching its peak over the period 2016-2020 with an estimated contribution of 11.4%. However, a significant decrease was recorded over the period 2006-2010 with a contribution of 7.1% despite the implementation of the 2nd generation of the Poverty Reduction Strategy Paper (PRSP II) over the period.

EHDI occupies the 3rd place with a progressively increasing contribution to the DDMI with 6.4% (2001-2005), 6.6% (2006-2010), 9.2% (2011-2015) and 10.2% respectively over the period 2016-2020. This progressive contribution is amply justified by the implementation since 2000 of policies, plans and programs for the development of education and health (PDEF, PAQUET-EF, PNDS, etc.).

The 4th place in terms of contribution to the DDMI, goes to the coverage of economic dependence, which has tended to increase overall except for the period 2006-2010 when there is a drastic decrease with a contribution of only 0.8%. The peak of the contribution of the EHDI is recorded over the period 2016-2020 with a value of 7.6%.

In the 5th and last position, is placed the "networks, territories and migrations" sub-dimension, whose contribution to the DDMI shows an upward trend over the entire period 2001-2020 with the best score recorded over the period 2016-2020, i.e. 5%.

Graphic 22: Evolution of the average five-year contributions of the components of the DDMI

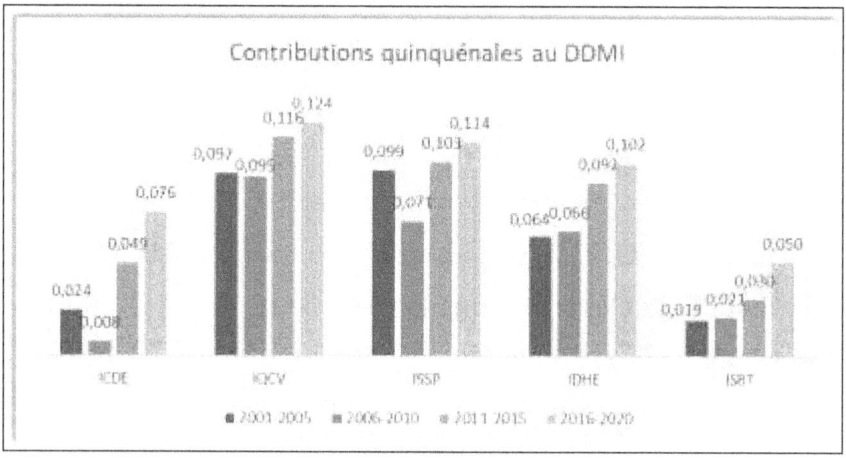

Source: CREG, ECA and Country Team calculations, 2023

4.3 Analysis of the functional budget series

The analysis of the series of the functional budget over the four sub-periods (2000-2004, 2005-2009, 2010-2014 and 2015-2021) shows overall that the five-year average contributions or shares of the eight (08) budgetary functions in the general budget have remained relatively stable over the period 2000-2021.

The share of the Economy function[11] in the general budget remains higher over the entire period 2000-2021 with a contribution that fluctuates between 33.3% and 35.2%. This preponderance of the contribution of the Economy-function proves the importance given by

[11] The contribution of the Economy function reflects the share of budget spending by the Economy sector (excluding construction and energy) in the general budget, which is referred to as the share of spending by other economic sectors.

the State to the financing of activities to produce public goods and services, sources of strong and sustained growth.

The Institutional Function and the Education Function are in 2nd and 3rd position respectively, with relatively stable average contributions over the four sub-periods. The contribution of the Institutional Function remained around 18% from 2000 to 2014 and subsequently decreased to 15.7% over the 2015-2021 sub-period, thus showing the impact of reforms in good governance, particularly the rationalization of public spending, carried out by the State as part of the Emerging Senegal Plan (PSE).

As for ***the education function***, its contribution remained around 17%, showing the interest given by the State in the development of skills but also the positive effects generated by the pressure of the frequent demands of the education system unions on the State.

The Building-Energy function comes in 4th place with a stable proportion in the general budget of about 13% over the first three sub-periods (2000-2004, 2005-2009, 2010-2014). This proportion reached 14.4% over the 2015-2021 sub-period, reflecting the efforts made by the State in the financing of public infrastructure and facilities as part of the implementation of the PSE.

The security function occupies 5th place and its share in the general budget has remained relatively stable over the period 2000-2021 with values fluctuating around 7% over the four sub-periods with a peak of 7.9% for the 2015-2021 sub-period. This peak can be explained by the efforts made by the State to properly equip the defense and security forces and consequently, to strengthen prevention against the terrorist threat in a hotbed of West African tension.

The health function occupies 6th place with a constant share of 4.3% in the overall budget over the first two sub-periods (2000-2004 and 2005-2009). This contribution of the health function gradually increased thereafter, reaching 4.4% over the 2010-2014 sub-period and 5% over the 2015-2021 sub-period, reflecting the efforts made by the State to improve the financial incentives of health personnel as well as the technical platform.

The Social Network function (7th) and the Professional Network function (8th) come in last place with a share of the general budget of between 3% and 4% and 1.8% and 2.3% respectively over the entire period from 2000 to 2021. The small shares of these two functions in the general budget show that spending on leisure or prestige and communication has not been a priority for the State over the last two decades.

Graphic 23: Evolution of contributions or five-year average shares of budgetary functions over the period 2000-2021

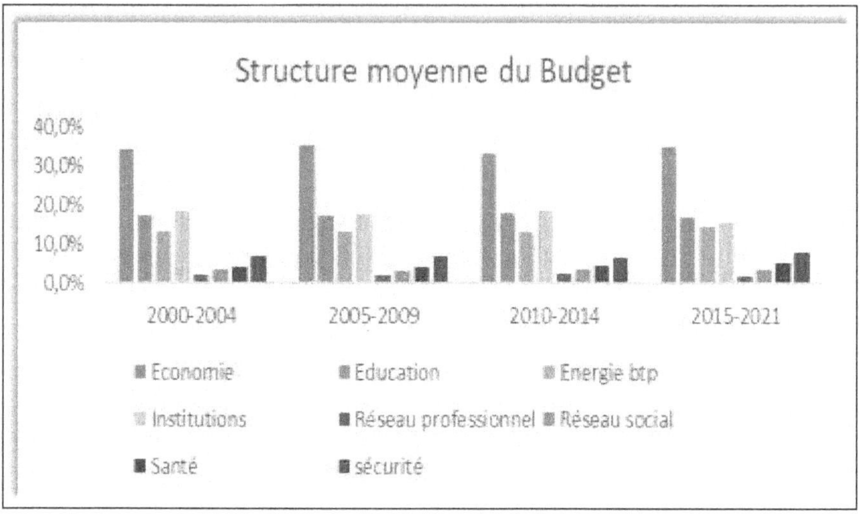

Source: Ministry of Finance and Budget
and Country Team calculations, 2023

4.4 Solutions for optimal control under budget constraints

Below are four scenarios for an optimal control solution under budget constraints. The optimal overall balanced structures show for each online solution the sectoral structures and in column the structures by type of expenditure that minimizes the standard (here the total cost of the budget) which allows to have an optimal performance of the DDMI. It should be noted that the structures are weights of each budgetary function and each type of expenditure in the overall cost of the Senegalese state budget.

The overall standard that serves as a reference for the optimization of the budget structure is 322.72. The optimal control solutions are obtained after several iterations. Each iteration corresponds to a possible optimal structure whose standard is lower than the global reference standard. Below we present the results of the last three iterations of optimal solutions.

Table 29: Solution 1 of optimal control with budget constraints

	Optimal overall balanced structure			
Norm= 319.08	FON	INV	TRF	TOTAL
Economic affairs	12,9%	2,3%	12,2%	27,4%
Education	8,6%	0,8%	5,7%	15,2%
Energy Building	4,1%	10,3%	11,0%	25,4%
Institutions	6,9%	0,2%	4,5%	11,7%
Professional network	0,5%	0,4%	0,9%	1,9%
Social network	2,1%	0,6%	1,5%	4,2%
Health	1,8%	1,8%	3,9%	7,5%
Security	3,9%	0,1%	2,6%	6,7%
Total	40,9%	16,6%	42,5%	100,0%

Source: CREG 2024

The first solution optimizes the budget structure according to a standard value of 319.08. This iteration reduces the total cost of the budget by 1.127% compared to the baseline total cost. In this structure, the expenditure on operations, investment and transfers of all eight economic functions represent 40.9%, 16.6% and 42.5% of the total cost respectively. According to solution 1, most of the resources are allocated to the economy, energy-Building, education and institutions. These are then the large amounts of expenditure in this budget structure. By allocating a substantial share of the resources allocated to the operating economy (12.9%) and transfers (12.2%), the government is making the option of positioning itself as an important force for demand for employment or for improving the conditions of workers in the economic affairs sector. It may also reflect the government's ability to improve the business climate through the awarding of public procurement. Expenditure items in the energy-Building sector are primarily intended for investments (10.3%) and transfers (11.0%). Investments in this sector finance the Building of public infrastructure (roads, airports, etc.), energy plants and telecommunications infrastructure. The education sector and the institutional function have similar structures to what is observed in the economic affairs sector. The dominant items are therefore operating and transfer expenditure. These expenditures represent 8.6% and 5.7% respectively in the education sector and 6.9% and 4.5% for the institutional function. However, it should be noted that investment in human capital remains the poor relation of this optimal solution. The resources allocated to investments in education and health are very low (0.8% and 1.8% of the budget respectively). These allocations do not, for example, allow the government to cover the needs for school equipment, health equipment and quality training for teachers and health workers. This portfolio leaves less room for Research and Development (R&D), which receives almost no funding in these sectors (education and health). This structure does not allow the government to focus its economic development on the production of knowledge, innovation and technology. This is also confirmed by the almost marginal proportion (0.1%) reserved for defense and security investments. In a stable country such as Senegal, this budget item is much more used to purchase military equipment for the participation of the national army in peacekeeping missions in other regions of the continent and the world.

Table 30: Solution 2 of optimal control with budget constraints

	Optimal overall balanced structure			
Norm= 319.06	**FON**	**INV**	**TRF**	**TOTAL**
Economic affairs	13,0%	1,8%	12,6%	27,42%
Education	8,4%	0,9%	5,9%	15,17%
Energy Building	4,1%	10,7%	10,6%	25,43%
Institutions	6,9%	0,2%	4,5%	11,67%
Professional network	0,5%	0,4%	1,0%	1,91%
Social network	2,1%	0,6%	1,5%	4,21%
Health	1,8%	1,9%	3,9%	7,48%
Security	4,0%	0,1%	2,5%	6,70%
Total	40,94%	16,60%	42,45%	100,0%

Source: CREG 2024

Solution 2 minimizes the cost of the budget by 1.134% with a standard value of 319.06. The structure by type of expenditure is the same with operations, investments and transfers representing 40.94%, 16.60% and 42.45% of the total budget. It should also be noted that from the point of view of the large masses of expenditure described in the first solution, the difference is not significant. Thus, the analysis presented in solution 1 is also valid for this solution. On the other hand, there are some structural changes that deserve attention.

In terms of the structure of the economic affairs function, operating and transfer expenditure are increased by 0.1 percentage point and 0.4 percentage point respectively. This slight revaluation of operations can, for example, be used to improve working conditions in the sector, either by increasing salaries and wage components, or by a marginal increase in public orders. The increase in transfers implies an increase in subsidies to the economic affairs sector (e.g. the subsidy for agricultural fertilizers). However, investment spending has been revised downwards by 0.5 points respectively compared to the first solution, which can be a bad thing for the business environment and the promotion of the private sector in the country.

Option 2 proposes a reduction of 0.2 percentage points in operating expenditure, which is offset by an increase in investment and transfer expenditure of 0.1 percentage points and 0.2 percentage points. In addition to improving educational facilities, this change in structure can also be used to increase academic scholarships.

As far as the energy-Building function is concerned, the changes concern investment and transfer expenditure. The budget planner performs a zero-sum operation, subtracting transfer spending by 0.4 percentage points and then increasing capital spending by the same amount. This decision could result in an increase in the cost of certain energy products if the change concerns, for example, the reduction of subsidies on energy products, including oil, gas and electricity. On the other hand, it is possible to see an increase in tax revenues if this change affects the exemptions or incentives granted to companies in the energy-Building sector.

This solution also improves capital expenditure in the healthcare sector by 0.1 percentage point. This increase is undoubtedly in favor of improving the health technical platform, which is known to be deficient in many developing countries such as Senegal.

Table 31: Solution 3 of optimal control with budget constraints

	Optimal overall balanced structure			
Norm= 318.53	**FON**	**INV**	**TRF**	**TOTAL**
Economic affairs	12,7%	2,4%	12,3%	27,42%
Education	8,5%	0,8%	5,9%	15,17%
Energy Building	3,6%	9,4%	12,4%	25,43%
Institutions	6,8%	0,1%	4,8%	11,67%
Professional network	0,5%	0,4%	1,0%	1,91%
Social network	2,1%	0,8%	1,3%	4,21%
Health	1,7%	1,4%	4,4%	7,48%
Security	4,9%	1,3%	0,6%	6,70%
Total	40,94%	16,60%	42,45%	100,0%

Source: CREG 2024

It is important to emphasize first that on a purely mathematical level, the most efficient optimal solution is the last solution because it optimizes the DDMI at the lowest possible cost. This cost corresponds to a standard of 318.53 for the last iteration (solution 3). This standard represents a reduction in the budgetary cost of 1.30% compared to the overall reference standard. However, it is important to clarify that policy- or strategically, decision-makers may opt for a budget structure that is different from the optimal one.

This optimal structure remains like the first solution in many ways. However, it is less in favor of energy policy and strengthening the health system. For example, a reduction in energy investment expenditure in favor of increased transfers has a greater influence on consumers' purchasing power instead of encouraging an increase in geographical coverage, service or electrification rates, which are the main objectives of energy policy.

A final remark concerns the institutional function, which has hardly varied across the different solutions. Even at the level of the last solution where we have observed a change, it is a modification in favor of transfer expenditure. This observation expresses an institutional reality linked to the cumbersome system of governance, the bureaucracy, and the complexity of the political system in the country. This also poses problems of effectiveness and efficiency of state institutions. This situation exposes the country to an increase in corruption and a delay in the implementation and transmission of public decisions.

Summary of results

The results of solutions 1, 2 and 3 show that there is convergence in the optimal structure of the budget functions. The Economic affairs and Energy-Building functions represent 27.42% and 25.43% of the budget respectively, while over the period 2000-2021, these functions contributed to about 33.3% and 35.2% for the Economic affairs function and 13.4% (or 14.4%) for the Energy-Building function. Thus, the optimal balanced structures reveal an overfinancing of economic affairs to the detriment of the underfinancing of the Energy-Building function.

A slight downward reassessment of the Education function is envisaged in the optimal solutions, bringing the contribution of this function to the budget at 15.17% compared to 17% allocated on average over the last twenty years. As regards the health function, although the Maputo targets have not been met (15%), the balanced optimal solutions devote more resources to health, at least 2.48 percentage points more, as over the period 2000-2021 the allocation of resources to this function varied between 4.4% and 5%.

According to the analysis of the average structures of the functional budget, the Institution function represents the second allocation item, with a contribution that varies between 15% and 18% of the budget. The four optimal solutions converge with a contribution of 11.67%, i.e. a minimum decrease of 3.03 percentage points. In terms of security, despite the expansion of jihadist groups in the Sahel region, particularly in neighboring countries, territorial integrity is preserved in Senegal. This situation could provide flexibility to consider a slight decrease in the contribution of the Security function. Thus, this contribution, which varies between 7% and 7.9%, can be reduced to 6.70%.

The public policies implemented in recent years have given very little importance to social and professional network functions. On average, they capture barely 5% of the available resources. Allocations to the social network, for example, over the period 2000-2021 vary between 3% and 4%. The contribution of the professional network is less important and varies between 1.8% and 2.3%. This low allocation can be explained by the fact that the contribution of these functions to the creation of national wealth is negligible. However, these functions play a major role in the economy because they guarantee social cohesion, national unity and improve the sense of belonging of vulnerable and excluded populations. To this end, the reassessment and maintenance of the contribution of social and professional network functions at 6% is a social imperative in Senegal.

Conclusion

This chapter dealt with the problem of the functional allocation of the Senegalese State budget which optimizes the well-being of the population under budgetary constraints. The productive function of well-being is apprehended by the Sustainable Development and Demographic Dividend Monitoring Index. An analysis of the budget was carried out over the period from 2000 to 2021 with an average structure of the budget comprising eight functions, namely: Economic affairs, Energy-Building, Education, Health, Institutional, Security, Social and Professional Network function.

Based on Pontryagin's theories of optimal control (1959), we designed an optimization program with optimal control, under budgetary constraint to generate solutions of balanced optimal overall structures. This program has made it possible, after several iterations, to select four possible solutions.

A comparative analysis of the three solutions shows that there is not much flexibility in restructuring the budget from one scenario to another because the budget structures are rigid. The results of the solutions also show that there is convergence in the optimal structure of the budget functions. In addition, it should be stressed that there is no *"best solution"* because the statistically intuitive solution can be politically and socially ineffective. Thus, the scenario to be adopted should be the one that best achieves the country's development objectives. This solution must then be compatible with the government's development agenda and the vision of the leaders.

Bibliographical references

Adli, Z., et Akacem, K., (2012). LE CONSENSUS DE WASHINGTON, LE FMI ET L'ALGERIE.

Aguey, S. (2020). INVESTIMENT PUBLIC ET CHANGEMENT STRUCTUREL : UNE ANALYSE EN EQUILIBRE GENERAL DYNAMIQUE. Annale des Sciences Economiques et de Gestion, 20(1).

Bellman, R. 1953. An introduction to the theory of dynamic programming.Technical report.

Bozio, A., et Grenet, J. (Eds.). (2010). Economie des politiques publiques. La Découverte.

Creel, J. (2001). Faut-il contraindre la politique budgétaire en Union monétaire : Les enseignements d'une maquette simulée. Revue de l'OFCE, no<(sup> 77), 199-249. https://doi.org/10.3917/reof.077.0199

Creel, J., et Sterdyniak, H. (1998). Du bon usage des politiques monétaire et budgétaire en Europe. Revue d'économie financière, (45), 167-196.

Dramani, L., Akpo, E., Oga, J. B., Guidimé, C. D., Konan, S., Agbahoungba, S., ... & Mabika, C. (2022). Demographic Dividend Monitoring Index Conceptual Framework and Case Studies in Africa. In The Routledge Handbook of African Demography (pp. 654-675). Routledge.

Ffrench-Davis, R. (2010). Latin America: The structural fiscal balance policy in Chile: A move toward counter-cyclical macroeconomics. Journal of Globalization and Development, 1(1).

Guèye T.N. (2021). Effets des dépenses publiques d'éducation, la fiscalité et la corruption sur la croissance économique en Afrique de l'ouest : une analyse empirique sur données de panel. European Scientific Journal, ESJ, 17 (38), 160. https://doi.org/10.19044/esj.2021.v17n38p160

Kalman, R. (1959). On the general theory of control systems. IRE Transactions on Automatic Control, 4(3), 110-110.

Kalman, R. E. (1960). A new approach to linear filtering and prediction problems.

Kane, C. S. (2018). Cyclicité des politiques budgétaires dans l'Union Economique et Monétaire Ouest Africaine (UEMOA). REVUE CEDRES-ETUDES, 7(66).

Kuate Fotue, L. (2015). Allocation des dépenses publiques pour la transformation structurelle.

Llorca, M. (2016). Défis à relever pour la politique budgétaire en Amérique latine en matière de stabilisation et de redistribution. Cuadernos de Economía, 35(SPE67), 119-147.

Lyapunov, A. M. (1992). The general problem of the stability of motion. International journal of control, 55(3), 531-534.

Mankiw G. N., et Taylor M. P., (2013). Principe de l'économie. De Boeck supérieur.

Mtiraoui, A., (2015). L'impact de l'action du pouvoir public sur le Développement économique : Application au Secteur de l'éducation dans la région MENA.

Musgrave, R. A. (1959). The Theory of Public Finance: A Study in Public Economy. New York: McGraw Hill.

Pontryagin, L. S. (1959). Optimal regulation processes. Uspekhi Matematicheskikh Nauk, 14(1), 3-20.

Rota-Graziosi, G., Caldeira, E., Dama, A. A., Djoufelkit, H., & Ehrhart, H. (2021). La qualité de la dépense publique dans les pays en développement : mesure et déterminants.

Trinnou, G. M., (2021). ANAYSE DES FACTEURS EXPLICATIFS DE L'EFFORT FISCAL ET DU POTENTIEL FISCAL DANS LES PAYS DE L'UEMOA, Document d'Etude et de Recherche N° COFEB/DER/2021/03.

CHAPTER 8

ANALYSIS OF PARTIAL BALANCE BUDGET SENSITIVITY-LINKAGE

Introduction

The principles of public economy

Since the end of the economic transition, with the transition from a planned economy to a market economy and the globalization of free trade in factors of production, there has been a renewed interest in the place of the state in the economy and the importance of its interventions. It was therefore important to put into perspective the role of the state, the extent of its interventions, and the effectiveness of its actions beyond the simple analytical framework that highlights the contrasts between the main currents of economic thought, in particular the Keynesians who are in favor of state intervention, and the classics who militate for the policy of laissez-faire. It is in this context that public economics has emerged as the most holistic objective alternative for dealing with issues of the state, its role and its actions in the contemporary economy.

- **Public economics: definition and purpose**

Public economics is the discipline of economics that is concerned with public intervention in the broad sense (Bozio et al., 2010). Indeed, public intervention refers to all the actions by which a government or a public authority intervenes in the economic sphere. The concept of public authority in this context extends to local authorities and social security bodies to form the trio that the national accounts refer to as public administrations (APUs). Its purpose is therefore the evaluation, production and maintenance of public goods (Hébert, 1994).

Theories of public economics contribute to economic analysis through two complementary approaches. The first approach is said to be positive and makes it possible to assess the impacts of public policies on the economy, and the second approach, which is prescriptive, informs decision-makers about the most effective policy according to the objectives previously defined.

○ The concept of service and public goods and their characteristics

General equilibrium theory studies the production and exchange of private goods. Private goods are both rivals and excludable. The principle of rivalry implies that the quantity consumed by one consumer reduces the quantity available to other consumers by the same amount. As for the criterion of excludability, it is the possibility of excluding or preventing any individual from using goods. Thus, as opposed to private property, public property is neither exclusionary nor rival (Mankiw and Taylor, 2013). The two above-mentioned criteria are valid for characterizing all goods and services produced in an economy and allow them to be classified into four main families, namely: private goods, communal goods, public goods and club goods. The table below summarizes the typology of properties classified according to the criteria of rivalry and excludability.

Table 32: Typology of properties

	With exclusion of use	**Without exclusion of use**
Rival	Private property Ex: apple	Communal property E.g. pasture
Non rival	Club Properties Ex: encrypted TV	Public goods E.g. national defense

According to Mankiw and Taylor (2013), the three most important public goods are national defense, basic research and the fight against poverty. For Bozio et al., 2010, public action is not limited to the sovereign functions of the State but is now expanding to the provision of goods and services in education, health, social protection and the reduction of inequalities.

○ The role (functions) of the State in the economy (R. Musgrave)

In their book entitled "Public finance in theory and practice", Musgrave et Musgrave, (1989) have defined four (04) functions of the State in the economy. These are (a) the allocation function, (b) the redistribution function, (c) the stabilization function and finally (d) the fiscal policy coordination function.

- **The allocation function**

The State intervenes in the allocation of resources, i.e. in their use. It spends money to finance its sovereign functions consisting of maintaining order internally (police and judicial activity) and externally (defense activity). It is also a producer of non-market services (education, health, social housing) and controls public companies placed in the market sector.

- **The redistribution function**

Income redistribution is the set of measures taken by the state to change the distribution of income by levying taxes and contributions (compulsory levies) and distributing transfer income. This redistribution allows the coverage of social risks (sickness, maternity, unemployment and old age) and acts on inequalities and poverty in the name of social justice.

- **The stabilization function**

The State's mission is to stabilize the economy, i.e. to preserve economic equilibrium (full employment, price stability, foreign trade balance) and to achieve sustained growth by implementing short-term economic policies adapted to the current economic situation. The two main instruments for stabilizing the economy available to the State are monetary policy and fiscal policy.

- **The Fiscal Policy Coordination Function**

Fiscal policy has several distinct objectives, but these overlap in practice, making it difficult to design effective policy. For example, when expansionary policy is needed, the government has the choice between increasing public spending or reducing the level of taxation on the one hand and reducing public spending or increasing the level of taxation on the other. Thus, the function of coordinating fiscal policy would require that state intervention guarantee the neutrality of stabilization measures in relation to the objectives of resource allocation and redistribution. This function also ensures that fiscal policy is consistent with the government's policy objectives. In the context of a monetary union, this function becomes more important because fiscal policy is now the only instrument at the State's disposal to cushion fluctuations in activity and support growth. The European Union's Stability and Growth Pact and the WAEMU Convergence Pact are examples of fiscal policy coordination instruments.

- **The main budgetary principles**

To guarantee compliance with the fundamental principles of clarity, sincerity and transparency in the management of public resources, four (04) main budgetary rules,[12] namely annuality, unity, universality and specialty, have been enacted.

- **Annuality**

This principle expresses the idea that the budgetary authorization given to the executive to collect public revenues and execute expenditures through the finance law is only valid for one year.

- **The Principle of Unity**

The principle of budgetary unity means that all the State's revenue and expenditure must be included in a single document called the budget. The budget must be presented to the national representation and must be balanced (the total revenue during a financial year must be the total expenditure).

- **The principle of universality**

The principle of universality is complementary to that of unity and includes two rules, namely non-allocation and non-compensation. The rule of non-allocation consists of allocating all revenue to all expenditure. It is therefore not allowed to allocate a particular revenue to a particular expenditure. As for the rule of non-offsetting, sometimes referred to as the rule of gross revenue, it consists of prohibiting the offsetting of an expenditure by a receipt.

- **The principle of speciality**

According to this principle, the appropriations which are made available by finance law are allocated to specific expenditures. The authorization given by parliamentarians to the government in terms of spending is not given in a lump sum, in a global way. The spending authority is detailed for each vote category. The consequence is that appropriation can only be used to finance the expenditure for which it was planned. Consequently, each appropriation voted has a destination, and the government during the financial year cannot in principle change this destination.

---

[12] http://www.vie-publique.fr/fiches/21823-quels-sont-les-grands-principes-budgetaires ("What are the main budgetary principles?" 2022).

The Economy of Well-being

The economics of well-being is a field that explores the measurement and evaluation of the well-being of individuals and societies, complementing traditional economic indicators such as gross domestic product (GDP) or national income. It is a branch of economics that aims to assess social situations and guide public decision-making (Baujard, 2017). His approach is essentially welfarist in that the analyses are generally oriented towards the individual preferences of the members of society.

o The Economics of Well-Being: Debates, Contributions and Policies to Improve the Well-Being of Individuals and Societies

It aims to analyze the well-being of individuals and societies, as well as to formulate economic policies to improve their overall well-being. In this context, many authors have engaged in in-depth discussions to better understand the concept and identify appropriate measures to help policymakers promote collective well-being.

Arthur Pigou, a neoclassical economist, was interested in the development of an economic policy aimed at improving the social situation of all. In his book "The Economics of Welfare" (1920), Pigou introduced the central concept of "economic well-being" and proposed tools for measuring and evaluating well-being within a society. The author considers that economic well-being can be improved by allocating resources efficiently and equalizing marginal costs and benefits. Thus, he suggested that government intervention, through taxes or subsidies, could help improve collective welfare. In the same vein, Amartya Sen has played a key role in the development of the welfare economy. His book "Choice, Welfare and Measurement" (1982) marked an important step forward in redefining well-being and proposing alternative measures. Sen criticized traditional approaches that focus on income and consumption, pointing out that they neglect essential aspects of well-being. He introduced the concept of *"capabilities"* to assess well-being, focusing on the actual abilities of individuals to achieve their aspirations. According to Sen, well-being encompasses dimensions such as health, education, freedom of choice, and social relationships. He advocated economic policies aimed at expanding individual capabilities and promoting social equity to improve collective well-being. Sen's approach has had a significant impact by broadening the view of well-being to include non-monetary aspects and emphasizing the reduction of inequalities. His work has helped shape economic debates and policies by highlighting real outcomes for individuals and proposing more comprehensive measures of well-being.

After Amartya Sen's work, other major authors have made significant contributions to the economics of well-being. We can cite among others the work of Martha Nussbaum (2000) who developed the concept of "human capabilities" by emphasizing rights and freedoms as drivers of well-being. Richard Layard et al (2014) formulated the theory of the economics of happiness, emphasizing the importance of mental health, quality social relationships, and equity in determining well-being. Joseph Stiglitz and Jean-Paul Fitoussi (2009) led a commission that proposed new indicators of well-being, considering dimensions such as health, education, the environment and inequality. These contributions have enriched the understanding of well-being and influenced economic debates and policies by focusing on more significant aspects of people's well-being.

Through these contributions and theoretical approaches, we can see the importance of the state in improving the well-being of the population. Moreover, the Keynesian approach emphasizes the role of the state in regulating the economy and providing public goods, which are essential for the well-being of the population (Vivien, 2007). According to this perspective, the state can intervene proactively to correct market failures and ensure an efficient allocation of resources. Approaches such as welfare economics and political economy emphasize social justice and equity in the allocation of goods and resources. These approaches see the state as playing a crucial role in redistributing income and reducing inequality to improve the overall well-being of the population. The analyses show the diversity of approaches, which in turn is accompanied by a diversity of measures (Perron, 2019).

- **Diverse perspectives on assessing well-being**

Amartya Sen (82) proposes assessing the well-being of individuals by measuring their access to essential elements such as health, education and freedom of choice. Martha Nussbaum (2000) suggests a list of fundamental abilities, such as good health, social relationships, and self-actualization, that should be considered in measuring well-being. Richard Layard (2005) emphasizes the subjective assessment of well-being by using surveys to assess individuals' life satisfaction. Ruut Veenhoven (1984), David Bartram (2012) and Simon Langlois (2014) agree that satisfaction with life has a cognitive dimension, while happiness refers to the emotional dimension of well-being. Ed Diener

(1994) considers subjective well-being to include long-term levels of affectivity, a lack of unpleasant effects, and life satisfaction. Michel Forsé and Maxime Parodi (2014) identify three determinants of satisfaction with one's own life: individual resources, employment and the quality of professional life, as well as the different aspects of emotional and social life. Joseph Stiglitz, Jean-Paul Fitoussi, and Amartya Sen (2009) suggested including indicators such as health, education, the environment, income inequality, and citizen participation to assess well-being beyond GDP. The Human Development Index (HDI), developed by the United Nations Development Program (UNDP), combines indicators such as life expectancy, education and income to measure the level of human development in a country. In addition, the Gross National Happiness (GNH), proposed by Bhutan, considers dimensions such as mental health, spirituality, environmental preservation, culture and governance to assess national well-being (Dasho et al, 2012).

In conclusion, welfare economics offers an alternative and complementary perspective to traditional economics by focusing on the well-being of individuals and societies. It proposes more comprehensive approaches and measures to assess and improve well-being, recognizing that economic progress can only be fully appreciated when it is accompanied by an improvement in human well-being.

Section 1: Literature Review of the Relationship Between Budget Functions and DDMI Components

- **Education and the components of the DDMI**

Niang (2005) sought to analyze the impact of public expenditure on education on poverty in Senegal. He compared the concentration curves of this government spending to that of household consumption. The results show that public expenditure on primary education is relatively better distributed in terms of equity between social groups than that of households. However, public spending on technical and vocational education appears to be of little benefit to the poorest households (20% of the least wealthy).

In the same vein, Lanjouw et al. (2001) conducted a static analysis of the impact of public expenditure on education and health on poverty in Indonesia. They found that spending on basic education and primary health care is generally more pro-poor. On the other hand, spending on higher education and hospitals is less beneficial to this social category.

Afonso et al. (2008), on the other hand, sought to analyze the impact of public spending, education and institutions on income distribution in advanced countries, using a non-parametric tool in this case the DEA (Data Envelopment Analysis) models. The results of the study show that public policies significantly affect the distribution of income through social spending, and indirectly through highly skilled training or human capital and sound economic institutions.

Using a model of simultaneous equations, Fan et al. (1999) sought to estimate the direct and indirect effects of different types of public expenditure on rural poverty and productivity in India. The results of their research showed that public investment in rural infrastructure such as roads, research and development in agriculture, and spending on education has a very significant positive impact on poverty reduction and productivity increases. However, for other types of expenditure, such as irrigation, water and soil conservation, health, and rural and community development, the respective contributions to poverty reduction and productivity growth remain relatively modest. In the same vein, Fan et al. (2002) conducted similar studies in China, and found that public spending directed at education has the greatest impact on reducing rural poverty and regional inequality, in addition to the significant effect on increasing production. The authors add that the increase in rural non-farm employment largely explains this decline.

In addition, Dabla-Norris and Matovu (2002) sought to measure the effects of government spending, in the form of public transfers in the education and infrastructure sectors, on household decisions about enrolling children in school or accumulating assets. Using a dynamic intergenerational model, the authors found that an increase in public spending on primary and secondary education has a positive impact on poverty reduction and the economy, despite a decline in infrastructure investment. In addition, the impact of public transfers on macro-economic aggregates and poverty depends strongly on their magnitude. In other words, if they are substantial enough and target the most disadvantaged groups, then considerable effects could be expected on poverty reduction and economic growth. However, small transfers would have a marginal impact on poverty and the economy.

In another vein, Balma et al. (2010) used a CGE model to assess the direct and indirect impacts of public education policies on well-being, poverty and income distribution in Burkina Faso. The results of the simulations indicate that a uniform 40% increase in public spending on basic education, offset by an increase in the sales tax (an additional tax on consumer goods), would result not only in improved welfare but also in a lower incidence of poverty for wage households. However, the results show that under these conditions of high unit cost of education among farm households, their situation would not improve in terms of well-being and poverty, while the structure of income distribution would remain unchanged.

- **Health and the components of the DDMI**

Early theoretical work in health economics adopted the neoclassical approach. According to this approach, people are considered substantially rational and make their own personal decisions in terms of market exchanges. In the private medicine sector, we therefore have a producer-consumer model where the doctor plays the role of a producer, and where the patient is considered as a consumer or an investor in his or her health capital. This approach now has many limitations, including independence of supply and demand and consumer governance. While the physician would have a discretionary power that would allow him to use the request for his personal services. Since the 1970s, the supply-induced demand hypothesis has been an important pillar of the use of the neoclassical model in ambulatory medicine (Evans, 1974). From this perspective, health expenditure is dissociated from financial responsibility, in other words, doctors and patients do not intervene in determining the total cost of their decisions; consequently, the role of price is reduced. These models also have additional limitations, including conflicts of interest and informational asymmetry between the different groups of staff in the hospital (medical staff, patients, administrative staff, nurses, etc.) that are not included in the analysis (Khaldi, N., & Arib, F. 2022).

The contributions of agency theory (normative and positive) in health economics make it possible to overcome some of the limitations of neo-classical theory, thus offering elements that can help make decisions in terms of economic policy.

In terms of agency relations, the theoretical contribution of the approach to the health care system is essentially manifested in the explicit consideration of divergences of interests, information asymmetries and risks associated with economic activity. According to Bejean, 1997, the relationships between the staff of the health system are modelled in terms of multiple agency relationships, in particular between the attending physician and the patient in outpatient medicine, between the insured and the insurer in the field of health insurance, between the medical staff and the managing administrator of the hospital, between this administrator and his supervisory authorities (...) ». In terms of economic policy, the main contribution of the agency theory is to demonstrate that certain rules of reward or budget allocation are over-manipulated by agents. Therefore, incentives must be introduced to limit the opportunistic behavior of actors. The application of agency theory in health economics, however, has limitations in the theoretical model itself and its assumptions.

The economics of conventions theoretically make it possible to overcome the limits of the contractual approach by suggesting very realistic explanations of economic behavior. It provides additional elements necessary for the analysis suggested by the theory of agency, particularly in terms of economic policy. At the theoretical level, the theory of the economics of conventions and the assumption of procedural rationality provide a good understanding of behavior and decision-making measures in the health sector.

Empirically, the first models for measuring the sources of economic growth began with Solow (1957) and Denison (1962). These authors did not consider the health factor. However, Bloom et al (2001) and Sala-i-martin (2001) considered health to be one of the main sources of growth. Indeed, a healthy population plays a driving role in economic growth. These authors perceived health as a product of the growth process. They stipulate that, people with high incomes are healthy because they have easier access to goods and services that promote good health. In addition, according to Ulmann (2003), the improvement of health status depends on technological progress and medicine. He notes that economic growth leads to higher household incomes. Access to better living conditions improves health (good nutrition, healthy housing, etc.), but also health spending increases. This author insists on the fact that at the national level, the improvement of the state of health of the population will only be achieved if there is an egalitarian distribution of wealth.

Frenk (2004) argues that health performance is highly dependent on the economy, but also on the health systems themselves. He insists on the importance of taking this link into account in the science and economics of health. Indeed, investing in health is not only desirable, but also essential in most societies. In other words, health systems are facing difficult and complex challenges, including new pressures from an ageing population, the rise of chronic diseases and the intensive use of expensive but life-saving medical technologies. Thus, the need to design health financing policies and determine corresponding investments considering interactions with the economy is a key idea.

According to the work of the World Health Organization's (WHO) Commission on Macroeconomics and Health, health performance and economic performance are interdependent. Thus, poverty, malnutrition and infant mortality cause a reduction in life expectancy. For this reason, people in rich countries enjoy better health than those in poor countries. Also, national income directly influences the development of health systems, particularly through the insurance system and public spending. While national income mainly determines the level of health spending, it is increasing, however, at a higher rate, a reality highlighted by Miniar Ben A. S.et Sami H. in 2015.

Health economists therefore consider public health to be an important factor in growth and well-being. It represents both consumer goods and capital. As capital, it allows everyone to generate income on the labor market. As consumer goods, it allows individuals to increase their well-being and gives them the freedom to pursue their interests. From an economic point of view, health is a factor of human capital and therefore a driver of economic development. In fact, health status is increasingly integrated into theories of economic growth as a factor of dynamism.

- **The "Institutions" and the components of the DDMI**

In the United States, until 1945, institutionalism competed very largely with marginalism. Driven by Thorstein Veblen at the end of the nineteenth century, economic institutionalism became a veritable school of thought at the beginning of the nineteenth century around Wesley C. Mitchell at Columbia University (New York) and especially John R. Commons at the University of Wisconsin. This early interest in institutions experienced a prolonged eclipse until the 1970s. Institutions are then neglected and treated as a given (an exogenous variable) both by neoclassical synthesis and by monetarism. It was not until the publication of Markets and Hierarchies in 1975 that Oliver E. Williamson called for the birth of a new institutional economics (New Institutional Economics), of which the company then became the privileged object of his writing. Under the impetus of Douglass C. North, also a Nobel Prize winner, this microeconomic approach to institutions was subsequently extended to the analysis of the factors of growth and development (Gilles M. 2010).

In addition, the development policies advocated by the Washington Consensus have shown their limits since the early 1990s. As a result, reflection has refocused on institutional factors, which are increasingly considered to be the priority target of development aid policies. While sociologists are wondering about the decline of the latter, institutions are in vogue among economists, as evidenced by the awarding of the 2009 Nobel Prize in Economics to Oliver E. Williamson and Elinor Ostrom for their work on economic governance.

To demonstrate the vital role that institutions play in economic development and growth, numerous studies have been conducted based on this new paradigm highlighting the influence of institutional environments on the effectiveness of sectoral reforms (Edison, 2003).

The work of Demetriades and Law (2006) remains to some extent pioneering in assessing the effect of financial development on growth as a function of the quality of institutions. Using a sample of 72 countries over the period 1978-2000, the authors show the positive effects of financial development on growth in middle-income countries with sound institutions. In low-income countries, where institutions are of low quality, financial development does not generate growth. Following Demetriades and Law (2006), Law et al. (2013) deepen the analysis of institutional quality thresholds in the finance-growth relationship on a sample of 85 countries over the period 1980-2008. The authors suggest that the impact of finance on growth is positive and significant only beyond a certain threshold of institutional development. Below this threshold, the relationship is non-significant. A re-examination of this relationship is proposed by Law et al. (2018) using a quadratic model on a dynamic panel. The results show that the financial "curse" occurs when institutions are altered. For example, institutions play an important role in the link between financial development and growth, and countries with better institutional quality benefit greatly from the development of the banking sector. In addition, financial markets that are integrated within a sound institutional framework are more effective in ensuring sustainable economic development.

EBO'OH NTJEN, S. D., NEBA, C. Y., (2021) show that a good quality policy institutional framework lowers the threshold level of quality of economic institutions that can improve the effect of financial development on economic growth in sub-Saharan Africa. Using a sample of 30 sub-Saharan African countries over the period 1996 to 2018, they used a non-linear model of endogenous growth to develop an estimate by cointegration on panel data. Their results show that financial development has a negative effect in the short term and a positive effect in the long term. Institutions change the effect of financial development on growth. Thus, an improvement in the quality of political institutions from the average of sub-Saharan African countries to that of more stable economies (Senegal), raises the economic institutional threshold from 15.7089 points to 10.3423; a decrease of 5.3666. Similarly, when the quality of economic institutions is varied from the average of sub-Saharan African economies to that of an economy with a high quality of economic institutions (South Africa), a 1% increase in the standard deviation of financial development results in a 0.0018% margin of productive efficiency gain.

The analysis by Gasmi et al (2006) shows through an econometric study that certain characteristics describing the political sphere, more particularly "political accountability", have a significant impact on the regulatory performance of the telecommunications sector, which these authors measure by the economic performance of this sector.

According to Pouvourville and Contandriopoulos (2000), there are three practices of economic analysis in the field of health economics: the study of the interrelations between health and social development, the analysis of the impact of the determinants of health on the health status of individuals, and the analysis of the impact of this dimension on development through human capital, which contributes to the improvement of the quality of the factors of production.

For example, Acemoglu & Johnson (2005) found that institutions that affect all sectors of the economy have a significant direct effect on financial development. They have shown that property rights and contracting institutions are important determinants of financial development. Chauffour (2011) argued that institutions, measured by economic freedom and civil and political liberties, determine why some countries achieve and sustain better economic growth. Baier et al., (2012) noted that in the immediate post-crisis period, there is generally a decrease in economic freedom that stems from increased regulation, which portends slower economic growth in the future. Hafer, (2013) showed that countries with a higher level of initial economic freedom reveal on average higher levels of development of financial intermediaries in the following years. Nawaz, (2015) also established that institutions play an important role in determining the economic growth of developed economies relative to developing economies.

For the study region, Ben Naceur & al. (2014) showed that the quality of institutions, particularly the rule of law, promoted financial development by signaling confidence in the quality of the legal system in support of economic activity. Gazdar & Cherif (2015) reported that finance is more likely to support economic growth in MENA countries with sound institutional environments.

Sghaier, (2018) found, using dynamic panel analysis (GMM), that financial development has a positive effect on economic growth. The author also argues that institutions seem to work in addition to financial development and that the effect of financial development is more pronounced in the presence of the institutional quality variable. Accordingly, the author recommends that particular importance be given to the implementation of policies that lead to the deepening of financial systems. Thus, by promoting the development of a country's financial system, economic growth will be accelerated.

In the same vein, Minea and Villieu (2010) endogenize institutions through a simple model of endogenous growth with public spending (with reference to Barro, 1990), in which they assume that the quality of institutions is assessed by the collection costs associated with mobilizing tax revenues. The authors suggest, among other things, that there are threshold effects in the relationship between finance and growth, associated with differences in institutional quality. Financial development has a positive influence on economic growth when institutional quality exceeds a certain threshold, while below it has a negative impact.

- **"Security" and the components of the DDMI**

In recent years, "security" has become a very central issue. Faced with a multitude of potential threats ranging from terrorism and computer viruses to fraud and organized crime, the world is perceived by many as increasingly dangerous. As a result, security has received more attention and the demand for security goods and services has steadily increased, resulting in a wide and diversified range of economic activities, both public and private, that make up the emerging security economy (Barrie S, 2004)

It is certain that war is one of the social phenomena that are difficult to sustain and that are likely to result in something other than entropy: human losses, material destruction, problematic demobilizations, pensions for the disabled and the families of the victims, massive debts, interruptions of economic circuits, and finally, in the event of defeats, territorial amputations and war indemnities for the benefit of the victor (Diebolt C. and Jaoul M. 2004). Marxists add to the misdeeds of open conflicts the accumulation of capital burdened by the state monopolization of private fortunes in the form of loans. The history of mankind gives many examples of nations ruined by war, naturally when it ends in a military disaster and even sometimes, in the event of victory, when the country has had to make too great an effort to win.

According to Miller et al. (1996), victims incur three types of costs of crime: (1) out-of-pocket expenses such as medical bills and property losses, (2) decreased productivity, and (3) non-monetary losses, including fear, suffering, and loss of quality of life (from Pamela E, 2010).

The question arises as to what the specific weight of economic factors and underdevelopment in the explanation of conflicts is and in the process of spiraling and unregulated propagation that characterize them. War must be financed and can be motivated by the capture of wealth. Conflicts are fostered by economic underdevelopment, youth unemployment, poverty and the impossibility for states to perform sovereign functions. According to the World Bank, 2003), 80% of LDCs have experienced conflicts. It also estimates that a per capita income is twice as high as half the risk of war.

In their theoretical model on which their empirical tests are based, Collier and Hoeffler (2000) place themselves in the utilitarian framework of Grossman (1991). They oppose rebellion, a form of organized crime characterized by greed, to the supposedly legitimate government that receives grievances. The most significant variables are economic. Conflicts are more likely when the level of per capita income is low, the share of raw materials in exports is high and the country is polarized around two major ethnic groups. These factors have since been refined and supplemented. The nature of raw materials is central and subsoil resources, particularly hydrocarbons, are more factors of conflict than agricultural raw materials (Bannon, Collier, 2003). Questions of the credibility of power and redistributive measures vis-a-vis excluded groups are central to explaining conflicts (Azam, 2000). Numerous studies on Africa have sought to specify the economic factors of conflict (Annan, 1998; Elbadawi, Sambanes 2000; Hugon, 2003; Nour Abdel Lotif, 1999). According to Anyawu's (2002) tests, the main explanatory factors of African civil wars are the low GDP growth rate, the importance of natural resources, the duration of peace, social fragmentation and the number of inhabitants (Hugon P, 2006).

The economic effects of insecurity and armed conflict manifest themselves in the destruction or devaluation of physical capital (infrastructure, equipment), human capital and social capital based on trust, rules or networks of relationships. International comparisons show that wars cause per capita income to fall by 15%, cut the growth rate by two percentage points, and lead to capital flight affecting an average of 20% of the working population (Hugon P, 2006).

According to the same author, military spending has no ripple effects and innovations insofar as, except for South Africa, sub-Saharan Africa is an importer of arms. Conflicts also have negative cross-border impacts, impacts that unfortunately statistics drawn up in national frameworks, do not capture very well. War can also have a high cost in terms of military spending and foreign debt, but in most cases the military technologies used are simple, and therefore inexpensive.

- **The "social network" and the components of the DDMI**

The "social network" budget function is closely related to dimension 2 of the DDMI in its sub-dimension of "social ties". In this sense, a review of the literature on social ties and its impacts on different domains can be carried out.

This is the case in the field of employment, in which Bunel and Lenoir (2004) were interested in the specific case of young Moroccan graduates. Faced with the decreasing impact of the level of qualification on access to employment and a high salary, our authors, faced with the mobilization by university leavers of job search methods such as the social network, sought to analyze the impact of the network of family and friends on the probability of finding a job and on the remuneration obtained five years after leaving university. This allowed them to draw the main conclusion that while the social network increases the probability of finding a job, it leads to lower-paid jobs.

Ouellet (2008) focused on another specific area, namely the field of migration. Indeed, his study on the place of the social and support network in the migratory and integration journey of immigrants living in Rivière-du-Loup. From this study, it emerges that it is mainly the migrants' desire to achieve their potential, and not the involvement of the social network, that has guided them in their migratory and integration journeys. Moreover, creating a social network has proven to be a more complex process than simply making new contacts with people through individuals or institutions.

The framework of SMEs and the relationship with the social network was also discussed. This was the case of the study on "the social network of the manager of small and medium-sized enterprises: a strategic tool for his communication" carried out by Brassier-Rodrigues and Brassier (2010). Faced with the need for SME managers to think about a strategic approach to their communication that allows them to meet market expectations in an appropriate and responsive way, our authors consider the manager's social network to be an advantageous communication tool. And at the end of their analyses, they conclude that SMEs have an interest in developing a communication strategy based on traditional communication tools, while creating and maintaining a social network for "industrial" business partners.

- **The "professional network" and the components of the DDMI**

The "professional networks" budget function is mainly associated with Dimension 2 of the DDMI. Indeed, this budgetary function is closely linked to the Quality of the Living Environment Index (QLEI), particularly with its sub-dimensions "Work-life balance" and "Subjective well-being" because of the potential impact that a budgetary variation of "professional networks" can have on these two sub-dimensions. And the latter have also been the subject of various studies because of their importance as a factor in the development of the population's living environment.

Indeed, the sub-dimension of work-life balance is already a vast subject of reflection that has generated vast literature based on various questions. Among these questions, we find the question of the achievability of the objective of work-life balance. This has been studied in South Africa by Malherbe (2020) following the 2018 expansion of the scope of South African legislation on leave and social security benefits for employed parents. The main finding of the study is that the work-life balance of parents and carers has not received the necessary attention in the South African legislative program, despite the generosity of the Constitution. South African policymakers and legislators could therefore draw on the provisions of Directive 2019/1158 on parental leave and childcare to develop a single South African framework to ensure work-life balance for parents and carers. From another angle, Zahra (2020) also looked at the issue of work-life balance by studying its impact on job performance. Through this study, it was possible to observe that high levels of role overload and interference between work and family have an impact on the recruitment and retention efforts of organizations, which often has negative effects on their profitability.

The sub-dimension of subjective well-being, like the sub-dimension of work-life balance, has also been the subject of a large literature on it. Langlois (2014) was interested in the question of well-being by linking it to happiness and the feeling of justice. The main results of his study are that the measure of happiness and the measure of satisfaction with the life led are not completely interchangeable, although they are strongly correlated; the well-established relationship between income and the feeling of well-being cannot be analyzed without taking into account the social representation that social actors have of their situation; and finally that it is important to take into account the sense of justice in the assessment of well-being, distinguishing between the judgment made on one's personal situation and the judgment made on society as a whole. This notion of subjective well-being has also been the subject of more recent studies, including that of Richard (2022). It focused on the relationship between subjective well-being and transitions into and out of poverty. To this end, it finds that the subjective well-being of individuals is correlated with entry and exit from poverty in terms of living conditions, but that individuals do not seem to be affected by transitions to and from income poverty at 60% of median income. Only crossing the monetary threshold corresponding to 80% of median income is perceived as significant by the individuals interviewed, which makes it a subjective line of poverty.

- **The "Building and Energy" and the components of the DDMI**

The budget function of the Building-energy sector is related to various components of the DDMI, namely mainly, dimension 2 (QLEI) through its sub-dimension "housing conditions" and dimension 5 (NTSI) through its sub-dimensions "urbanization" and "infrastructure" and can contribute to their evolution and consequently to the improvement of the DDMI. These sub-dimensions are therefore of real importance in the evolution of the index and therefore of the growth of countries. This importance is also noted long before in the existing literature on these sub-dimensions.

Indeed, as far as housing is concerned, there are relatively many studies, particularly those highlighting its relationship with economic growth. This is the case of Poirier (2000), who researched the role of the housing sector in the development of national economies and its influence on economic growth. And which concluded at the end of its work that the quality, and not the quantity, of housing influences the increase in workers' productivity significantly. Moreover, this influence of housing also extends to many other aspects of economic and social life such as education and health. The same is true for Bigot, Daudey and Hoibian (2014) who, at the request of the Union Sociale pour l'Habitat (USH), asked themselves whether housing, and more specifically social housing, is an asset or a handicap for growth. In response to this question, they find that the hypertrophy of the housing sector could be the cause of less economic dynamism and a loss of competitiveness in countries, such as France, where real estate inflation is high.

The infrastructure sector is not to be outdone in terms of studies carried out. This is evidenced by this recent study by Traoré and Traoré (2022) on infrastructure and economic growth in Mali. And the main findings of this study are that (i) transport infrastructure is a positive and significant determinant of GDP per capita growth in the short and long term; (ii) an increase in water and sanitation infrastructure stocks leads to a significant increase in GDP per capita in the short term but not in the long term; and (iii) energy infrastructure and telecommunications stocks do not have a significant effect on economic growth in the short or long term. Ultimately, the main conclusion to be drawn is that it would therefore be worthwhile investing more in physical infrastructure. Increased investment in physical infrastructure and the mobilization of significant resources for infrastructure maintenance can be a powerful driver of economic growth.

- **The Economics and Components of the DDMI**

The "economy" budget function encompasses a wide range of areas. Hence its link with all the components of the DDMI. There is therefore no shortage of literature on the different fields linking the economy and the DDMI.

Among these different areas, the area of poverty stands out, particularly from the point of view of inputs and outputs, robustness and vulnerability, but also from the perspective of the effects of fiscal policies on poverty. Regarding the dynamics of poverty in terms of inflows and outflows, Mededji (2007) was strongly interested in the specific context of the urban environment of Benin. He concludes from his study that the proportion of short-term poor households is higher than that of the long-term poor, and that among the short-term poor, inflows are greater than outflows. The framework of robustness and vulnerability to poverty has also aroused the interest of various authors, including Akhenaten (2016). The latter, following his work in the DRC, observes that rural households are slightly more vulnerable to poverty than urban households and household poverty is transmitted from generation to generation and is not the result of isolated events. Poverty is therefore chronic. Ihnach et al. (2020), on the other hand, looked at the effects of fiscal policies on poverty and inequality in Morocco. And this study found that all deciles are net beneficiaries of fiscal policy except for the richest two deciles where taxes paid exceed benefits received. The poorest decile is the largest net beneficiary, benefiting from free public services in the form of education and health, and from transfers and subsidies on consumer products.

Other areas also link the budgetary function of the economy to the DDMI. This is the case of the environment, which has been the subject of studies, including that of Obringer (2007) on the link between Chinese economic growth and the environment, which has highlighted the seriousness of the environmental damage that was necessary for China's meteoric growth, and which today represents an obstacle to this growth. This has led to an increase in the requirements of controls and standards related to the environment. This is also the case in the field of infrastructure, for which we take the example of Thiao's (2019) study on the link between public infrastructure spending and economic growth in Senegal. The results of his study mainly suggest that economic activity is more sensitive to the decline than to the increase in public infrastructure spending. And as a result, maintaining relatively high levels of public infrastructure spending is hurting Senegal's economic growth.

Section 2: Methodology for Fiscal Sensitivity Analysis

The Demographic Dividend Monitoring Index (DDMI) is an indicator used to measure the capture of the demographic dividend in synergy with sustainable development. It allows a country or territory to be able to assess its progress in the production of well-being.

The DDMI focuses on five (05) dimensions: (i) economic dependence, (ii) quality of the living environment, (iii) transitions into poverty, (iv) expanded human capital and (v) networks and territories. Each dimension covers one (01) to seven (07) fields or sub-dimensions. In turn, the sub-dimensions are made up of several elementary indicators that are specific to them.

The methodology used in the first dimension is the National Transfer Accounts (NTA) approach. The purpose of this method is to produce a measure, both individual and aggregate, of the acquisition and distribution of economic resources at different ages. This consists of introducing age into National Accounts. These accounts are intended to understand how economic flows flow between different age groups of a population for a given country and for a given year. They indicate at each age the different sources of income and the different uses of this income in terms of consumption, whether private or public, and savings. They thus make it possible to study the economic consequences of changing the age structure of the population (United Nations, 2013).

Dimension 2 (or Quality of the living environment) is inspired by the Better Life Index methodology developed by the OECD (2011). In its standard formulation, the living environment covers eleven (11) sub-dimensions considered essential to well-being. But in the context of DD monitoring, only seven (Civic Engagement, Social Ties, Environment; Work-life balance and Security) of the eleven are retained the analysis of the living environment, the other four (04) being considered by the other dimensions. Each sub-dimension of the living environment is measured using one to four indicators. Within each subdimension, the basic indicators that make up the sub-dimension are averaged with the same weighting, with the latter being normalized beforehand. The Quality of Living Environment Indicator (QLEI) is a weighted average of the sub-dimensional composite indicators.

The analysis of poverty dynamics carried out at the level of dimension 3 is based on a new approach to measuring transitions in poverty by Dang and Lanjouw (2013).

The latter have developed a method for constructing pseudo-panels and estimating the transition matrix on two or more poverty surveys. The idea is to follow cohort of individuals (or households) over time.

Dimensions 4 and 5 are inspired by the HDI and Clusters method respectively. Based on the three classic sub-dimensions of the HDI, dimension 4 introduces fertility into the Building of the indicator to consider aspects relating to demography and the sustainability of development. As for dimension 5, it covers four (04) sub-dimensions: urbanization, migration, infrastructure and financial flows. Each sub-dimension has several indicators to quantify it. The indicators are normalized so that the values are between 0 (the worst score) and 1 (the best score). The sub dimensional index is obtained by the geometric mean of the indicators that make up the subdimension. The Synthetic Indicator of Networks and Territories (NTSI) also represent the geometric mean of the sub dimensional indices.

By design, the DDMI is unitless and its value varies between 0, which indicates a terrible situation, and 1, which indicates an excellent situation. It is obtained by the geometric mean of the synthetic indicators resulting from the five (05) dimensions mentioned above. Its formula is as follows:

$$\boldsymbol{DDMI = \sqrt[5]{EDCI * QLEI * PESI * EHDI * NTSI}}$$

Where:

EDCI is the indicator of coverage of economic dependency,

QLEI is the indicator of the quality of the living environment,

PESI is the synthetic indicator of exit from poverty,

EHDI is the Broader Human Development Index, and

NTSI is the indicator for networks and territories

Its interpretation is made through a given grid. In this grid, countries or territories are divided into three categories according to the value of the indicator. Thus, when the indicator has a value below 0.50, the situation of the country or territory is qualified as weak. However, the situation is considered average when the indicator has a value between 0.5 and 0.8. Finally, when the value of the indicator is greater than or equal to 0.8, the situation of the country or territory will be classified as good (or high or better).

Budget Transformation Methodology

The methodology of fiscal transformation requires, in the first place, that the national budget be distributed in accordance with the dimensions of the demographic dividend. These functions, of which there are four, are as follows:

– The "Human Capital" budget function includes all operating and investment expenditure related to health and education. This is precisely the total expenditure on health and education carried out by the State (all ministries combined).

– The "Governance" budget function which includes operating and investment expenditure related to institutions and security. More specifically, it is all institutional[13] and security expenditure [14] carried out by the State (all ministries combined)

– The "Structure of the economy" function: This function includes operating and investment expenditure related to BTA/Energy and other production sectors (primary, secondary and tertiary) carried out by all ministries.

– the "Professional and Social Network" function: grouping together all the operating, operating and investment expenses related to Communication and Leisure carried out by all the ministerial departments.

DDMI Retropolation and Connection Methodology

The methodology for backcasting and linking DDMI consists first in calibrating the DDMI of the years in which the survey data are available, and secondly, through the calibration method of linking the DDMI of the other years between two consecutive surveys. This allows for a continuous series of DDMIs.

1. Backcasting or Calibrating DDMI Remote Points

The first step here is to identify all the years for which survey data are available. The objective of this exercise is to calculate the DDMIs for these years to have the distant points.

2. Calibration and calibration

The connection is based on the calibration method. In this step, the DDMI will be calculated over several years to have sufficient information for the alignment of the budget and the calculation of the elasticities. The indicators making up the DDMI will therefore be calculated based on survey data and statistical yearbooks for the national level. In summary, it is a question of linking the DDMI over

---

[13] The "Institutions" budget function takes into account all operating and investment expenses related to the country's institutional architecture. These include the expenses of institutions such as the Presidency, the Prime Minister, the Parliament, the Ministry of Foreign Affairs, the Economic and Social Council, the Senate, the High Council of Local Authorities, etc.

[14] The "Security" budget function takes into account all operating and investment expenses related to security. These include the expenses of institutions such as the Ministry of the Interior, the Ministry of the Armed Forces, the Ministry of the Environment (Water and Forests), etc.

the past 10 to 15 years through a calibration process to have sufficient data for statistical robustness.

Alignment of DDMI Functional Budget methodology

1. **DDMI Mapping and Budget Functions: Transit Table**

The strategic axes of economic and social development of the States of the countries studied are summarized in 04 dimensions, namely (i) Human Capital, (ii) Governance, (iii) Professional and Social Networks and finally (iv) the structure of the economy.

Each dimension is composed of two sub-components as shown in the following representation:

Figure 11: The dimensions of the DDMI

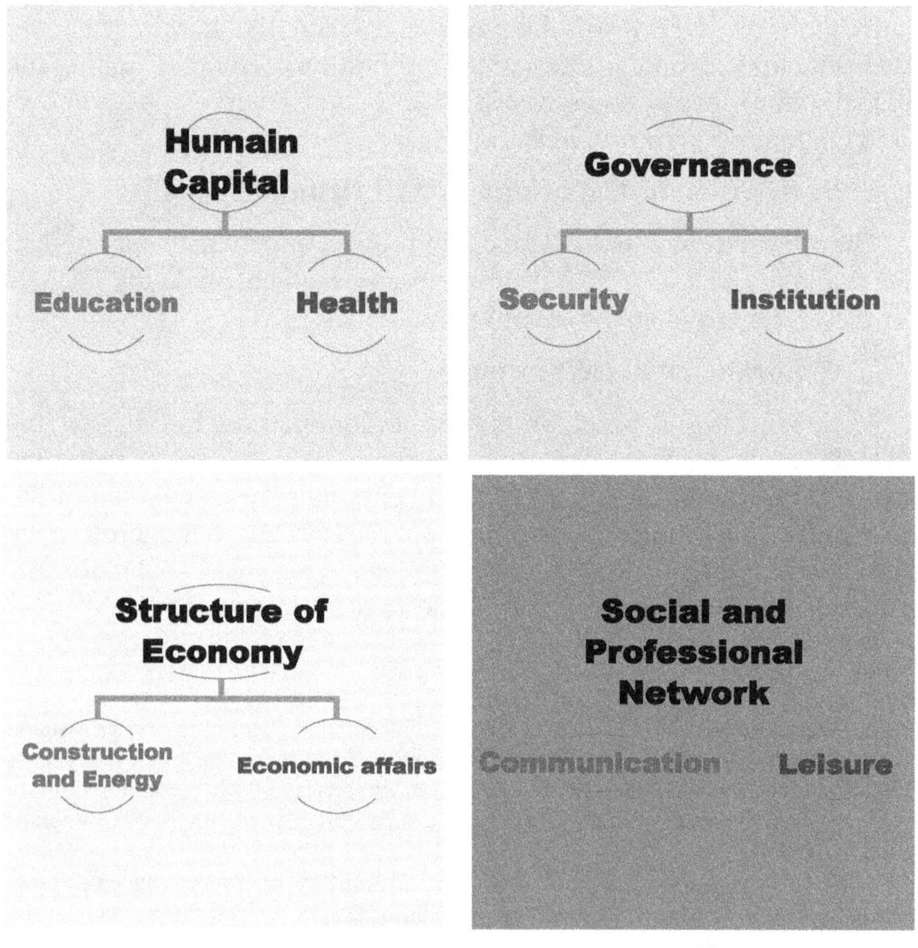

Source: CREG 2023

The Demographic Dividend Monitoring Index (DDMI) covers the aspects of economic and social life that go into capturing the demographic dividend:

1. **Link between the 8 budget functions and the dimensions of the DDMI**

Need to explain the links between budgetary functions and the dimensions of the DDMI (Determinants of budgetary functions) see in the literature.

Starting from the 24 sub-dimensions to feed the budgetary functions.

2. **Stages of stowage**

Step 1: Audits of the Budget and DDMI series

At this stage, it is a question of combing through all the series of the budget and the DDMI previously calculated in the previous steps of the process. The objective is to check the overall consistency of the quantities and to carry out quality control of the series before the descriptive analysis and estimation phase.

Step 2: Transit **table** – build the DDMI accounts corresponding to the budgetary functions –

The Institutions Budget function is followed by the DDMI indicator, civic engagement.

Table 32: Transit table - build the DDMI accounts corresponding to the budget functions

Development Components	Budget Functions	Dimensions du DDMI	Characteristics
Human Capital	Education	Education	Non-composite
	Health	Health	Non-composite
Governance	Institutions	Civic Engagement	Non-composite
	Security	PESI (Poverty Exit Synthetic Index[15]) + Security	Composite
Professional and Social Networks	Social network	Social network	Non-composite
	Professional Networks	Work-life balance + subjective well-	Composite

[15] Those excluded from growth.

Development Components	Budget Functions	Dimensions du DDMI	Characteristics
		being (literature review)	
Structure of the economy	Building and Energy	Urbanization + infrastructure + housing+	Composite
	Economics affairs	EDCI + PESI + Standard of Living + Migration + Infrastructure + Environment	Composite

Step 3: **Building of budgetary indices, structural indices or Base 100 indices, with a reference**.

For reasons of equivalence between the DDMI, which is in the form of an index, it is important to transform public and private spending into indices. It is necessary to remember that the expenditure indices can be in a structural form or in a base 100 form considering a base year.

Step 4: **Graphical analysis of the DDMI series and budget functions**.

Graphic analysis, also known as descriptive analysis, is a step that precedes econometric tests. The objective of the latter is to intuitively understand the relationship that could exist between macroeconomic quantities. It also allows you to track trends across different series to identify inflection points and outliers.

Step 5: **Econometric analysis of each series – Correlogram, Unit root test**

Preliminary tests are important in any econometric study. In time series where the risk of fallacious regressions is regular, these preliminary tests on series allow us to know the nature and properties of series.

Step 6: **Specification of the Macro Fiscal Theoretical Model**

The theoretical macro-fiscal model is inspired by different economic theories. Here, in the framework of this model, we draw inspiration from the classical Cobb Douglas model by specifying DDMI functions as production functions that can be explained by a set of so-called explanatory variables.

Step 7: Specification of the empirical model and estimation of budget elasticities via an ensemble model.

Once the empirical model or framework has been defined, step 7 is devoted to the empirical specification of the model. The aim here is to clearly identify the variables that will be used in the modelling. We will have two types of variables, namely explanatory variables and explained variables

Step 8: Empirical Model Estimation and Econometric Results Analysis

Once the empirical model has been specified, the next step is to mobilize the appropriate econometric methods for the estimation of the model parameters. The results of this estimation will therefore be the subject of an econometric analysis which consists first in seeing the overall significance of the model, in other words the explanatory power of the model. In a second step, it will be a question of interpreting the results by giving them meaning in the real sphere. This will make it possible to draw implications for economic policies.

Step 9: Robustness and predication test of the business model

This is a crucial step in any empirical study. It allows to give scientific validity to the results obtained and in which the model allows to predict the values of the dependent variable. Thus, once the model has been estimated, it is subjected to a battery of robustness tests.

Step 10: In-depth analysis of the validated results and design of the Policy briefs.

The last stage of the linkage is devoted to the economic analysis of the results regarding the different hypotheses formulated (expected signs) and theories. It consists of interpreting the coefficients and amplitude of the different explanatory variables.

3. Specification of Macro Budget Modeling

Production function

Let Y be the Demographic Dividend Monitoring Index (DDMI). In its economic function, we assume that it is the combination of private and public expenditure.

$$Y = AK^{\alpha}L^{\beta}$$

A Cobb Douglas production function.

We consider the economic and budgetary functions retained in the budgetary transformation.

Framed 3: The Cobb-Douglass Production Function

In general, a production function is a specification of how the quantity of production behaves based on the inputs used in production. This concept can be applied at the level of individual companies, industries or entire economies.

In economics, the Cobb-Douglas functional form of production functions is widely used to represent the relationship between production and inputs. It was proposed by Knut Wicksell (1851 - 1926) and tested based on statistical data by Charles Cobb and Paul Douglas in 1928.

The function used by the authors to model production is as follows:

$$P(L,K) = AL^{\alpha}K^{\beta}$$

where:

- P = total output (the dollar value of all goods produced in a year)

- L = labor input (the total number of person-hours worked in a year)

- K = capital contribution (the monetary value of all machinery, equipment and buildings)

- Total factors of productivity

- are the production elasticities of labor and capital, respectively. These values are constantly determined by the available technology. α *et* β

The elasticity of production measures the responsiveness of production to a change in the levels of labor or capital used in production, all other things being equal.

Capital used in production, all other things being equal. For example, if α = 0.15, a 1% increase in labor will result in an increase of about 0.15% in output.

In addition, if:

$\alpha + \beta = 1$, the production function has constant returns to scale. In other words, if L and K each increase by 20%, P increases by 20%.

Returns to scale are a technical property of production that examines changes in output following a proportional change in output (where all inputs increase by a constant factor).

If output increases in the same proportion, then there are constant returns on the scale, sometimes referred to simply as returns to scale. If output increases less than this proportional change, there are diminishing returns to scale. If production increases by more than this proportion, there are increasing returns to scale (DRI).

However, if

$\alpha + \beta < 1$, the returns to scale are diminishing, and if

$\alpha + \beta > 1$, the returns to scale are increasing.

On the assumption of perfect competition, it can be shown that α and β are the shares of labor and capital in production.

For each function, the following production function will be used:

$$Y = AK^{\alpha}L^{\beta}$$

More specifically for the function:

Function 1: Macro-budget modelling of the health sector

$Y_1 = A_1\, K_{1Pr}^{\lambda 1}\, K_{1Pu}^{\alpha 1}\, L_1^{\beta 1}$ **(1)**

$\boldsymbol{K_{1Pr}}$Represents private investment in economic function (1).

$\boldsymbol{K_{1Pu}}$Represents public investment in the economic function (1).

Thus, the production of well-being in a particular function is conditioned by the allocation of resources to produce the goods and services that derive well-being. We can then write:

$$Y_1 = A_1\, K_{1Pr}^{\lambda_1}\, K_{1Pu}^{\alpha 1}\, L_1^{\beta_1}$$

At the public level, expenditure (DEP) is characterized by 03 budgetary natures, including:

- Operation *(Function)*
- Investment *(Inv)*
- Transfers *(Trf)*

Considering these three budgetary natures, equation (1) becomes:

$Y_1 = A_1\, K_{1Pr}^{\lambda_1}\, Fonc_1^{\alpha_{11}}\, Inv_1^{\alpha_{12}}\, Trf_1^{\alpha_{12}}\, L_1^{\beta_1}$ **(2)**

By linearizing, we obtain:

$\log Y_1 = \log A_1 + \lambda_1 logK_{1Pr} + \alpha_1 logFonc_1 + \alpha_2 logInv_1 + \alpha_3 logTrf_1 + \beta_1 \log L_1$ **(3)**

With: $\lambda_1\ \alpha_1;\alpha_2;\ \alpha_3\ et\ \beta_1 > 0$

$$\mathrm{I}(Fon_1) = \frac{Fonc_1}{DEP_1} \quad \textbf{(4)}$$

$$\mathrm{I}(Inv_1) = \frac{Inv_1}{DEP_1} \quad \textbf{(5)}$$

$$\mathrm{I}(\mathrm{Trf}_1) = \frac{Trf_1}{DEP_1} \quad \textbf{(6)}$$

$\log Y_1 = \log A_1 + \lambda_1 logK_{1Pr} + \alpha_1' logDEP_1 + \beta_1 \log L_1$ **(7)**

$\alpha_1' = \alpha_1 + \alpha_2 + \alpha_3$ **(8)**

$DEP_1 = Fonc_1 + Inv_1 + Trf_1$ **(9)**

The DDMI is designed as a wellness feature. It is equivalent to an output (verified by an external validity test between the evolution at the level of DDMI / GDP or evolution of the growth rate DDMI and GDP or between Log DDMI and LOG GDP.

As a result, the validation of the test confirms the equivalence of DDMI and GDP. Thus, DDMI can be used as a global output function. This is equivalent to saying that the production functions of the global output are equivalent to the functions of the global output of well-being.

However, the innovation in this model is to identify the nature or source of well-being.

Of the above we can write:

$DDMI_1 \equiv Y_1$ **(10)**

The DDMI is an index between 0 and 100 while the expenses are in monetary units. To respect the equivalence of equation (10), all variables in monetary values will be transformed into indices. Thus, we will have:

$\log DDMI_1 = \log A_1 + \lambda_1 logI(K_{1Pr}) + \alpha_1 logI(Fonc_1) + \alpha_2 logI(Inv_1) + \alpha_3 logI(Trf_1) + \beta_1 \log I(L_1)$ **(11)**

$I(K_{1Pr})$= index of private expenditure in the function (1) **(12)**

$I(L_1)$= index of the stock of labour in the function (1). **(13)**

Function 2: Macro-budgetary modelling of the education sector

$Y_2 = A_2\, K_{2Pr}^{\lambda_2}\; Fonc_2^{\alpha_4}\, Inv_2^{\alpha_5}\, Trf_2^{\alpha_6}\, L_2^{\beta_2}$ **(14)**

$\log Y_2 = \log A_2 + \lambda_2 logK_{2Pr} + \alpha_4 logFonc_2 + \alpha_5 logInv_2 + \alpha_6 logTrf_2 + \beta_2 \log L_2$ **(15)**

$$\mathrm{I}(Fon_2) = \frac{Fonc_2}{DEP_2} \quad \textbf{(16)}$$

$$\mathrm{I}(Inv_2) = \frac{Inv_2}{DEP_2} \quad \textbf{(17)}$$

$$\mathrm{I}(\mathrm{Trf}_2) = \frac{Trf_2}{DEP_2} \quad \textbf{(18)}$$

$\log Y_2 = \log A_2 + \lambda_2 logK_{2Pr} + \alpha_2' logDEP_2 + \beta_2 \log L_2$ **(19)**

$\alpha_2' = \alpha_4 + \alpha_5 + \alpha_6$ **(20)**

$DEP_2 = Fonc_2 + Inv_2 + Trf_2$ **(21)**

$DDMI_2 \equiv Y_2$ **(22)**

$\log DDMI_2 = \log A_2 + \lambda_2 logI(K_{2Pr}) + \alpha_4 logI(Fonc_2) + \alpha_5 logI(Inv_2) + \alpha_6 logI(Trf_2) + \beta_2 \log I(L_2)$ **(23)**

$I(K_{2Pr})$= index of private expenditure in the function (14) **(24)**

$I(L_2)$= index of the stock of labour in the function (14). **(25)**

Function 3: Macro-budgetary modelling of the institutional sector

$Y_3 = A_3\, K_{3Pr}^{\lambda_3}\; Fonc_3^{\alpha_7}\, Inv_3^{\alpha_8}\, Trf_3^{\alpha_9}\, L_3^{\beta_3}$ **(26)**

$\log Y_3 = \log A_3 + \lambda_3 logK_{3Pr} + \alpha_7 logFonc_3 + \alpha_8 logInv_3 + \alpha_9 logTrf_3 + \beta_3 \log L_3$ **(27)**

$$\mathrm{I}(Fon_3) = \frac{Fonc_3}{DEP_3} \quad \textbf{(28)}$$

$$\mathrm{I}(Inv_3) = \frac{Inv_3}{DEP_3} \quad \textbf{(29)}$$

$$\mathrm{I}(\mathrm{Trf}_3) = \frac{Trf_3}{DEP_3} \quad \textbf{(30)}$$

$\log Y_3 = \log A_3 + \lambda_3 logK_{3Pr} + \alpha_3' logDEP_3 + \beta_3 \log L_3$ **(31)**

$\alpha_3' = \alpha_7 + \alpha_8 + \alpha_9$ **(32)**

$DEP_3 = Fonc_3 + Inv_3 + Trf_3$ **(33)**

$DDMI_3 \equiv Y_3$ **(34)**

$\log DDMI_3 = \log A_3 + \lambda_3 logI(K_{3Pr}) + \alpha_7 logI(Fonc_3) + \alpha_8 logI(Inv_3) + \alpha_9 logI(Trf_3) + \beta_3 \log I(L_3)$ **(35)**

$I(K_{3Pr})$= index of private expenditure in the function (26) **(36)**

$I(L_3)$= index of the stock of labour in the function (26). **(37)**

Function 4: Macro-budget modelling of the security sector

$Y_4 = A_4\, K_{4Pr}^{\lambda_4}\, Fonc_4^{\alpha_{10}}\, Inv_4^{\alpha_{11}}\, Trf_4^{\alpha_{12}}\, L_4^{\beta_4}$ **(38)**

$\log Y_4 = \log A_4 + \lambda_4 logK_{4Pr} + \alpha_{10} logFonc_4 + \alpha_{11} logInv_4 + \alpha_{12} logTrf_4 + \beta_4 \log L_4$**(39)**

$$\mathrm{I}(Fon_4) = \frac{Fonc_4}{DEP_4} \quad \mathbf{(40)}$$

$$\mathrm{I}(Inv_4) = \frac{Inv_4}{DEP_4} \quad \mathbf{(41)}$$

$$\mathrm{I}(\mathrm{Trf}_4) = \frac{Trf_4}{DEP_4} \quad \mathbf{(42)}$$

$\log Y_4 = \log A_4 + \lambda_4 logK_{4Pr} + \alpha'_4 logDEP_4 + \beta_4 \log L_4$ **(43)**

$\alpha'_4 = \alpha_{10} + \alpha_{11} + \alpha_{12}$ **(44)**

$DEP_4 = Fonc_4 + Inv_4 + Trf_4$ **(45)**

$DDMI_4 \equiv Y_4$ **(46)**

$\log DDMI_4 = \log A_4 + \lambda_4 logI(K_{4Pr}) + \alpha_{10} logI(Fonc_4) + \alpha_{11} logI(Inv_4) + \alpha_{12} logI(Trf_4) + \beta_4 \log I(L_4)$ **(47)**

$I(K_{4Pr})$= index of private expenditure in the function ('38) **(48)**

$I(L_4)$= index of the stock of labour in the function (38). **(49)**

Function 5: Macro-budgetary modelling of the professional networks sector

$Y_5 = A_5\, K_{5Pr}^{\lambda_5}\, Fonc_5^{\alpha_{13}}\, Inv_5^{\alpha_{14}}\, Trf_5^{\alpha_{15}}\, L_5^{\beta_5}$ **(50)**

$\log Y_5 = \log A_5 + \lambda_5 logK_{5Pr} + \alpha_{13} logFonc_5 + \alpha_{14} logInv_5 + \alpha_{15} logTrf_5 + \beta_5 \log L_5$**(51)**

$$\text{I}(Fon_5) = \frac{Fonc_5}{DEP_5} \quad \textbf{(52)}$$

$$\text{I}(Inv_5) = \frac{Inv_5}{DEP_5} \quad \textbf{(53)}$$

$$\text{I(Trf}_5) = \frac{Trf_5}{DEP_5} \quad \textbf{(54)}$$

$$\log Y_5 = \log A_5 + \lambda_5 logK_{5Pr} + \alpha_5' logDEP_5 + \beta_5 \log L_5 \quad \textbf{(55)}$$

$$\alpha_5' = \alpha_{13} + \alpha_{14} + \alpha_{15} \quad \textbf{(56)}$$

$$DEP_5 = Fonc_5 + Inv_5 + Trf_5 \ \textbf{(57)}$$

$$DDMI_5 \equiv Y_5 \quad \textbf{(58)}$$

$$\log DDMI_5 = \log A_5 + \lambda_5 logI(K_{5Pr}) + \alpha_{13} logI(Fonc_5) + \alpha_{14} logI(Inv_5) + \alpha_{15} logI(Trf_5) + \beta_5 \log I(L_5) \qquad \textbf{(59)}$$

$I(K_{5Pr})$= index of private expenditure in the function (50) **(60)**

$I(L_5)$= index of the stock of labour in the function (50). **(61)**

Function 6: Macro-budget modelling of the social media sector

$$Y_6 = A_6 \, K_{6Pr}^{\lambda_6} \, Fonc_6^{\alpha_{16}} \, Inv_6^{\alpha_{17}} \, Trf_6^{\alpha_{18}} \, L_6^{\beta_6} \qquad \textbf{(62)}$$

$$\log Y_6 = \log A_6 + \lambda_6 logK_{6Pr} + \alpha_{16} logFonc_6 + \alpha_{17} logInv_6 + \alpha_{18} logTrf_6 + \beta_6 \log L_6 \textbf{(63)}$$

$$\text{I}(Fon_6) = \frac{Fonc_6}{DEP_6} \quad \textbf{(64)}$$

$$\text{I}(Inv_6) = \frac{Inv_6}{DEP_6} \quad \textbf{(65)}$$

$$\text{I(Trf}_6) = \frac{Trf_6}{DEP_6} \quad \textbf{(66)}$$

$$\log Y_6 = \log A_6 + \lambda_6 logK_{6Pr} + \alpha_6' logDEP_6 + \beta_6 \log L_6 \quad \textbf{(67)}$$

$$\alpha_6' = \alpha_{16} + \alpha_{17} + \alpha_{18} \quad \textbf{(68)}$$

$$DEP_6 = Fonc_6 + Inv_6 + Trf_6 \ \textbf{(69)}$$

$$DDMI_6 \equiv Y_6 \quad \textbf{(70)}$$

$$\log DDMI_6 = \log A_6 + \lambda_6 logI(K_{6Pr}) + \alpha_{16} logI(Fonc_6) + \alpha_{17} logI(Inv_6) + \alpha_{18} logI(Trf_6) + \beta_6 \log I(L_6) \qquad \textbf{(71)}$$

$I(K_{6Pr})$= index of private expenditure in the function (62) **(72)**

$I(L_6)$= index of the stock of labour in the function (62). **(73)**

Function 7: Macro-budget modelling of the Building and energy sector

$Y_7 = A_7\, K_{7Pr}^{\lambda_7}\, Fonc_7^{\alpha_{19}}\, Inv_7^{\alpha_{20}}\, Trf_7^{\alpha_{21}}\, L_7^{\beta_7}$ **(74)**

$\log Y_7 = \log A_7 + \lambda_7 logK_{7Pr} + \alpha_{19} logFonc_7 + \alpha_{20} logInv_7 + \alpha_{21} logTrf_7 + \beta_7 \log L_7$**(75)**

$$\mathrm{I}(Fon_7) = \frac{Fonc_7}{DEP_7} \quad \textbf{(76)}$$

$$\mathrm{I}(Inv_7) = \frac{Inv_7}{DEP_7} \quad \textbf{(77)}$$

$$\mathrm{I}(\mathrm{Trf}_7) = \frac{Trf_7}{DEP_7} \quad \textbf{(78)}$$

$\log Y_7 = \log A_7 + \lambda_7 logK_{7Pr} + \alpha'_7 logDEP_7 + \beta_7 \log L_7$ **(79)**

$\alpha'_7 = \alpha_{19} + \alpha_{20} + \alpha_{21}$ **(80)**

$DEP_7 = Fonc_7 + Inv_7 + Trf_7$ **(81)**

$DDMI_7 \equiv Y_7$ **(82)**

$\log DDMI_7 = \log A_7 + \lambda_7 logI(K_{7Pr}) + \alpha_{19} logI(Fonc_7) + \alpha_{20} logI(Inv_7) + \alpha_{21} logI(Trf_7) + \beta_7 \log I(L_7)$ **(83)**

$I(K_{7Pr})$= index of private expenditure in the function (74) **(84)**

$I(L_7)$= index of the stock of labour in the function (74). **(85)**

Function 8: Macro-fiscal modelling of the economic sector

$Y_8 = A_8\, K_{8Pr}^{\lambda_8}\, Fonc_8^{\alpha_{22}}\, Inv_8^{\alpha_{23}}\, Trf_8^{\alpha_{24}}\, L_8^{\beta_8}$ **(86)**

$\log Y_8 = \log A_8 + \lambda_8 logK_{8Pr} + \alpha_{22} logFonc_8 + \alpha_{23} logInv_8 + \alpha_{24} logTrf_8 + \beta_8 \log L_8$**(87)**

$$\mathrm{I}(Fon_8) = \frac{Fonc_8}{DEP_8} \quad \textbf{(88)}$$

$$\mathrm{I}(Inv_8) = \frac{Inv_8}{DEP_8} \quad \textbf{(89}$$

$$\mathrm{I}(\mathrm{Trf}_8) = \frac{Trf_8}{DEP_8} \quad \textbf{(90)}$$

$\log Y_8 = \log A_8 + \lambda_8 logK_{8Pr} + \alpha'_8 logDEP_8 + \beta_8 \log L_8$ **(91)**

$\alpha'_8 = \alpha_{22} + \alpha_{23} + \alpha_{24}$ **(92)**

$DEP_8 = Fonc_8 + Inv_8 + Trf_8$ **(93)**

$DDMI_8 \equiv Y_8$ **(94)**

$\log DDMI_8 = \log A_8 + \lambda_8 logI(K_{8Pr}) + \alpha_{22} logI(Fonc_8) + \alpha_{23} logI(Inv_8) + \alpha_{24} logI(Trf_8) + \beta_8 \log I(L_8)$ **(95)**

$I(K_{8Pr})$= index of private expenditure in the function (86) **(96)**

$I(L_8)$= index of the stock of labour in the function (86). **(97)**

Looping the model

Since we have 08 functions, and each function requires 12 equations, we will have a total of 6x12 for a total of 96 equations.

In addition, for each year, we must have the following convergence identities:

$\sum_{J=1}^{8} DEP_j = Budget\ exécuté$ (98)

$\sum_{J=1}^{8} K_{jPr} = Dépenses\ privées$ (99)

$\sum_{J=1}^{8} L_j = Stock\ de\ main\ d'oeuvre$ (100)

$\prod_{J=1}^{8} DDMI_j = DDMI$ (101)

Estimation via the simultaneous equation model or via the Eviews model module.

Section 3: Analysis of sectoral fiscal elasticities

The parameters of the macro-fiscal model are estimated from the actual data of two countries that we will refer to as *country Y* and *country Z* for the purposes of the illustration. For each economic function by country, we have four coefficients. On the one hand, there is an alpha coefficient (α) for each budgetary type (operating, investment, transfer), which makes it possible to assess the effect and amplitude of the types of expenditure on the well-being indicator at the sectoral level, particularly the DDMI of the sector concerned. On the other hand, we have the beta coefficient (β), which allows us to measure the effects and amplitude of the sector's total spending on the sector index. Roughly speaking, we have thirty-two (32) coefficients for each country, including 24 parameters that are coefficients (α) and 8 beta coefficients (β). The confidence level of the results is represented in the table by asterisks (*). The 90%, 95% and 99% confidence levels are represented by one, two and three asterisks, respectively.

Table 33: Budgetary elasticities of the human capital component

FUNCTIONS	Coefficient α						Coefficient β	
	FON		INV		TFR		COUNTRY Y	COUNTRY Z
	COUNTRY Y	COUNTRY Z	COUNTRY Y	COUNTRY Z	COUNTRY Y	COUNTRY Z		
Education	0,484**	0,829***	0,234***	-0,01	0,300	-0,023	0,467***	0,113***
Health	0,366***	0,121***	0,591***	0,084***	0,247***	0,908***	-0,012	0,008

Source: CREG estimates, 2024

The functional transformation of the budget that we have previously discussed makes it possible to determine the budget allocated to each economic function to produce well-being in a sector. A priori, an increase in budget allocations should contribute to an improvement in the sector's well-being indicator. When we analyze the coefficients (β) of countries Y and Z, an increase in the total budget significantly influences the DDMI for some sectors, which is not the case for other sectors. For example, a 10% change in the total budget of the education sector leads to an improvement in the DDMI education index of 4.67% in country Y and a smaller increase, estimated at 1.13% for country Z. When we reason by budgetary nature, operating expenditure significantly influences the sector's indicator, while transfer expenditure is significantly zero. By increasing the operating budget by 10%, countries Y and Z can expect an average increase in the sector's well-being, indicator of 4.84% and 8.29%. Moreover, investment spending in the education sector is effective only in the case of country Y and can contribute to improving the performance indicator by 2.34%, as this item of expenditure benefits from an additional allocation of 10%.

Regarding the second dimension of the human capital component, it must be noted that the mechanical increase in the total allocation of the sector does not guarantee an improvement in the health DDMI. At this level, budget reallocation strategies must exclusively consider the budgetary nature of the health sector's DDMI. Thus, in both countries, any change in the allocation of the sector's budget, regardless of the budgetary nature, leads to a positive improvement in the health DDMI. On the other hand, the magnitude of the induced effects varies from one country to another, and even from one item of expenditure to another. While a 10% increase in the operating budget improves the health DDMI by 3.66% in country Y, the average increase in country Z is only 1.21%. If the two countries decide to increase their health investment spending by 10%, country Y will be more efficient because the effects on its sectoral DDMI are much greater than that of country Z. Country Y will record an improvement in its indicator of 5.91% on this operation, against a marginal increase of 0.84% for country Z. Conversely, country Z would be more efficient if the same experiment was repeated, but this time with transfer spending. For this country, the induced effect of transfer expenditure on the health sector's DDMI is almost proportional, i.e. an increase of 9.08% compared to only 2.47% for country Y.

Table 34: Budgetary elasticities of the structure of the economy

FUNCTIONS	Coefficient α						Coefficient β	
	FON		INV		TFR		COUNTRY Y	COUNTRY Z
	COUNTRY Y	COUNTRY Z	COUNTRY Y	COUNTRY Z	COUNTRY Y	COUNTRY Z		
Construction & Energy	-0,197***	0,061***	0,351***	0,787***	0,861***	0,082***	0,113***	0,0004
Economic Affairs	0,368***	0,708***	0,223***	0,266***	0,529***	0,079	0,022	0,094***

Source: CREG estimates, 2024

The Building- Energy and economic affairs sectors play a central role in the production of well-being. The purpose of this component is to produce goods and services to strengthen the structure of the economy and provide the population with basic infrastructure. The total budget allocated to energy and basic infrastructure services in country Y significantly influences the DDMI of the Building-energy sector, while its effect is significantly non-zero in the case of country Z. When country Y increases the total budget of the energy-Building sector by 10%, the sector's DDMI improves by an average of 1.13%. Budget allocations by type of expenditure are also effective, except for the operating expenditure of country Y, which has a negative influence on the DDMI Building-energy. This result is particularly controversial because it reveals that this item of expenditure contributes to the deterioration of the DDMI of the energy-Building sector. This inefficiency of the operating budget in the Building-energy sector can hide several dysfunctions. The most recurrent failures in this sector are often linked to the implementation of a poor recruitment policy, a dominance of precarious and temporary jobs, low wages, the viscosity of wages or high wage disparities, etc. On the other hand, the operating budget of this sector contributes slightly, but positively, to the improvement of the sector's performance indicator. This improvement is estimated to average 0.61 percentage points for an additional budget allocation of 10%. Capital spending is more efficient in country Z compared to country Y, where the magnitude is smaller. Thus, when the two countries increase their energy-Building investment budgets by 10%, the sectoral DDMI increases by 7.87 percentage points in country Z compared to 3.51 points in country Y. Contrary to what is observed with the investment budget, as far as the transfer budget is concerned, it is rather country Y that is the most efficient. For the same level of change, the DDMI energy-Building could increase by an average of 8.61% in country Y and by 0.82% in country Z.

The DDMI of the economic affairs sector is weakly sensitive to an increase in the total budget of the sector in country Z, while in country Y there is no significant influence. A 10% increase in the budget allocations of the economic affairs sector leads to an average increase of 0.94% in the DDMI of this sector. This indicator is also sensitive to the operating and investment budget in both country Y and country Z. An upward allocation of the operating budget of 10% leads to an increase in the index sector of 3.68% and 7.08% respectively in countries Y and Z, while a similar allocation applied to the investment budget improves the indicator by 2.23% in Y and 2.66% in country Z. We deduce that in the economic affairs sector, the operating and investment expenses of country Z are then more efficient. Transfers from the economic affairs sector in developing countries are often dominated by subsidies to the agricultural sector and exemptions on international trade activities (import or export), etc. This item of expenditure can then contribute to the collective well-being by supporting the purchasing power of individuals. We note a substantial improvement of 5.29% in the sector's well-being index when we increase the economic affairs budget of country Y by 10%. In contrast to what is observed in country Z, *cash transfers or subsidies to support the economy* are more effective in country Y.

Table 35: Budgetary elasticities of the governance component

FUNCTIONS	Coefficient α						Coefficient β	
	FON		INV		TFR		COUNTRY Y	COUNTRY Z
	COUNTRY Y	COUNTRY Z	COUNTRY Y	COUNTRY Z	COUNTRY Y	COUNTRY Z		
Institution	0,051	0,744***	-0,181***	0,004	0,981***	0,252	-0,281***	0,030
Security	0,976***	0,902***	0,018	0,015***	0,004	-0,032**	0,132***	0,076

Source: CREG estimates, 2024

Governance essentially uses financial resources to produce public goods and services related to the institutional management and security of the country. Developing countries are known to have *budget-hungry* institutions. The bad judgement of institutions, rightly or wrongly, is somewhat confirmed in the case of countries Y and Z. Indeed, the DDMI of the institutional function is not sensitive to the increase in the total budget allocated to the sector. The situation is much more worrying in the example of country Y, because not only is the total budget significantly associated with the DDMI institution, but it has a negative influence on the sector index. This inverse relationship means that when the total budget dedicated to institutions in country Y increases by 10%, the sector's well-being index decreases by 2.81%. The expenditure allocated to the functions of the institutions is effective only at the level of country Z and contributes to increasing the sector's DDMI by 7.44%. On the other hand, investment expenditure in this sector has no influence in the case of country Z and its inverse associated with the sector's DDMI in the case of country Y. Thus, a decrease in the institutional sector well-being index (DDMI Institution) of 1.81% is induced by a 10% increase in the investment budget. Transfer spending is only effective in country Y and contributes on average to an almost proportional improvement in the DDMI sector of 9.81%.

The security sector is a strategic function of the State. Indeed, no social institution can sustain its actions and ensure well-being in a sustainable way in a potentially unstable and volatile environment. It is then up to each State to find the means to ensure the security of individuals and to guarantee the integrity of its territory. The sector's financing strategy is therefore appropriate to achieve its objectives in an area as sensitive as security. The inefficiency of total security spending in country Z is ample evidence that increasing the sector's overall allocation is not enough to improve people's sense of security. In addition, in country Y, an increase in the total security budget significantly improves the sense of security of individuals by 1.32%. In addition, an improvement in the pay of security and defense agents and their working conditions has a positive influence on the security DDMI and improves the feeling of security in the two countries (Y and Z) by 9.76% and 9.02% respectively. The acquisition of new military and security equipment (army vehicles, patrol cars, weapons, etc.) improves the general level of security of individuals by 0.15% in country Z. Conversely, in country Y, these investments do not reassure individuals too much about their general level of security in that country. A significant portion of the relocation costs in the security sector are allocated to staff training. The fact that the increase in the budget allocated to this item of expenditure does not influence individuals' sense of security can be problematic (example of country Y). But this situation is even more worrying when, as in the case of country Z, there is a significant inverse relationship between the transfer budget and the DDMI of the sector. This means that individuals' sense of security deteriorates as the State increases its efforts to train staff, for example. This rather atypical evidence is the expression of various flaws in the system of allocation of transfers to security, which should be the subject of an in-depth analysis.

Table 36: Budgetary elasticities of the professional and social network component

FUNCTIONS	Coefficient α						Coefficient β	
	FON		INV		TFR			
	PAYS Y	*PAYS Z*	*PAYS Y*	*PAYS Z*	*PAYS Y*	*PAYS Z*	*PAYS Y*	*PAYS Z*
Professional Network	0,016	0,667***	0,025*	0,128***	0,045***	0,387***	0,011***	0,004***
Social Network	0,875***	0,180***	0,227***	0,056	0,101***	0,933***	0,004	0,005

Source: CREG estimates, 2024

The social and professional network is somewhat considered the poor relation of the budget allocation system. Although the importance of these sectors for strengthening social cohesion and individuals' sense of belonging is well established, the fact is that the social and professional network sectors continue to receive the lowest benefits. However, the total budget of the professional network sector has a small positive influence on the sector's DDMI. In country Y and Z, a budget reallocation in favor of an increase in the total budget of 10% leads to an improvement in the sector's DDMI of 0.11% and 0.04%, respectively. The operating budget of country Z is efficient and promotes an improvement in the index of 6.67% while there is no effect in country Y. A 10% change in capital expenditure leads to an increase in the professional network DDMI of 0.25% in country Y and 1.28% in country Z. In the same dynamic, it can be observed that transfer spending in the sector is more efficient in country Z with an improvement in the index of 3.87% against 0.45%.

As for the total budget of the social network sector, it has no significant influence on the sector's well-being indicator for both country Y and country Z. This inefficiency of total budget allocations can be explained, for example, by threshold problems, as the sector's allocations remain relatively low compared to other sectors. As a stimulus, the operating budget contributes to effectively improving the DDMI social network by 8.75 percentage points in country Y and only 1.80 percentage points in country Z. In contrast to what is observed in terms of operating expenditure, it turns out that country Z's transfer expenditure in the sector is more efficient than that of country Y. An increase in the transfer budget of 10% leads to an almost proportional increase of 9.33% in country Z compared to a small increase of only 1.01% in country Y. Only this country guarantees an efficiency of investment spending in the sector with an average improvement in the DDMI social network index of 2.27%.

Conclusion

The economic analysis of public expenditure in partial equilibrium can be done by using a macro-fiscal model to assess the sensitivity of budget allocations to the well-being indicator (DDMI). Determining the way in which public spending initiated by the government in each sector impacts the quality of public services and in turn the well-being of the population makes it possible to assess the effectiveness of public policies. The direction, magnitude and significance of the variations measured by the fiscal elasticities are used to identify sectoral policies that are favorable to the well-being of the population, those that are unfavorable and those that have no effect on collective well-being. Nevertheless, at this stage it should be noted that the output of the analysis only allows us to make observations, to have evidence, etc. Thus, to initiate reforms or implement new policies because of this evidence, it would be useful to complete this analysis with a prospective study (the simulation of public policies) of new initiatives.

Bibliographical references

Arthur Pigou (1920), The Economics of Welfare, Macmillan and Co. Ltd.

Vivien, Franck-Dominique. "II. The confidence of standard economic theory in sustainable growth", Franck-Dominique Vivien ed., Le développement soutenable. La Découverte, 2007, pp. 31-56.

Baujard, Antoinette. "The economy of well-being is dead." Long live the economy of well-being! ", Gilles Campagnolo ed., Economic Philosophy. An inventory of the situation. Éditions Matériologiques, 2017, pp. 77-128.

Bartram, D. (2012). Economic Migration and Happiness: Comparing Immigrants' and Natives' Happiness Gains from Income. Social Indicators Research, 108(3), 361-376.

Dasho Karma Ura, Sabina Alkire, Tshoki Zangmo, and Karma Wangdi (2012). "A Short Guide to Gross National Happiness Index." The Centre for Bhutan Studies.

Layard, R., & Clark, A. E. (2014). What predicts a successful life? A life-course model of well-being. The Economic Journal, 124(580), F720-F738.

Langlois, S. (2014). Subjective Well-Being and Cultural Values: Evidence from Latin America. Social Indicators Research, 116(2), 357-378

Michel Forsé and Maxime Parodi (2014), Subjective Well-Being and Sense of Social Justice. https://www.jstor.org/stable/43998535

Nussbaum, M. C. (2000). Women and Human Development: The Capabilities Approach. Cambridge University Press.

Perron Zoé, Buzaud Julia, Diter Kevin, Martin Claude. Approaches to well-being. A multidimensional field of research. In: Revue des politiques sociales et familiales, n°131-132, 2019.

Stiglitz, J., Sen, A., & Fitoussi, J. (2009). Report on the measurement of economic performance and social progress. Commission on the Measurement of Economic Performance and Social Progress.

Veenhoven, R. (1984). Conditions of Happiness. Dordrecht: D. Reidel Publishing Company.

Bozio, A., Grenet, J., Bach, L., Carbonnier, C., 2010. Economics of Public Policies, La découverte. ed. Repères, Paris.

Hébert, R.F., 1994. Foundations and developments of public economics. Eighteenth Century 26, 37–49. https://doi.org/10.3406/dhs.1994.1966

Mankiw, N.G., Taylor, M.P., 2013. Principles of Economics. De BoeckP, Paris.

Musgrave, R., Musgrave, P., 1989. Public finance in theory and pratice, 5th ed, Finance series. McGraw-Hill Book Co, New York.

What are the main budgetary principles? [WWW Document], 2022... vie-publique.fr. URL http://www.vie-publique.fr/fiches/21823-quels-sont-les-grands-principes-budgetaires (accessed 6.14.23).

Economic growth and the housing sector: a statistical study of the relationship between housing stock and labour productivity in industrialised countries. 2002. Doctoral thesis.

BUNEL, Matthieu and LENOIR, Magali. The social network of Moroccan graduates: a guarantee for employment but not for salary. Junuary, Laboratoire du GATE-Université Lumière Lyon, 2004.

MEDEDJI, Damien. Dynamics of urban poverty in Benin: an analysis in terms of inputs and outputs. 2007.

OBRINGER*, Frédéric. China's economic growth at the risk of the environment: a difficult realization. Hérodote, 2007, no. 2, p. 95-104.

OUELLET, Maude. The place of the social and support network in the migratory and integration journey of migrants living in Rivière-du-Loup. 2008. Doctoral thesis. Laval University.

BRASSIER-RODRIQUES, C. and BRASSIER, Pascal. The social network of the manager of small and medium-sized companies: a strategic tool for his communication. Le grand livre de l'économie PME, Gilles Lecointre (Dir.), Gualino, Paris, 2010, p. 171-189.

HOIBIAN, R. Bigot-E. Daudey-S. Is social housing an asset or a handicap for growth? 2014.

LANGLOIS, Simon. Happiness, subjective well-being and a sense of social justice in Quebec. L'Année sociologique, 2014, vol. 64, no 2, p . 389-420.

AKHENATON, I. Z. U. Analysis of robustness and vulnerability to poverty in the DRC. 2016.

THIAO, Abdou. Public Infrastructure Spending and Economic Growth in Senegal: A NARDL Model Approach. Revue Economie & Kapital, 2019, no 15.

EHRHART, Hélène, IHNACH, Houssine, EL ANSARY, Abdenbi, et al. The effects of fiscal policy on poverty and inequality in Morocco. 2020.

MALHERBE, Kitty. Work-life balance in South Africa: an unachievable goal?. Revue de droit comparé du travail et de la sécurité sociale, 2020, no 3, p. 144-157.

ZAHRA, Djebaili. Work-life balance and its impact on work performance. Revue Chercheur Economique/Volume, 2020, vol. 7, no 1, p. 178-193.

LAMINE, Traoré, SOUAÏBOU, SAMBA and MODIBO, Traoré. Infrastructure and economic growth: the case of Mali. International Journal of Accounting, Finance, Auditing, Management and Economics, 2022, Vol. 3, No. 2-2, p. 118-138

RICHARD, Éléonore. Becoming Poor: From Income to Feeling: Transitions to and from Poverty and Subjective Well-Being. Revue des politiques sociales et familiales, 2022, no 1, p. 23-45.

CHAPTER 9

SIMULATION OF PUBLIC POLICIES IN GLOBAL BUDGET EQUILIBRIUM

Introduction

Global equilibrium policy simulations are analyses that assess the impact of different economic policies on the global economy. These simulations often use complex economic models and empirical data to predict how changes in monetary, fiscal, trade, or other policies could influence key economic variables such as economic growth, employment, inflation, exchange rates, and international trade.

In the context of developing countries, economic policy simulations play a crucial role in the implementation of economic and social development projects. Indeed, many economic issues cannot be satisfactorily dealt with in partial equilibrium, i.e. at the level of a sector of activity or a market taken into isolation (Décaluwé et al, 2001). Will we try to see the effects of investments in the education sector on economic growth? The direct and induced effects of a tax policy on the removal of tax barriers? These are all questions about the consequences of the policies implemented on the economy and the well-being of the population in general, the answers to which in a general balance framework are more satisfactory because they give an overview of the channels through which the implementation of a granted policy. General equilibrium models are, so to speak, essential for the achievement of the development objectives of both industrialized and developing countries.

It is in this context that many models have been developed to identify the transmission channels of the different economic policies. The best-known models are the computable general equilibrium models (Adelman and Robinson (1978), Shoven and Walley (1984), Decaluwe and Martens 1988), ...) which are instruments of mesoeconomical analysis, halfway between microeconomics and macroeconomics or combining the two. These models are carried out according to well-defined political objectives and economic parameters.

However, the rapid economic development of Asian dragons, South Korea, Taiwan, Singapore and Hong Kong, has highlighted an important factor that is the demographic structure of their respective populations.

This rapid growth, also known as the demographic dividend, was facilitated by the demographic structure of these countries, which had a large working-age population that supported economic growth at the time. Thus, with a smaller population in charge, there is a certain reallocation of public resources from the social sectors (education and health) to sectors with high potential for economic growth.

The demographic factor is thus the poor relation of economic policy, as it is not considered in the national accounts, particularly the social accounting matrices, the main tool for the simulation models of the computable general equilibrium model.

As a result, new accounting models have been developed to account for the limitations of the social accounting matrix, the National Transfer Accounts (NTAs) developed by Lee and Mason (2011). The latter model introduces age into the system of national accounts. It describes how resources are acquired, consumed and shared between generations at each age and makes it possible to calculate the demographic dividend for a given country. This demographic dividend makes it possible to see the share of economic growth that goes to the structure of the population. Thus, the introduction of age into the system of national accounts was a decisive turning point in the production of a normative framework for the optimal exploitation of the economic growth potential of countries with a population structure conducive to achieving accelerated economic growth. This normative framework developed by the Regional Consortium for Research in Generational Economics (CREG) is known as the Demographic Dividend Monitoring Index (DDMI).

The DDMI is a synthetic index that represents the different dimensions of economic and social life in five main dimensions. Dimension 1, the Life Cycle Deficit, represents the ability of a given population to meet its consumption needs using the labor income generated by the economy. It thus makes it possible to study the economic consequences linked to the modification of the age structure of the population. The quality of the living environment dimension makes it possible to measure the conformity of the living environment in its security aspects, subjective well-being, and non-monetary poverty in general. Dimension 3, poverty dynamics, makes it possible to determine the inflows and exits of income poverty between two periods. It thus makes it possible to assess vulnerability as well as stability in situations of poverty and non-poverty. Dimension 4, expanded human development, assesses the level of education and health of a given population. And finally, dimension 5, networks and territories, assesses the state and structure of space in terms of infrastructure and mobility of human and monetary resources and goods and services.

In Niger, the current demographic structure characterized by its youth, of which about 68% of the population is under 25 years old (48.68% are under 14 years old and 19.36% are in the 15-24 age group), is not yet favorable to the capture of the demographic dividend. This is evidenced by the country's economic support ratio, which is 37% in 2010 and estimated at 34% and 38% in 2030 and 2050 respectively; This is a ratio much lower than the ratio of other comparable African countries.

In Guinea, the demographic structure is also marked by a predominance of the young population with 55.5% under 20 years old, and 64.1% under 25 years old. The latter, resulting in a high dependency ratio of 92% in 2021, is therefore, as for Niger, not yet favorable to the capture of the demographic dividend. With an economic support ratio of 42% in 2020 and estimated at 46% and 50% in 2035 and 2050 respectively, Guinea is expected to experience growth in the number of effective producers per 100 consumers, a factor in improving the potential of the demographic dividend.

Faced with the demographic situation of these two countries, it remains essential for them to act in favor of an optimal exploitation of the demographic structure to capture the demographic dividend, which is favorable to the economy and well-being. In this sense, a major concern may be: What is the effect of public policies on the sectors affecting the demographic dividend? To this end, a macro-fiscal simulation model has been developed, the Budgeting Sensitive to Demographic Dividend (BSDD), which makes it possible to see the channels through which government action affects the dimensions that make it possible to increase the demographic dividend.

In the following developments, we will first draw up the economic and social context of Senegal and make a brief review of the literature on public policy simulations, then we will present the BSDD methodology and finally the results and discussions.

Section 1: Socio-economic context

Geographical and demographic situation

The Economic Community of West African States (ECOWAS), an area covering an area of 6.4 million km2, is a regional inter-governmental organization founded on May 28, 1975, by the Treaty of Lagos. It includes 15 West African countries: Benin, Burkina Faso, Cape Verde, Côte d'Ivoire, Gambia, Ghana, Guinea, Guinea-Bissau,

Liberia, Mali, Niger, Nigeria, Senegal, Sierra Leone and Togo. Its headquarters are in Abuja, Nigeria.

In 2019, the population of ECOWAS was estimated at 393.4 million, an increase of 118% compared to 1990 (180.8 million). Nigeria, with 203.3 million people, accounted for more than half of this population, followed by Ghana (31.5 million) and Côte d'Ivoire (26.2 million) (AFI, 2025). Based on ECOWAS data, the total population of the ECOWAS region is estimated in 2022 at about 419.5 million inhabitants, including 26.1 million inhabitants in Niger and 13.9 million in Guinea.

The population of ECOWAS is predominantly young, with 43.4% under the age of 15 in 2019, and a regional average age of 18. Niger (with a population under 25 years of age representing nearly 70% of the total population according to the last RGPH-2012) has the lowest median age in the region (15.4 years) while Cape Verde has the highest (26.6 years). The proportion of young people aged 15 to 29 was 47.5% in 2019 and will remain high in the coming decades, reaching 42.3% in 2043 (AFI, 2025). In Guinea, 44.7% of the Guinean population is made up of children aged 0 to 14 years (INS, 2019). This large youth population (although an asset) and the slow pace of demographic transition limit the decline in the fertility rate, which maintains high pressure on health and education infrastructure.

In 2019, 53% of the population lived in rural areas, although this rate has been declining since 1990 (70%). Countries such as Niger (83.5%), Burkina Faso (70%) and Guinea (63.5%) remain overwhelmingly rural. Rapid urbanization, particularly in Nigeria, Côte d'Ivoire and Ghana, is leading to poorly planned urban growth: 47% of urban dwellers live in slums (AFI, 2025).

Human Capital

– Education

Education is a key pillar of human and economic development in the ECOWAS region. However, it faces structural, logistical and security challenges that hinder its full expansion, particularly in rural and unstable areas.

Across the region, school enrolment rates have increased over the decades, but remain below international standards, particularly at the secondary and tertiary levels. The gross primary enrolment ratio is generally above 70% in most member countries, with countries such as Ghana and Cape Verde exceeding 90% while secondary school enrolment remains lower, with averages hovering around 45%, according to ECOWAS estimates. Gender inequalities and rural/urban disparities persist, with lower girls' enrolment in rural areas, aggravated by early marriages and precarious households.

In Niger, the primary school completion rate was 54% in 2021 for girls and 61% for boys. However, lower secondary completion rates show a considerable drop, with only 14.8 per cent of girls and 17.1 per cent of boys. In 2017, gross enrolment ratios in secondary education were 20% for girls and 27% for boys. The gross enrolment ratio in tertiary education was 3% for women in 2020, compared to 6% for men (UNESCO, 2024).

In Guinea, despite progress in education, there is still educational poverty, i.e. the proportion of children unable to read and understand an age-appropriate text at the age of 10, which is quite high at 83%. As a result, with 98% of children enrolled in primary school who could have a low level of learning, the result is a fairly low primary school completion rate of 56% in 2021 for girls and 70% for boys. In addition, lower secondary completion rates show a considerable drop, with only 30.8 per cent of girls and 39.3 per cent of boys. Gross enrolment ratios in secondary education reveal a gender gap, with 31 per cent of girls enrolled compared to 41 per cent of boys. The gross enrolment rate in tertiary education was 9% for women in 2021, compared to 4% for men.

These low levels of education observed in the ECOWAS region, particularly in Niger and Guinea, particularly affect girls. This is due in part to the relatively high rates of child marriage and early pregnancy.

– Health

Health is a central issue for human and economic development in the ECOWAS region. Member countries face profound structural challenges in health care, marked by limited access, low quality of services, and high exposure to communicable and noncommunicable diseases. These challenges persist despite national and regional efforts in health policies.

Health systems in the ECOWAS region suffer from a widespread deficit in human, infrastructural, medical and financial resources, which severely limits their ability to meet the growing needs of populations (DFAT, 2020). The epidemiological burden in the region is particularly high, with persistent communicable diseases (malaria, multidrug-resistant tuberculosis, neglected tropical diseases), non-communicable diseases on the rise (hypertension, diabetes, cardiovascular diseases) and malnutrition (DFAT, 2020).

Malaria remains the leading cause of morbidity and mortality, followed by tuberculosis and diarrheal infections. The situation is aggravated by high rates of infants and maternal mortality. Among the leading causes of death for children under 5 years of age are pneumonia, intrapartum complications, diarrhea and malaria, often aggravated by malnutrition (DFAT, 2020).

The ECOWAS region has some of the highest maternal and infant mortality rates in the world. This is largely the result of insufficient access to quality care, particularly in rural areas, and shortcomings in the management of obstetric emergencies (DFAT, 2020). The COVID-19 pandemic has also revealed the structural vulnerability of health systems, although its direct impact has been relatively limited due to the youth of the population and lower international exposure (EREO, 2023).

As of August 2020, ECOWAS had approximately 28,000 active COVID-19 cases and 2,296 deaths, but humanitarian NGOs believed that these figures were underestimated due to limited testing capacities (DFAT, 2020). This pandemic has amplified the pressures on already fragile health systems, leading to interruptions in essential services (immunization, maternal care, nutrition).

In addition, there is a low public expenditure per capita on health, well below international standards, highlighting that the region is far from meeting the requirements of Sustainable Development Goal 3 (good health and well-being) (AFI, 2025). In 2019, more than 65% of the multidimensional poor population in sub-Saharan Africa lived in West Africa, increasing the health vulnerability of the population (AFI, 2025).

Geographical and socio-economic inequalities in access to care are also significant in the region. Rural areas and marginalized groups, including women and youth, face more barriers to accessing health services. Social practices such as female genital mutilation, which are still prevalent in several member countries, are also a public health and human rights problem (DFAT, 2020). In addition, mental and reproductive health services remain largely underdeveloped, despite their growing importance, especially among young women, who are often affected by early pregnancies and obstetric complications (DFAT, 2020).

It should be noted that chronic insecurity in some areas, particularly in the Sahel (Burkina Faso, Mali, Niger) and northern Nigeria, has caused the closure of hundreds of health centers, leaving thousands of people without access to essential services. In 2019, nearly 2,000 schools and health centers were closed in these countries due to insecurity (EREO, 2023). This has a lasting threat to health coverage and the achievement of regional human development goals.

- Demography

Regarding mortality, it is still marked by high rates overall in the ECOWAS zone. For example, it is observed that in Niger, the maternal mortality rate is still high, estimated at 441 per 100,000 live births in 2020. The neonatal mortality rate increased from 24 to 43 deaths per 1000 live births between 2012 and 2021 (WHO, 2025). In addition, in 2021, only 43% of births were attended by qualified health personnel, which reveals the urgency of improving access to care. According to the 2023 Perinatal Maternal Death Surveillance and Response (PRDS) report, the main direct causes of maternal death in Niger include hemorrhage (34%), hypertension disorders (28%), infections (24%), and difficult deliveries (3%). Although these causes are largely preventable, many women still give birth at home, far from health facilities. This situation is accentuated by a low health coverage of 55.45% (National Health Information System-SNIS, 2023).

In Guinea, maternal mortality also remains high, with an estimated rate of 614 per 100,000 live births, including 530 in urban areas and 657 in rural areas (INS, 2017). Also, out of 1000 children born alive, 92 die before reaching their first birthday with a higher risk of mortality in rural areas (100 per 1000) than in urban areas (71 per thousand). The under-5 mortality rate increased from 123 to 111 per 1,000 live births from 2012 to 2018 and the neonatal mortality rate remained almost stationary from 33 to 32 per 1000 (DHS 2018).

About fertility, it is noted that the ECOWAS (Economic Community of West African States) region is characterized by some of the highest fertility levels in the world, particularly in some Sahelian countries. This has profound implications for the demographic transition, human capital development, pressure on social services and economic growth. This high level of fertility is reflected in a high Total Fertility Rate (TFR) in the region, with strong disparities between countries. Niger has the highest fertility rate, with about 6.8 children per woman in 2022, making it the country with the highest fertility in the world (UNFPA, 2023). Guinea, on the other hand, has a TFR of 4.30 children per woman in 2022 (World Bank, 2023).

As for family planning in the ECOWAS region, it remains a major challenge for public health policies. However, it is an essential lever for reducing maternal mortality, improving reproductive health, strengthening women's empowerment and supporting the demographic transition. Contraceptive prevalence rates remain low in many ECOWAS countries, especially for modern methods with an average rate of use of modern contraceptive methods in the region below 20%, with significant differences between countries (EREO, 2023). In addition, access to family planning services is often limited by structural factors: shortage of skilled personnel, stock-outs, cultural taboos, and social pressures. Niger has one of the lowest contraceptive prevalence rates in the world with a contraceptive prevalence rate of modern methods of around 10% in 2021 (Republic of Niger, 2023). Indeed, the use of family planning (FP), recognized as the main means of controlling fertility, has not made significant progress in Niger. The results of the 2012 EDSNMICS IV highlighted a low level of use of modern contraceptives among women in union, which fell from 12% in 2012 to 10% in 2021 despite a high level of knowledge of contraceptive methods and the fact that they have been free of charge in public health facilities since 2006 (Konaté, Maiga and Chen, 2014) (Republic of Niger, 2023).

Guinea also has a low situation in terms of family planning in the region, which has a modern contraceptive prevalence rate of 11% (DHS, 2018), with a slight increase in urban areas. However, the rate remains well below the targets set by the National Reproductive Health Strategy. Among the determinants of these low rates, we have: the low enrolment of girls; early marriages; and women's low decision-making autonomy in reproductive health (DFAT, 2020).

Economy

According to the ANSD's report on the economic and social situation, at the international level, the year 2019 is marked by a slowdown in global economic activity with a growth rate of 2.8%, after 3.5% a year earlier.

At the level of the ECOWAS economy, ECOWAS GDP was estimated at US$633.1 billion, or 25.5% of the total GDP of the African continent in 2019. Nigeria dominated the regional economy with 61.8% of regional GDP, followed by Ghana and Côte d'Ivoire. The economic growth rate was 3.6% in 2019 but fell due to the COVID-19 pandemic. As for Niger, the GDP growth rate increased from 2.0% in 2023 to 8.4%

in 2024 (4.9% per capita) thanks to the lifting of sanctions and a 48.5% increase in exports, particularly oil. This growth was driven by agriculture (+11.1%) after a good season, and by industrialization (+12.1%), supported by oil production (World Bank, 2025). And in Guinea, GDP grew by an estimated 5.7% in 2023 compared to 4% in 2022. This growth is driven by agriculture and mining (AEO, 2024).

As for the informal sector, it accounted for 37.8% of regional GDP, or USD 279.6 billion, with an average of 65.6% of the working population. Countries such as Mali (81.8%) and Benin (74.9%) have the highest levels of informality, while Cape Verde (35.7%) and Ghana (49.4%) are below the regional average (AFI, 2025). In Niger, the informal sector represents between 55% and 60% of the country's GDP in 2022, mainly through the trade and agriculture sectors, while in Guinea, the sector contributes nearly 57.5% of GDP in 2019 (Directorate General of the Treasury, 2024, 2025) and 42% of GDP in 2023 (INS, 2024).

Poverty remains a major challenge in the region, with strong disparities between states. Projections show that by 2043, despite a relative reduction in poverty to 16 percent, the absolute number of poor people will reach 117.1 million. According to 2016 data, 65.3% of the multidimensional poor in sub-Saharan Africa live in West Africa. In 2019, 27.2% of the population lived below the international monetary poverty line (USD 2.15/day), or about 106.8 million people. Countries such as Niger, Nigeria, Liberia, Togo and Sierra Leone have rates above 25%, while Cape Verde (3.4%), Senegal (9.2%) and Côte d'Ivoire (11.1%) have the lowest rates (AFI, 2025). In 2024, Niger has an extreme poverty rate of 45.3%; a rate that is expected to decline to 35.8% by 2027, driven by projected strong growth in the agricultural sector (World Bank, 2025). Guinea, on the other hand, has a poverty rate of 51.9% due to higher inflation and insufficient job creation in the non-mining sector (World Bank, 2025).

As for the labor market in the ECOWAS region, it is characterized by a strong predominance of the informal sector, a high unemployment rate among young people and a low capacity of economies to create decent jobs, especially for the young and fast-growing population.

In 2020, the unemployment rate for young people aged 15 to 24 in the ECOWAS region was estimated at 11.9%. This rate is relatively moderate at first glance, but it does not consider the quality of jobs, as a large part of this population works in precarious conditions in the informal sector. If the latter were excluded, the unemployment rate would be considerably higher (AFI, 2025). In Niger, the unemployment rate for young people aged 15 to 24 fell from 3.85% in 2012 to 0.42% in 2023; while in Guinea, this rate has increased, from 6.43% in 2012 to 7.10% in 2023 and 8.46% in 2020 (World Bank, 2025).

The informal sector accounts for the bulk of economic activity and employment in the region. In 2019, about 65.6% of the labor force was employed in the informal sector. This rate is the third highest in Africa, after those of the East African Community (EAC) (72.3%) and the Economic Community of Central African States (ECCAS) (68.6%). In Niger, almost all jobs are informal and in Guinea, these informal jobs are estimated at 96% of the country's jobs in 2019 (Directorate General of the Treasury, 2024, 2025).

Section 2: Selective Literature Review

The use of Computable General Equilibrium (CGE) models. Indeed, despite their own limitations, they remain particularly appropriate for studying the repercussions of macroeconomic policies on a country and its economy.

Estache et al. (2007) conducted a study on the impact of infrastructure spending in Mali using a computable general equilibrium analysis. For example, a 20% increase in public investment in infrastructure led to an increase in GDP of 0.84 percentage points and wages of 0.76 percentage points, as well as here, considering productivity gains. This wage increase is a consequence of the increase in output in the labor-intensive Building sector.

Dumont and Mesplé-Somps (2000) assessed the impact of public infrastructure on competitiveness and growth in Senegal using a sequential dynamic CGME. They assume that public investment constitutes a positive externality on total factor productivity (TFP), the effect of which is measured through the ratio between the stock of public capital and the stock of private capital. The authors conclude that, as far as Senegal is concerned, it should be noted that even if the devaluation of the CFA franc in 1994 has enabled the growth of the Senegalese economy to resume, mainly as a result of the development of the Building and fishing sectors, and to correct some of the handicaps to competitiveness, the fact remains that for its effect to last, it is necessary to combat the downward trend in productivity factors. Ba and Sy (2015) analyze the impact of a reallocation of public spending in the process of structural transformation of the Senegalese economy over the period 2015-2035. Using an inter-temporal Computable General Equilibrium Model (CGEM), they show that a reallocation of public spending would lead to an increase in growth of 0.2 percentage points more than the PES Priority Action Plan forecast of 7.1% over the period 2015-2018. Their results show an increase in the share of employment in the secondary sector, which rose successively to 17.2%, 20.7%, 25.1% and 26.7% over the respective periods of 2015-2020, 2021-2025, 2026-2030 and 2031-2035, to the detriment of the primary and tertiary sectors.

Mboup et al. (2018), analyzing the impact of EPAs on women's employment in Senegal through a dynamic MEGC, simulated an accompanying policy involving a 10% increase in public investment. The results show that public investment has effects that mitigate the negative impact of the EPAs on the labor market (a decrease in the unemployment rate of 2.98%). The decrease in the unemployment rate is 2.84% and 3.12% respectively for women and men with the accompanying policy compared to 1.73% and 2.09% with the EPAs without public investment.

Fall et al. (2013) studied the effects of agricultural policy on growth through increased agricultural productivity using a CGME. Their results show an average annual increase of 10.7% in agricultural activity over the period 2014-2023. However, this performance could be halved if investment expenditure becomes inefficient or if the investment monitoring and maintenance mechanism is weak.

Public investment thus has a significant impact on the economy. More specifically, economic literature teaches us, with the work of Agénor (2007), that public infrastructure plays a catalytic role in the economy through its positive effect on factor productivity and private capital formation. These combined effects promote job creation and therefore a gender-sensitive policy should result in an increase in the number of jobs for women and men. To this end, numerous empirical studies have shown the importance of public investment, and more particularly of public social infrastructure, on women's employment. However, there is no consensus on the positive effect of physical investments on women's employment, but studies agree on the reduction of domestic work hours. Our present study approaches the same approach based on the empirical evidence obtained through computable general equilibrium models. Through the Senegalese government's public investments in the second phase of the PSE, we will empirically analyze their effects on job creation in general, for women and youth, considering factors such as rainfall.

Section 3: Methodology

Estimating fiscal elasticities is the seventh step in the demographic dividend-sensitive budgeting process. This step takes place after the specification of the macro-budgetary theoretical model. It is important to note that the basic theoretical model remains unchanged. Below is the specification of the augmented macro-fiscal theoretical model:

Specification of Macro Budget Modeling

Production function

Let Y be the Demographic Dividend Monitoring Index (DDMI). We assume that the production of public goods and services takes the form of a Cobb-Douglas function. Thus:

$$Y = AK^{\alpha}L^{\beta}$$

A Cobb Douglas production function.

We consider the economic and budgetary functions retained in the budgetary transformation.

Box 2: The Cobb Douglass Production Function

In general, a production function is a specification of how the quantity of production behaves based on the inputs used in production. This concept can be applied at the level of individual companies, industries or entire economies.

In economics, the Cobb-Douglas functional form of production functions is widely used to represent the relationship between production and inputs. It was proposed by Knut Wicksell (1851 - 1926) and tested based on statistical data by Charles Cobb and Paul Douglas in 1928.

The function used by the authors to model production is as follows:

$$P(L,K) = AL^{\alpha}K^{\beta}$$

where:

- P = total output (the dollar value of all goods produced in a year)

– L = labor input (the total number of person-hours worked in a year)

– K = capital contribution (the monetary value of all machinery, equipment and buildings)

– Total factor productivity

– are the production elasticities of labor and capital, respectively. These values are constantly determined by the available technology. α et β

The elasticity of production measures the responsiveness of production to a change in the levels of labor or capital used in production, all other things being equal.

Capital used in production, all other things being equal. For example, if $\alpha = 0.15$, a 1% increase in labor will result in an increase of about 0.15% in output.

In addition, if:

$\alpha + \beta = 1$ The production function has constant returns to scale. In other words, if L and K each increase by 20%, P increases by 20%.

Returns to scale are a technical property of production that examines changes in output following a proportional change in output (where all inputs increase by a constant factor).

If output increases in the same proportion, then there are constant returns on the scale, sometimes referred to simply as returns to scale. If output increases less than this proportional change, there are diminishing returns to scale. If production increases by more than this proportion, there are increasing returns to scale (DRI).

However, if

$\alpha + \beta < 1$, the returns to scale are diminishing, and if

$\alpha + \beta > 1$, the returns to scale are increasing.

On the assumption of perfect competition, it can be shown that α and β are the shares of labor and capital in production.

For each function, the following production function will be retained $Y = AK^{\alpha}L^{\beta}$

More specifically for the function:

Function 1: Macro-budget modelling of the health sector

$Y_1 = A_1\, K_{1Pr}^{\lambda 1}\, K_{1Pu}^{\alpha 1}\, L_1^{\beta 1}$ **(1)**

$\boldsymbol{K_{1Pr}}$Represents private investment in economic function (1).

$\boldsymbol{K_{1Pu}}$Represents public investment in the economic function (1).

Thus, the production of well-being in a particular function is conditioned by the allocation of resources to produce the goods and services that derive well-being. We can then write:

$$Y_1 = A_1\, K_{1Pr}^{\lambda_1}\, K_{1Pu}^{\alpha 1}\, L_1^{\beta_1}$$

At the public level, expenditure (DEP) is characterized by 03 budgetary natures, including:

- Operation *(Function)*
- Investment *(Inv)*
- Transfers *(Trf)*

Considering these three budgetary natures, equation (1) becomes:

$Y_1 = A_1\, K_{1Pr}^{\lambda_1}\, Fonc_1^{\alpha_{11}}\, Inv_1^{\alpha_{12}}\, Trf_1^{\alpha_{12}}\, L_1^{\beta_1}$ **(2)**

By linearizing, we obtain:

$\log Y_1 = \log A_1 + \lambda_1 logK_{1Pr} + \alpha_1 logFonc_1 + \alpha_2 logInv_1 + \alpha_3 logTrf_1 + \beta_1 \log L_1$ **(3)**

With: $\lambda_1\ \alpha_1; \alpha_2;\ \alpha_3\ et\ \beta_1 > 0$

$$\text{I}(Fon_1) = \frac{Fonc_1}{PIB} \times \frac{PIB}{DEP_1} \quad \textbf{(4)}$$

$$\text{I}(Inv_1) = \frac{Inv_1}{PIB} \times \frac{PIB}{DEP_1} \quad \textbf{(5)}$$

$$\text{I}(\text{Trf}_1) = \frac{Trf_1}{PIB} \times \frac{PIB}{DEP_1} \quad \textbf{(6)}$$

$\log Y_1 = \log A_1 + \lambda_1 logK_{1Pr} + \alpha_1' logDEP_1 + \beta_1 \log L_1$ **(7)**

$\alpha_1' = \alpha_1 + \alpha_2 + \alpha_3$ **(8)**

$DEP_1 = Fonc_1 + Inv_1 + Trf_1$ **(9)**

The DDMI is designed as a wellness feature. It is equivalent to an output (verified by an external validity test between the evolution at the level of DDMI / GDP or evolution of the growth rate DDMI and GDP or between Log DDMI and LOG GDP.

As a result, the validation of the test confirms the equivalence of DDMI and GDP. Thus, DDMI can be used as a global output function. This is equivalent to saying that the production functions of the global output are equivalent to the functions of the global output of well-being.

However, the innovation in this model is to identify the nature or source of well-being.

Of the above we can write:

$DDMI_1 \equiv Y_1$ **(10)**

The DDMI is an index between 0 and 100 while the expenses are in monetary units. To respect the equivalence of equation (10), all variables in monetary values will be transformed into indices. Thus, we will have:

$$\log DDMI_1 = \log A_1 + \lambda_1 logI(K_{1Pr}) + \alpha_1 logI(Fonc_1) + \alpha_2 logI(Inv_1) + \alpha_3 logI(Trf_1) + \beta_1 \log I(L_1) \qquad \textbf{(11)}$$

$I(K_{1Pr})$= index of private expenditure in the function (1) **(12)**

$I(L_1)$= index of the stock of labour in the function (1). **(13)**

Replacing equations (4), (5) and (6) in equation 11 we obtain:

$$\log DDMI_1 = \log A_1 + \lambda_1 logI(K_{1Pr}) + \alpha_1 \log (\frac{Fonc_1}{PIB} \times \frac{PIB}{DEP_1}) + \alpha_2 \log (\frac{Inv_1}{PIB} \times \frac{PIB}{DEP_1}) + \alpha_3 \log (\frac{Trf_1}{PIB} \times \frac{PIB}{DEP_1}) + \beta_1 \log I(L_1) \qquad \textbf{(14)}$$

$$\log DDMI_1 = \log A_1 + \lambda_1 logI(K_{1Pr}) + \alpha_1 \log\left(\frac{Fonc_1}{PIB}\right) + \alpha_1 \log\left(\frac{PIB}{DEP_1}\right) + \alpha_2 \log\left(\frac{Inv_1}{PIB}\right) + \alpha_2 \log\left(\frac{PIB}{DEP_1}\right) + \alpha_3 \log\left(\frac{Trf_1}{PIB}\right) + \alpha_3 \log (\frac{PIB}{DEP_1}) + \beta_1 \log I(L_1) \qquad \textbf{(15)}$$

$$\log DDMI_1 = \log A_1 + \lambda_1 logI(K_{1Pr}) + \alpha_1 \log\left(\frac{Fonc_1}{PIB}\right) + \alpha_2 \log\left(\frac{Inv_1}{PIB}\right) + \alpha_3 \log\left(\frac{Trf_1}{PIB}\right) + (\alpha_1 + \alpha_2 + \alpha_3) \log (\frac{PIB}{DEP_1}) + \beta_1 \log I(L_1) \textbf{(16)}$$

If we ask:

$$\frac{Fonc_1}{PIB} = Fonc_1' \; ; \; \frac{Inv_1}{PIB} = Inv_1' \; ; \quad \frac{Trf_1}{PIB} = Trf_1' \quad \textbf{(17)}$$

Equation 16 becomes:

$$\log DDMI_1 = \log A_1 + \lambda_1 log I(K_{1Pr}) + \alpha_1 \log(Fonc_1') + \alpha_2 \log(Inv_1') + \alpha_3 \log(Trf_1') + (\alpha_1 + \alpha_2 + \alpha_3)\log\left(\frac{PIB}{DEP_1}\right) + \beta_1 \log I(L_1) \qquad \textbf{(18)}$$

Function 2: Macro-budgetary modelling of the education sector

$$Y_2 = A_2 \, K_{2Pr}^{\lambda_2} \, Fonc_2^{\alpha_4} \, Inv_2^{\alpha_5} \, Trf_2^{\alpha_6} \, L_2^{\beta_2} \qquad \textbf{(19)}$$

$$\log Y_2 = \log A_2 + \lambda_2 log K_{2Pr} + \alpha_4 log Fonc_2 + \alpha_5 log Inv_2 + \alpha_6 log Trf_2 + \beta_2 \log L_2 \quad \textbf{(20)}$$

$$\mathrm{I}(Fon_2) = \frac{Fonc_2}{PIB} \times \frac{PIB}{DEP_2} \quad \textbf{(21)}$$

$$\mathrm{I}(Inv_2) = \frac{Inv_2}{PIB} \times \frac{PIB}{DEP_2} \quad \textbf{(22)}$$

$$\mathrm{I}(\mathrm{Trf}_2) = \frac{Trf_2}{PIB} \times \frac{PIB}{DEP_2} \quad \textbf{(23)}$$

$$\log Y_2 = \log A_2 + \lambda_2 log K_{2Pr} + \alpha_2' log DEP_2 + \beta_2 \log L_2 \quad \textbf{(24)}$$

$$\alpha_2' = \alpha_4 + \alpha_5 + \alpha_6 \quad \textbf{(25)}$$

$$DEP_2 = Fonc_2 + Inv_2 + Trf_2 \quad \textbf{(26)}$$

$$DDMI_2 \equiv Y_2 \quad \textbf{(27)}$$

$$\log DDMI_2 = \log A_2 + \lambda_2 log I(K_{2Pr}) + \alpha_4 log I(Fonc_2) + \alpha_5 log I(Inv_2) + \alpha_6 log I(Trf_2) + \beta_2 \log I(L_2) \qquad \textbf{(28)}$$

$I(K_{2Pr})$= index of private expenditure in the function (14) **(29)**

$I(L_2)$= index of the stock of labour in the function (14). **(30)**

Replacing equations (21), (22) and (23) in equation 11 we obtain:

$$\log DDMI_2 = \log A_2 + \lambda_2 log I(K_{2Pr}) + \alpha_4 \log\left(\frac{Fonc_2}{PIB} \times \frac{PIB}{DEP_2}\right) + \alpha_5 \log\left(\frac{Inv_2}{PIB} \times \frac{PIB}{DEP_2}\right) + \alpha_6 \log\left(\frac{Trf_2}{PIB} \times \frac{PIB}{DEP_2}\right) + \beta_2 \log I(L_2) \qquad \textbf{(31)}$$

$\log DDMI_2 = \log A_2 + \lambda_2 logI(K_{2Pr}) + \ \alpha_4 \log\left(\frac{Fonc_2}{PIB}\right) + \alpha_4 \log\left(\frac{PIB}{DEP_2}\right) + \ \alpha_5 \log\left(\frac{Inv_2}{PIB}\right) + \alpha_5 \log\left(\frac{PIB}{DEP_2}\right) + \ \alpha_6 \log\left(\frac{Trf_2}{PIB}\right) + \alpha_6 \log\left(\frac{PIB}{DEP_2}\right) + \beta_2 \log I(L_2)$ **(32)**

$\log DDMI_2 = \log A_2 + \lambda_2 logI(K_{2Pr}) + \ \alpha_4 \log\left(\frac{Fonc_2}{PIB}\right) + \alpha_5 \log\left(\frac{Inv_2}{PIB}\right) + \alpha_6 \log\left(\frac{Trf_2}{PIB}\right) + (\alpha_4 + \alpha_5 + \alpha_6) \log\left(\frac{PIB}{DEP_2}\right) + \beta_2 \log I(L_2)$**(32)**

$\log DDMI_2 = \log A_2 + \lambda_2 logI(K_{2Pr}) + \ \alpha_4 \log(Fonc_2') + \alpha_5 \log(Inv_2') + \alpha_6 \log(Trf_2') + (\alpha_4 + \alpha_5 + \alpha_6) \log\left(\frac{PIB}{DEP_2}\right) + \beta_2 \log I(L_2)$ **(33)**

Function 3: Macro-budgetary modelling of the institutional sector

$Y_3 = A_3 \, K_{3Pr}^{\lambda_3} \, Fonc_3^{\alpha_7} \, Inv_3^{\alpha_8} \, Trf_3^{\alpha_9} \, L_3^{\beta_3}$ **(34)**

$\log Y_3 = \log A_3 + \lambda_3 logK_{3Pr} + \ \alpha_7 logFonc_3 + \ \alpha_8 logInv_3 + \alpha_9 logTrf_3 + \beta_3 \log L_3$ **(35)**

$$\mathrm{I}(Fon_3) = \frac{Fonc_3}{PIB} \times \frac{PIB}{DEP_3} \quad (35)$$

$$\mathrm{I}(Inv_3) = \frac{Inv_3}{PIB} \times \frac{PIB}{DEP_3} \quad (36)$$

$$\mathrm{I}(\mathrm{Trf}_3) = \frac{Trf_3}{PIB} \times \frac{PIB}{DEP_3} \quad (37)$$

$\log Y_3 = \log A_3 + \lambda_3 logK_{3Pr} + \ \alpha_3' logDEP_3 + \beta_3 \log L_3$ **(38)**

$\alpha_3' = \alpha_7 + \alpha_8 + \alpha_9$ **(39)**

$DEP_3 = Fonc_3 + \ Inv_3 + \ Trf_3$ **(40)**

$DDMI_3 \equiv Y_3$ **(41)**

$\log DDMI_3 = \log A_3 + \lambda_3 logI(K_{3Pr}) + \ \alpha_7 logI(Fonc_3) + \alpha_8 logI(Inv_3) + \ \alpha_9 logI(Trf_3) + \beta_3 \log I(L_3)$ **(42)**

$I(K_{3Pr})$= index of private expenditure in the function (26) **(43)**

$I(L_3)$= index of the stock of labour in the function (26). **(44)**

$\log DDMI_3 = \log A_3 + \lambda_3 log I(K_{3Pr}) + \alpha_7 \log (\frac{Fonc_3}{PIB} \times \frac{PIB}{DEP_3}) + \alpha_8 \log (\frac{Inv_3}{PIB} \times \frac{PIB}{DEP_3}) + \alpha_9 \log (\frac{Trf_3}{PIB} \times \frac{PIB}{DEP_3}) + \beta_3 \log I(L_3)$ **(45)**

$\log DDMI_3 = \log A_3 + \lambda_3 log I(K_{3Pr}) + \alpha_7 \log \left(\frac{Fonc_3}{PIB}\right) + \alpha_7 \log \left(\frac{PIB}{DEP_3}\right) + \alpha_8 \log \left(\frac{Inv_3}{PIB}\right) + \alpha_8 \log \left(\frac{PIB}{DEP_3}\right) + \alpha_9 \log \left(\frac{Trf_3}{PIB}\right) + \alpha_9 \log (\frac{PIB}{DEP_3}) + \beta_3 \log I(L_3)$ **(46)**

$\log DDMI_3 = \log A_3 + \lambda_3 log I(K_{3Pr}) + \alpha_7 \log \left(\frac{Fonc_3}{PIB}\right) + \alpha_8 \log \left(\frac{Inv_3}{PIB}\right) + \alpha_9 \log \left(\frac{Trf_3}{PIB}\right) + (\alpha_7 + \alpha_8 + \alpha_9) \log (\frac{PIB}{DEP_3}) + \beta_3 \log I(L_3)$**(47)**

$\log DDMI_3 = \log A_3 + \lambda_3 log I(K_{3Pr}) + \alpha_7 \log(Fonc_3') + \alpha_8 \log(Inv_3') + \alpha_9 \log(Trf_3') + (\alpha_7 + \alpha_8 + \alpha_9) \log (\frac{PIB}{DEP_3}) + \beta_3 \log I(L_3)$ **(48)**

Function 4: Macro-budget modelling of the security sector

$Y_4 = A_4\, K_{4Pr}^{\lambda_4}\, Fonc_4^{\alpha_{10}}\, Inv_4^{\alpha_{11}}\, Trf_4^{\alpha_{12}}\, L_4^{\beta_4}$ **(49)**

$\log Y_4 = \log A_4 + \lambda_4 log K_{4Pr} + \alpha_{10} log Fonc_4 + \alpha_{11} log Inv_4 + \alpha_{12} log Trf_4 + \beta_4 \log L_4$**(50)**

$$\mathrm{I}(Fon_4) = \frac{Fonc_4}{PIB} \times \frac{PIB}{DEP_4} \quad \textbf{(51)}$$

$$\mathrm{I}(Inv_4) = \frac{Inv_4}{PIB} \times \frac{PIB}{DEP_4} \quad \textbf{(52)}$$

$$\mathrm{I}(\mathrm{Trf}_4) = \frac{Trf_4}{PIB} \times \frac{PIB}{DEP_4} \quad \textbf{(53)}$$

$\log Y_4 = \log A_4 + \lambda_4 log K_{4Pr} + \alpha_4' log DEP_4 + \beta_4 \log L_4$ **(54)**

$\alpha_4' = \alpha_{10} + \alpha_{11} + \alpha_{12}$ **(55)**

$DEP_4 = Fonc_4 + Inv_4 + Trf_4$ **(56)**

$DDMI_4 \equiv Y_4$ **(57)**

$\log DDMI_4 = \log A_4 + \lambda_4 log I(K_{4Pr}) + \alpha_{10} log I(Fonc_4) + \alpha_{11} log I(Inv_4) + \alpha_{12} log I(Trf_4) + \beta_4 \log I(L_4)$ **(58)**

$I(K_{4Pr})$= index of private expenditure in the function ('38) **(59)**

$I(L_4)$= index of the stock of labour in the function (38). **(60)**

$\log DDMI_4 = \log A_4 + \lambda_4 logI(K_{4Pr}) + \alpha_{10}\log(\frac{Fonc_4}{PIB} \times \frac{PIB}{DEP_4}) + \alpha_{11}\log(\frac{Inv_4}{PIB} \times \frac{PIB}{DEP_4}) + \alpha_{12}\log(\frac{Trf_4}{PIB} \times \frac{PIB}{DEP_4}) + \beta_4 \log I(L_4)$ **(61)**

$\log DDMI_4 = \log A_4 + \lambda_4 logI(K_{4Pr}) + \alpha_{10}\log\left(\frac{Fonc_4}{PIB}\right) + \alpha_{10}\log\left(\frac{PIB}{DEP_4}\right) + \alpha_{11}\log\left(\frac{Inv_4}{PIB}\right) + \alpha_{11}\log\left(\frac{PIB}{DEP_4}\right) + \alpha_{12}\log\left(\frac{Trf_4}{PIB}\right) + \alpha_{12}\log(\frac{PIB}{DEP_4}) + \beta_4 \log I(L_4)$ **(62)**

$\log DDMI_4 = \log A_4 + \lambda_4 logI(K_{4Pr}) + \alpha_{10}\log\left(\frac{Fonc_4}{PIB}\right) + \alpha_{11}\log\left(\frac{Inv_4}{PIB}\right) + \alpha_{12}\log\left(\frac{Trf_4}{PIB}\right) + (\alpha_{10} + \alpha_{11} + \alpha_{12})\log(\frac{PIB}{DEP_4}) + \beta_4 \log I(L_4)$**(63)**

$\log DDMI_4 = \log A_4 + \lambda_4 logI(K_{4Pr}) + \alpha_{10}\log(Fonc_4') + \alpha_{11}\log(Inv_4') + \alpha_{12}\log(Trf_4') + (\alpha_{10} + \alpha_{11} + \alpha_{12})\log(\frac{PIB}{DEP_4}) + \beta_4 \log I(L_4)$ **(64)**

Function 5: Macro-budgetary modelling of the professional networks sector

$Y_5 = A_5\, K_{5Pr}^{\lambda_5}\, Fonc_5^{\alpha_{13}}\, Inv_5^{\alpha_{14}}\, Trf_5^{\alpha_{15}}\, L_5^{\beta_5}$ **(65)**

$\log Y_5 = \log A_5 + \lambda_5 logK_{5Pr} + \alpha_{13} logFonc_5 + \alpha_{14} logInv_5 + \alpha_{15} logTrf_5 + \beta_5 \log L_5$**(66)**

$$\mathrm{I}(Fon_5) = \frac{Fonc_5}{PIB} \times \frac{PIB}{DEP_5} \quad \textbf{(67)}$$

$$\mathrm{I}(Inv_5) = \frac{Inv_5}{PIB} \times \frac{PIB}{DEP_5} \quad \textbf{(68)}$$

$$\mathrm{I}(\mathrm{Trf}_5) = \frac{Trf_5}{PIB} \times \frac{PIB}{DEP_5} \quad \textbf{(69)}$$

$\log Y_5 = \log A_5 + \lambda_5 logK_{5Pr} + \alpha_5' logDEP_5 + \beta_5 \log L_5$ **(70)**

$\alpha_5' = \alpha_{13} + \alpha_{14} + \alpha_{15}$ **(71)**

$DEP_5 = Fonc_5 + Inv_5 + Trf_5$ **(72)**

$DDMI_5 \equiv Y_5$ **(73)**

$\log DDMI_5 = \log A_5 + \lambda_5 log I(K_{5Pr}) + \alpha_{13} log I(Fonc_5) + \alpha_{14} log I(Inv_5) + \alpha_{15} log I(Trf_5) + \beta_5 \log I(L_5)$ **(74)**

$I(K_{5Pr})$= index of private expenditure in the function (50) **(75)**

$I(L_5)$= index of the stock of labour in the function (50). **(76)**

$\log DDMI_5 = \log A_5 + \lambda_5 log I(K_{5Pr}) + \alpha_{13} \log (\frac{Fonc_5}{PIB} \times \frac{PIB}{DEP_5}) + \alpha_{14} \log (\frac{Inv_5}{PIB} \times \frac{PIB}{DEP_5}) + \alpha_{15} \log (\frac{Trf_5}{PIB} \times \frac{PIB}{DEP_5}) + \beta_5 \log I(L_5)$ **(77)**

$\log DDMI_5 = \log A_5 + \lambda_5 log I(K_{5Pr}) + \alpha_{13} \log \left(\frac{Fonc_5}{PIB}\right) + \alpha_{13} \log \left(\frac{PIB}{DEP_5}\right) + \alpha_{14} \log \left(\frac{Inv_5}{PIB}\right) + \alpha_{14} \log \left(\frac{PIB}{DEP_5}\right) + \alpha_{15} \log \left(\frac{Trf_5}{PIB}\right) + \alpha_{15} \log (\frac{PIB}{DEP_5}) + \beta_5 \log I(L_5)$ **(78)**

$\log DDMI_5 = \log A_5 + \lambda_5 log I(K_{5Pr}) + \alpha_{13} \log \left(\frac{Fonc_5}{PIB}\right) + \alpha_{14} \log \left(\frac{Inv_5}{PIB}\right) + \alpha_{15} \log \left(\frac{Trf_5}{PIB}\right) + (\alpha_{13} + \alpha_{14} + \alpha_{15}) \log (\frac{PIB}{DEP_5}) + \beta_5 \log I(L_5)$**(79)**

$\log DDMI_5 = \log A_5 + \lambda_5 log I(K_{5Pr}) + \alpha_{13} \log(Fonc'_5) + \alpha_{14} \log(Inv'_5) + \alpha_{15} \log(Trf'_5) + (\alpha_{13} + \alpha_{14} + \alpha_{15}) \log (\frac{PIB}{DEP_5}) + \beta_5 \log I(L_5)$ **(80)**

Function 6: Macro-budget modelling of the social media sector

$Y_6 = A_6\, K_{6Pr}^{\lambda_6}\, Fonc_6^{\alpha_{16}}\, Inv_6^{\alpha_{17}}\, Trf_6^{\alpha_{18}}\, L_6^{\beta_6}$ **(81)**

$\log Y_6 = \log A_6 + \lambda_6 log K_{6Pr} + \alpha_{16} log Fonc_6 + \alpha_{17} log Inv_6 + \alpha_{18} log Trf_6 + \beta_6 \log L_6$**(82)**

$$\mathrm{I}(Fon_6) = \frac{Fonc_6}{PIB} \times \frac{PIB}{DEP_6} \quad \textbf{(83)}$$

$$\mathrm{I}(Inv_6) = \frac{Inv_6}{PIB} \times \frac{PIB}{DEP_6} \quad \textbf{(84)}$$

$$\mathrm{I}(\mathrm{Trf}_6) = \frac{Trf_6}{PIB} \times \frac{PIB}{DEP_6} \quad \textbf{(85)}$$

$\log Y_6 = \log A_6 + \lambda_6 log K_{6Pr} + \alpha'_6 log DEP_6 + \beta_6 \log L_6$ **(86)**

$\alpha'_6 = \alpha_{16} + \alpha_{17} + \alpha_{18}$ **(87)**

$DEP_6 = Fonc_6 + Inv_6 + Trf_6$ **(88)**

$DDMI_6 \equiv Y_6$ **(89)**

$\log DDMI_6 = \log A_6 + \lambda_6 logI(K_{6Pr}) + \alpha_{16} logI(Fonc_6) + \alpha_{17} logI(Inv_6) + \alpha_{18} logI(Trf_6) + \beta_6 \log I(L_6)$ **(90)**

$I(K_{6Pr})$= index of private expenditure in the function (62) **(91)**

$I(L_6)$= index of the stock of labour in the function (62). **(92)**

$\log DDMI_6 = \log A_6 + \lambda_6 logI(K_{6Pr}) + \alpha_{16}\log(\frac{Fonc_6}{PIB} \times \frac{PIB}{DEP_6}) + \alpha_{17}\log(\frac{Inv_6}{PIB} \times \frac{PIB}{DEP_6}) + \alpha_{18}\log(\frac{Trf_6}{PIB} \times \frac{PIB}{DEP_6}) + \beta_6 \log I(L_6)$ **(93)**

$\log DDMI_6 = \log A_6 + \lambda_6 logI(K_{6Pr}) + \alpha_{16}\log\left(\frac{Fonc_6}{PIB}\right) + \alpha_{16}\log\left(\frac{PIB}{DEP_6}\right) + \alpha_{17}\log\left(\frac{Inv_6}{PIB}\right) + \alpha_{17}\log\left(\frac{PIB}{DEP_6}\right) + \alpha_{18}\log\left(\frac{Trf_6}{PIB}\right) + \alpha_{18}\log(\frac{PIB}{DEP_6}) + \beta_6 \log I(L_6)$ **(94)**

$\log DDMI_6 = \log A_6 + \lambda_6 logI(K_{6Pr}) + \alpha_{16}\log\left(\frac{Fonc_6}{PIB}\right) + \alpha_{17}\log\left(\frac{Inv_6}{PIB}\right) + \alpha_{18}\log\left(\frac{Trf_6}{PIB}\right) + (\alpha_{16} + \alpha_{17} + \alpha_{18})\log(\frac{PIB}{DEP_6}) + \beta_6 \log I(L_6)$**(95)**

$\log DDMI_6 = \log A_6 + \lambda_6 logI(K_{6Pr}) + \alpha_{16}\log(Fonc_6') + \alpha_{17}\log(Inv_6') + \alpha_{18}\log(Trf_6') + (\alpha_{16} + \alpha_{17} + \alpha_{18})\log(\frac{PIB}{DEP_6}) + \beta_6 \log I(L_6)$ **(96)**

Function 7: Macro-budget modelling of the Building and energy sector

$Y_7 = A_7\, K_{7Pr}^{\lambda_7}\, Fonc_7^{\alpha_{19}}\, Inv_7^{\alpha_{20}}\, Trf_7^{\alpha_{21}}\, L_7^{\beta_7}$ **(97)**

$\log Y_7 = \log A_7 + \lambda_7 logK_{7Pr} + \alpha_{19} logFonc_7 + \alpha_{20} logInv_7 + \alpha_{21} logTrf_7 + \beta_7 \log L_7$**(98)**

$$\mathrm{I}(Fon_7) = \frac{Fonc_7}{PIB} \times \frac{PIB}{DEP_7} \quad \textbf{(99)}$$

$$\mathrm{I}(Inv_7) = \frac{Inv_7}{PIB} \times \frac{PIB}{DEP_7} \quad \textbf{(100)}$$

$$\mathrm{I}(\mathrm{Trf}_7) = \frac{Trf_7}{PIB} \times \frac{PIB}{DEP_7} \quad \textbf{(101)}$$

$\log Y_7 = \log A_7 + \lambda_7 logK_{7Pr} + \alpha_7' logDEP_7 + \beta_7 \log L_7$ **(102)**

$\alpha_7' = \alpha_{19} + \alpha_{20} + \alpha_{21}$ **(103)**

$DEP_7 = Fonc_7 + Inv_7 + Trf_7$ **(104)**

$DDMI_7 \equiv Y_7$ **(105)**

$\log DDMI_7 = \log A_7 + \lambda_7 logI(K_{7Pr}) + \alpha_{19} logI(Fonc_7) + \alpha_{20} logI(Inv_7) + \alpha_{21} logI(Trf_7) + \beta_7 \log I(L_7)$ **(106)**

$I(K_{7Pr})$= index of private expenditure in the function (74) **(107)**

$I(L_7)$= index of the stock of labour in the function (74). **(108)**

$\log DDMI_7 = \log A_7 + \lambda_7 logI(K_{7Pr}) + \alpha_{19}\log(\frac{Fonc_7}{PIB} \times \frac{PIB}{DEP_7}) + \alpha_{20}\log(\frac{Inv_7}{PIB} \times \frac{PIB}{DEP_7}) + \alpha_{21}\log(\frac{Trf_7}{PIB} \times \frac{PIB}{DEP_7}) + \beta_7 \log I(L_7)$ **(109)**

$\log DDMI_7 = \log A_7 + \lambda_7 logI(K_{7Pr}) + \alpha_{19}\log\left(\frac{Fonc_7}{PIB}\right) + \alpha_{19}\log\left(\frac{PIB}{DEP_7}\right) + \alpha_{20}\log\left(\frac{Inv_7}{PIB}\right) + \alpha_{20}\log\left(\frac{PIB}{DEP_7}\right) + \alpha_{21}\log\left(\frac{Trf_7}{PIB}\right) + \alpha_{21}\log(\frac{PIB}{DEP_7}) + \beta_7 \log I(L_7)$ **(110)**

$\log DDMI_7 = \log A_7 + \lambda_7 logI(K_{7Pr}) + \alpha_{19}\log\left(\frac{Fonc_7}{PIB}\right) + \alpha_{20}\log\left(\frac{Inv_7}{PIB}\right) + \alpha_{21}\log\left(\frac{Trf_7}{PIB}\right) + (\alpha_{19} + \alpha_{20} + \alpha_{21})\log(\frac{PIB}{DEP_7}) + \beta_7 \log I(L_7)$**(111)**

$\log DDMI_7 = \log A_7 + \lambda_7 logI(K_{7Pr}) + \alpha_{19}\log(Fonc_7') + \alpha_{20}\log(Inv_7') + \alpha_{21}\log(Trf_7') + (\alpha_{19} + \alpha_{20} + \alpha_{21})\log(\frac{PIB}{DEP_7}) + \beta_7 \log I(L_7)$ **(112)**

Function 8: Macro-fiscal modelling of the economic sector

$Y_8 = A_8\, K_{8Pr}^{\lambda_8}\, Fonc_8^{\alpha_{22}}\, Inv_8^{\alpha_{23}}\, Trf_8^{\alpha_{24}}\, L_8^{\beta_8}$ **(113)**

$\log Y_8 = \log A_8 + \lambda_8 logK_{8Pr} + \alpha_{22} logFonc_8 + \alpha_{23} logInv_8 + \alpha_{24} logTrf_8 + \beta_8 \log L_8$**(114)**

$$\mathrm{I}(Fon_8) = \frac{Fonc_8}{PIB} \times \frac{PIB}{DEP_8} \quad \mathbf{(115)}$$

$$\mathrm{I}(Inv_8) = \frac{Inv_8}{PIB} \times \frac{PIB}{DEP_8} \quad \mathbf{(116)}$$

$$\mathrm{I(Trf_8)} = \frac{Trf_8}{PIB} \times \frac{PIB}{DEP_8} \quad \mathbf{(117)}$$

$\log Y_8 = \log A_8 + \lambda_8 logK_{8Pr} + \alpha'_8 logDEP_8 + \beta_8 \log L_8$ **(118)**

$\alpha'_8 = \alpha_{22} + \alpha_{23} + \alpha_{24}$ **(119)**

$DEP_8 = Fonc_8 + Inv_8 + Trf_8$ **(120)**

$DDMI_8 \equiv Y_8$ **(121)**

$\log DDMI_8 = \log A_8 + \lambda_8 logI(K_{8Pr}) + \alpha_{22} logI(Fonc_8) + \alpha_{23} logI(Inv_8) + \alpha_{24} logI(Trf_8) + \beta_8 \log I(L_8)$ **(122)**

$I(K_{8Pr})$= index of private expenditure in the function (86) **(123)**

$I(L_8)$= index of the stock of labour in the function (86). **(124)**

$\log DDMI_8 = \log A_8 + \lambda_8 logI(K_{8Pr}) + \alpha_{22} \log (\frac{Fonc_8}{PIB} \times \frac{PIB}{DEP_8}) + \alpha_{23} \log (\frac{Inv_8}{PIB} \times \frac{PIB}{DEP_8}) + \alpha_{24} \log (\frac{Trf_8}{PIB} \times \frac{PIB}{DEP_8}) + \beta_8 \log I(L_8)$ **(125)**

$\log DDMI_8 = \log A_8 + \lambda_8 logI(K_{8Pr}) + \alpha_{22} \log \left(\frac{Fonc_8}{PIB}\right) + \alpha_{22} \log \left(\frac{PIB}{DEP_8}\right) + \alpha_{23} \log \left(\frac{Inv_8}{PIB}\right) + \alpha_{23} \log \left(\frac{PIB}{DEP_8}\right) + \alpha_{24} \log \left(\frac{Trf_8}{PIB}\right) + \alpha_{24} \log (\frac{PIB}{DEP_8}) + \beta_8 \log I(L_8)$ **(126)**

$\log DDMI_8 = \log A_8 + \lambda_8 logI(K_{8Pr}) + \alpha_{22} \log \left(\frac{Fonc_8}{PIB}\right) + \alpha_{23} \log \left(\frac{Inv_8}{PIB}\right) + \alpha_{24} \log \left(\frac{Trf_8}{PIB}\right) + (\alpha_{22} + \alpha_{23} + \alpha_{24}) \log (\frac{PIB}{DEP_8}) + \beta_8 \log I(L_8)$**(127)**

$\log DDMI_8 = \log A_8 + \lambda_8 logI(K_{8Pr}) + \alpha_{22} \log(Fonc'_8) + \alpha_{23} \log(Inv'_8) + \alpha_{24} \log(Trf'_8) + (\alpha_{22} + \alpha_{23} + \alpha_{24}) \log (\frac{PIB}{DEP_8}) + \beta_8 \log I(L_8)$ **(128)**

Looping the model

For each year, we must have the following convergence identities:

$\sum_{J=1}^{8} DEP_j = Budget\ exécuté$ (129)

$\sum_{J=1}^{8} K_{jPr} = Dépenses\ privées$ (130)

$\sum_{J=1}^{8} L_j = Stock\ de\ main\ d'oeuvre$ (131)

$\prod_{J=1}^{8} DDMI_j = DDMI$ (132)

Section 4: Simulations Shock Analysis

Niger: simulation of 17% of the total education budget on DDMI functions

Structurally, from 2004 to 2020, total expenditure actually allocated to education varied by an average of 17% in Niger. It is for this reason that in the case of this country, a 17% increase in the budget devoted to education was simulated.

The overall analysis of the effect of an increase in resources to produce education services makes it possible to observe the sensitivity of the other DDMI functions.

Year of Shock (2015)

– The allocation of 17% of the education budget resulted in an increase of 0.04% in the Education function of the DDMI. When we know that the bulk of the education budget is intended primarily for operations (50.6%), transfer (46.5%) and secondary investment (2.9%), we can conclude that this distribution does not substantially improve the education function of the DDMI and must therefore be corrected.

– As for the Building and energy function of the DDMI, the 17% increase in the education budget leads to a 2.92% decrease in its value. This suggests a drain on the Building and energy sector following the increase in education spending.

– The economics function of the DDMI recorded an increase of 0.37% following the shock on education, reflecting that education, as an element of human capital, is a real vector for improving the Economics function of the DDMI.

– The professional network function of the DDMI recorded a decrease of 0.28% following the 17% increase in expenditure executed for education. This situation shows, as for the building and energy function of the DDMI, that the increase in the education budget is a form of drain that has a negative effect on the professional network function of the DDMI.

– As far as the security function of the DDMI is concerned, the 17% increase in the education budget resulted in a 0.29% increase in the security function of the DDMI. This would not be unrelated to the effect of education on the components of security, both in terms of operation, investment and transfers.

– For the institutions function of the DDMI, the shock on education spending led to an improvement of 0.76%, compared to 0.42% for health. This means that once again, education is a real element of improvement of these two functions of the DDMI. This is not the case for the social network, which is not significantly affected by the 17% increase in education spending.

If in 2015, the 17% increase in the allocated budget impacted all the functions of the DDMI, the same is not true one year after the shock.

One year after the shock (2016)

The effects of an allocation of 17% of the education budget, one year after the shock, affected the functions of the DDMI differently.

– While the education function is positive and slightly affected, the building and energy function of the DDMI is the main beneficiary of the increase in the education budget. Indeed, there is an improvement of 1.04%, showing that instead of the increase benefiting education services, it is rather in the building sector that the effect has developed the most. Such a situation calls for investment in education to be directed towards teacher training, the acquisition of teaching and pedagogical materials at all levels of education. Transfers in terms of school canteen funding would facilitate the retention of learners in the education system.

– The functions of the DDMI professional network, safety and health are also positively affected by the increase of 17% of expenditure devoted to education, unlike the economy and institutions functions of the DDMI which are negatively affected.

Table 37: Effects of the 17% increase in the education budget

DDMI FUNCTIONS	2015	2016
Education	0,04%	0,02%
Building-energy	-2,92%	1,04%
Economic Affairs	0,37%	-0,20%
Professional network	-0,28%	0,19%
Security	0,29%	0,20%
Institution	0,76%	-0,22%
Health	0,42%	0,16%
Social network	0,00%	0,00%

Source: CREG, 2025

Guinea: simulation of 10% of the investment budget of each of the sectors on the functions of DDMI

The shock carried out in this simulation for Guinea consisted of increasing the investment budget of each of the eight sectors simultaneously by 10% over the period 2024-2027.

The overall analysis of the effect of an increase in resources for investment in the eight sectors makes it possible to observe the sensitivity of the different DDMI functions.

1st and 2nd Shock period (2024-2025 and 2025-2026)

A 10% increase in investment in the budget of the different sectors leads to a different variation in the DDMI depending on the sector. As a result, it is specifically observed that:

– Regarding human capital, a 10% increase in the investment budget instantly leads to an increase of 1.25% in the DDMI for education and 0.51% in the DDMI for health. In the following period, the same impacts observed in the first period were again observed in both sectors (1.25% for education and 0.51% for health).

– For the structure of the economy component, a 10% increase in investment in the budget of the various sectors instantly leads to an increase of 3.15% in the DDMI of the Building-Energy and 2.54% of the DDMI of the economy. For the second period, this increase in the budget leads to an increase in the DDMI of the Building-Energy and Economy sectors of 3.36% and 2.45% respectively.

– Regarding the governance component, a simultaneous increase in investment of 10% in the budget of the different sectors instantly leads to an increase of 0.59% in the institution's DDMI and 0.69% in the DDMI for security. The increase observed for these two functions of the IDD remains the same in the second period.

– Finally, in the network component, a 10% increase in investment in the budget of the various sectors is at the origin of an instant increase in the DDMI of the professional network by 1.91% and the DDMI of the social network by 1.09%. In the second period, the impact is around 1.93% for the professional network and 1.09% for the social network.

3rd Shock Period (2026-2027)

– At the level of human capital, the shock (increase in the investment budget of each sector) leads to an improvement in the DDMI of the education sector by 2.19%; and the DDMI of the health sector by

0.31%. In total, over the 2024-2027 simulation period, the simultaneous impact of the investment budget has a cumulative effect of 1.56% and 0.44% in the education and health sectors respectively.

– In the component of the structure of the economy, it is noted that the 10% increase in investment expenditure leads to an increase in the DDMI of 1.61% and 2.28% respectively for the Building-Energy and Economy sectors. In total, over the simulation period, the simultaneous impact of the investment budget has a cumulative effect of 2.71% and 2.42% in the Building-Energy and Economy sectors.

– Regarding governance, the increase in the investment budget is reflected in the third period, by an increase in the DDMI of 1.43% and 0.64% respectively in the institutions and security sector. In total, over the simulation period, the simultaneous impact of the investment budget has a cumulative effect of 0.87% and 0.67% respectively on these two sectors of institutions and security.

– Regarding the network component, the increase in the investment budget translates into an increase in well-being of 1.81% and 1.08% respectively in the professional and social sectors in period 3. Over the simulation period, the simultaneous impact of the investment budget has a cumulative effect of 1.88% in the education sector and 1.09% in the health sector.

Table 38: Effects of the 10% increase in the investment budget of each sector

Rank	DDMI FUNCTIONS	2024-2025	2025-2026	2026-2027
1er	Building-Energy	3,15%	3,36%	1,61%
2nd	Economic affairs	2,54%	2,45%	2,28%
3rd	Professional network	1,91%	1,93%	1,81%
4th	Education	1,25%	1,25%	2,19%
5th	Social network	1,09%	1,09%	1,08%
6th	Institution	0,59%	0,59%	1,43%
7th	Security	0,69%	0,69%	0,64%
8th	Health	0,51%	0,51%	0,31%

Source: CREG, 2025

Summary of results

The results of the analyses show that following a shock to the budget, the DDMI trend is generally upward in both Niger and Guinea. These results remain encouraging, especially since, as observed above, the Demographic Dividend has not yet been captured in these two countries. It is essential for these countries to reach the average level for the DDMI (0.5>DDMI<0.8).

Effective consideration of changes in the budget based on the simulations carried out should, as the results show, enable Niger and Guinea to move considerably closer to a level of DDMI favorable to capturing the demographic dividend. Indeed, by an improvement in the education budget of 17% in Niger; and an improvement in the investment budget of the eight sectors by 10% in Guinea, the level of the DDMI of each sector will be subject to a variation that should allow an overall improvement in well-being.

Based on these shock simulations, it is observed that:

In Niger, the DDMI function of health is the function that, on average, has seen the greatest improvement with 0.29% over the period, followed by the function of the institution with an average improvement of 0.27%. The improvement in the DDMI of the security function comes in third place with an average improvement over the period of 0.25%. This is followed respectively by the DDMI functions of economic affairs (0.09%), and education (0.03%). Finally, while the DDMI function of the social network is not significantly affected by this increase in the education budget, the DDMI functions of the Building-Energy and the professional network are experiencing a downward trend on average over the period with -0.94% and -0.05% respectively.

However, in Guinea, the State should rather give priority to the Building-Energy sector, whose impact on the DDMI, following an improvement in the investment budget of all sectors, is estimated at 2.71%. The economy sector is the second priority of the Guinean State with an impact on the DDMI of 2.42%, followed by the professional network sector with 1.88% and the education sector with 1.56%. Finally, the sectors of social network (1.09% impact on the DDMI), institution (0.87% impact on the DDMI), security (0.67% impact on the DDMI) and health (0.44% impact on the DDMI) close the list of priorities in Guinea.

These results highlight the priority sectors in which each of these two countries should invest to improve the efficiency of the overall level of well-being apprehended by the DDMI.

Conclusion

The implementation of the BSDD process is important for our leaders in their march towards capturing and even exploiting the demographic dividend. It makes it possible not only to transform the classic budget into a functional budget, but also to classify expenditure economically into three economic natures, namely investment, transfer and operation, de facto promoting a simplified and efficient analysis of the budget with a view to a more strategic orientation of State resources with a view to optimization.

Niger's results are indicative of a strategy for allocating resources to education that is not conducive to the quest to capture the demographic dividend. Indeed, most of the sector's budget is allocated to operations and transfers to the detriment of investment.

A trend that must change imperatively in view of the government's ambitions reflected in the national strategy documents (SDDCI[16] 2035, DPG[17], PDES 2022-2026).

The PDES[18] 2022-2026 provides for an allocation of 22% of budgetary resources to education.

In the context of the program budget, it is recommended to respect the linkage between planning and budgeting, in other words the orientations of the PDES must be rigorously reflected in budgeting, to ensure the successful implementation of public policies.

In Guinea, the results of the simulations call for a prioritization of investment in the Building-energy, economy, professional network and education sectors. This is in line with the major actions undertaken in the Building-energy sector such as the implementation of the master plans for Greater Conakry Vision 2040 and the redevelopment of Kaloum and the Loos Islands; in the economic sector, such as the development of the value chains of the main agricultural sectors (agriculture, livestock, fisheries, forestry), the revival of urban transport aimed at making the assets of the former Société Générale des

[16] SDCCI : Stratégie de Développement Durable et de Croissance Inclusive

[17] DPG: Dialogue Politique Générale

[18] PDES : Plan de Développement Economique et Social

Transports de Guinée (SOGETRAG) available to private investors in order to develop urban and inter-urban transport, but also the allocation of a 30-hectare site for the implementation of the pilot project of the industrial park in Guinea. Forécariah; and in the education sector, with the acquisition of important rolling stock and non-rolling stock, including textbooks and equipment for vocational centers.

With such political will, Niger and Guinea can hope to capture the demographic dividend as provided for in the DDMI profile.

Bibliographical references

Decaluwé, B., Dissou, Y., & Patry, A. (2001). Union douanière au sein de l'UEMOA. Revue économique, 52(4), 811-830.

Adelman, I., & Robinson, S. (1978). Income distribution policy in developing countries: A case study of Korea.

Shoven, J. B., & Whalley, J. (1984). Applied general-equilibrium models of taxation and international trade: An introduction and survey. Journal of Economic literature, 22(3), 1007-1051.

Decaluwé, B., & Martens, A. (1988). CGE modeling and developing economies: A concise empirical survey of 73 applications to 26 countries. Journal of Policy Modeling, 10(4), 529-568.

Bloom, D. E., Canning, D., & Graham, B. (2003). Longevity and life-cycle savings. The Scandinavian Journal of Economics, 105(3), 319-338.

Dumont, J. C., & Mesplé-Somps, S. (2000). L'impact des infrastructures publiques sur la compétitivité et la croissance : une analyse en EGC appliquée au Sénégal (No. DT/2000/08).

Mboup, S. D., Diédhiou, B. Y., Joshi, C. L., & Beaumais, O. (2018). Libéralisation, investissements publics, et emploi des femmes au Sénégal/Liberalization, public investment, and the employment of women in Senegal.

GENERAL CONCLUSION

This book discusses the importance of demographic dividend-sensitive budgeting in the context of sustainable development. It highlights the African Union's roadmap to capture the demographic dividend, which focuses on four strategic pillars: health and well-being, education and skills development, youth employment and entrepreneurship, and governance, peace and security. These pillars aim to create the conditions for inclusive and sustainable growth. The document highlights the need for strategic investments in key areas such as education, health and youth employment to maximize the benefits of the demographic transition. It also emphasizes the role of gender-responsive budgeting in ensuring equitable allocation of resources and addressing the specific needs of different population groups. The document provides a comprehensive framework for aligning public spending with demographic priorities to achieve long-term development goals.

This document is organized into nine separate chapters. The first chapter deals with the economic analysis of the national budget by presenting the structure and composition of the State budget, the instruments of budgetary policy and their roles in economic stability and the social impact of budgetary policy. The second chapter dealt with the principle of gender-responsive budgeting and the demographic dividend with a particular focus on the key concepts and foundations of the demographic dividend, its implementation process and the principles that frame the restatement of budget expenditures according to the demographic dividend monitoring index (DDMI). In the third chapter, we introduced the notion of the demographic dividend profile by presenting the profiles of some West and Central African countries. The next chapter (fourth chapter) presented the DDMI and GDDI indices and their sub-dimensions for these countries. The fifth chapter presented the methodology and results of the DDMI series obtained following a backcasting process. This method, which is a common technique for rebasing national accounts, made it possible to calibrate the DD index for the years between two national surveys. In the sixth chapter, we have studied in detail the methodology of the transformation of the classic State budget into a functional budget according to the sub-components of the DDMI. The seventh chapter introduced the optimal control model for the allocation of the state budget, proposing methods of optimizing public resources to maximize the benefits of the demographic dividend. The eighth chapter focused on the sectoral alignment of the budget with the DDMI, with an analysis of the sensitivity of the State budget to the demographic dividend index in a partial equilibrium model, and finally, the last chapter presents a case of economic policy simulation in a context of global equilibrium, illustrating the potential effects of different strategies on the capture of the demographic dividend and the budgetary balance. Through this structuring, the document provides a comprehensive analysis of the demographic dividend and its impact on economic and social development, particularly in Africa. It discusses the importance of demographically dividend-sensitive budgeting and implementing policies that align with demographic changes to maximize economic benefits.

The paper defines the demographic dividend as economic growth resulting from changes in the age structure of a population, with a focus on the need to invest in human capital, job creation, and good governance to realize this potential. As key pillars to capture the demographic dividend, the African Union's roadmap identifies four strategic pillars: health and well-being, education and skills development, employment and entrepreneurship, and governance, peace and security, which are key to fostering inclusive and sustainable growth.

Several African countries have developed national roadmaps to capture the demographic dividend, with a focus on strategic investments in education, health, youth employment and women's empowerment. In regions such as the Sahel, rapid population growth is leading to high dependency rates, which is straining public and family resources, and requiring a shift in budget allocation towards long-term investments in human capital and job creation. The demographic transition offers a unique opportunity to accelerate inclusive and accelerated economic growth, if countries can create enough jobs for the growing young workforce. Tools such as the Demographic Dividend Monitoring Index (DDMI) developed by the Regional Consortium for Research in Generational Economics (CREG) help track progress in capturing the demographic dividend by identifying sectors that need increased investment to optimize economic and social outcomes.

The national budget is an essential tool for resource allocation, influencing the success of public policies aimed at maximizing the demographic dividend through coherent and integrated sectoral investments. In analyzing the structure and composition of the national budget in the first chapter, we examined the distribution of resources and expenditures, as well as the classification of the different budget items. This first step allows us to understand how funds are allocated, and which sectors are receiving priority funding.

Gender-responsive budgeting helps ensure that financial resources are distributed equitably, meeting the diverse needs of men and women and promoting social and economic well-being. By recognizing and addressing the specific needs of men and women in the planning and allocation of resources, governments can help reduce gender inequalities, promote women's empowerment, and strengthen social cohesion. In addition, a gender-sensitive approach can foster more inclusive and sustainable economic growth, harnessing the full potential of the entire workforce. By investing in women's empowerment, eliminating gender discrimination, and strengthening gender analysis in the budget process, countries can truly harness the potential of demographic dividend for sustainable and equitable development.

The analysis of budget structures reveals that recurrent expenditure largely dominates in the eight countries studied, accounting for 44% of the total budget on average. In view of the results of the functional transformation of the budget, it is desirable to give pride of place not only to the structure of the economy but also to investments in the basic social sectors (health, education, standard of living); integrate the economic analysis of the functional budget into the State's decision-making process; promote the use of the BSDD tool in budget conferences for the implementation and evaluation of public policies; increase investments related to human capital (health, education, etc.) in the State budget.

Based on Pontryagin's theories of optimal control (1959), we designed an optimization program with optimal control, under budgetary constraint to generate solutions of optimal overall structures balanced by the functional budget of Senegal. This program has made it possible, after several iterations, to select four possible solutions. A comparative analysis of the three solutions shows that there is not much flexibility in restructuring the budget from one scenario to another because the budget structures are rigid. The results of the solutions also show that there is convergence in the optimal structure of the budget functions. In addition, it should be stressed that there is no "best solution" because the statistically intuitive solution can be politically and socially ineffective. Thus, the scenario to be adopted should be the one that best achieves the country's development objectives. This solution must then be compatible with the government's development agenda and the vision of the leaders.

The economic analysis of public spending in partial equilibrium was mentioned. The use of a macro-fiscal model allowed the assessment of the sensitivity of budget allocations to the indicator of well-being (DDMI). Assessing the effectiveness of public policies involves analyzing how government spending in various sectors influences the quality of public services, and by extension, the well-being of the population. The size, extent and relevance of the variations measured by fiscal elasticities are used to assess which public policies are effective in improving the well-being of the population, which do less so and which degrade the happiness of individuals. The general observation is that the structure of the budgetary nature is decisive for the effectiveness of the policy. Thus, specific sectoral financing policies (operating budget, investment budget and transfer budget) and targeted (Economic Affairs, Building-Energy, health, education, institutional, security, social network, and professional network) are more effective and preferable to globalizing and misguided policies.

Since reality is generally more complex than the representation of a model, the better public policies are not implemented in a compartmentalized context, by sector we found it useful in the sixth chapter to simulate policies in a context close to the conditions of the real economy. In the political, economic and social reality, the dimensions (sectors) of a nation's life are interconnected and interdependent. Thus, to initiate reforms or implement new policies based on this evidence, we have supplemented the partial equilibrium analysis with an overall equilibrium analysis. This assumption is better suited for forecasting and reforms and promotes the implementation of realistic public policies for capturing Africa's demographic dividend.

APPENDIX 1: Classification by Primary Functions

Line labels	Main functions	Code Section
Presidency of the Republic	Institution	1
Prime Minister	Institution	2
Department of National Defense	Security	3
Ministry of Territorial Administration and Decentralization	Security	4
Ministry of Security and Emergency Preparedness	Security	5
Department of Justice	Institution	6
Ministry of Foreign Affairs and Guineans Abroad	Institution	7
Ministry of Planning and Economic Development	Economy	8
Ministry of Economy and Finance	Economy	9
Ministry of Public Service and Labor	Institution	10
Ministry of Livestock	Economy	11
Ministry of Fisheries, Aquaculture and Maritime Economy	Economy	12
Ministry of Mines and Geology	Economy	13
Department of Public Works	Building-Energy	14
Ministry of Trade, Industry and SMEs	Economy	16
Ministry of Health	Health	18
Ministry of Social Action, Advancement of Women and Children	Social network	19
Ministry of Pre-University Education and Literacy	Education	20
Ministry of Technical Education, Vocational Training and Employment	Education	21
Ministry of Information and Communication	Professional network	22
Ministry of Youth and Youth Employment	Economy	23
National Assembly	Institution	24
Supreme court	Institution	25
High Authority for Communication	Institution	26
Economic and Social Council	Institution	27
General Secretariat of the Government	Institution	28
Ministry of Cooperation and African Integration	Institution	29

Line labels	Main functions	Code Section
General Secretariat for Religious Affairs	Social network	30
Ministry of the Environment, Water and Forests	Economy	31
Ministry of Transport	Economy	32
Grand Chancellery of the National Orders of Guinea	Institution	33
Ministry of Higher Education and Scientific Research	Education	34
Administration and Control of Major Projects	Institution	35
Ministry of Energy and Hydraulics	Building-Energy	36
Ministry of Posts, Telecommunications and Digital Economy	Economy	37
Min.Audi.Cont.Econ.F	Institution	38
Min.dec.deve.loca	Institution	39
Min.ElevaProtec.anim	Economy	40
Ministry of Industry, SMEs and Private Sector Promotion	Economy	41
Min.MFin.Empl.Thu.Fe	Economy	42
Ministry of Tourism, Hotels and Handicrafts	Economy	43
Min.Delegate Guin.Etr	Institution	44
General Secretariat of the Presidency in charge of Special Services, the Fight against Drugs	Security	46
Min. Security. President	Security	47
Min. Sec Perm. NDT	Security	48
Min. State Control	Institution	49
Administrative Region of Boké	Institution	51
Faranah Administrative Region	Institution	52
Administrative Region of Kankan	Institution	53
Administrative Region of Kindia	Institution	54
Administrative Region of Labé	Institution	55
Administrative Region of Mamou	Institution	56
Administrative Region of N'Zérékoré	Institution	57
S.E. Mission Quest.	Institution	60
Min. Alph., promo. Lan	Education	61
Min. Common.near PRG	Professional network	62
Ministry of Budget	Economy	64

Appendix 1: Classification by Primary Functions

Line labels	Main functions	Code Section
Min; Del.Aff.Soci	Social network	65
Min. Deleg.Secur Ref	Security	66
Ombudsman of the Republic	Institution	67
High Commission	Institution	68
Independent National Electoral Commission	Institution	69
Min.Law.Man	Institution	70
The Constitutional Court	Institution	72
The Court of Auditors	Institution	73
The High Court of Justice	Institution	74
The High Council of Local Authorities	Institution	75
Independent National Human Rights Institution	Institution	76
Ministry of Citizenship and National Unity	Social network	77
Ministry in charge of Investments and Public-Private Partnerships	Economy	78
Ministry of Hydrocarbons	Economy	79
Ministry of Sanitation and Hydraulics	Health	80
Ministry in charge of Investments and Public Private Sector	Economy	81
Ministry of Women's Rights and Empowerment	Institution	82
PRG Attached Structures	Institution	98
Common State expenditure	Institution	99

APPENDIX 2: Classification by Secondary Functions

CD_SECTION	LB_CHAPTER	MAIN FUNCTIONS	SECONDARY FUNCTIONS	LB_SUB-CHAPTER
18	Min. Public Health	Health	Health	Renf.Syst.Santé-Ens.N.V.--- Contrib.natio.BND
18	Min. Public Health	Health	Economy	Lut.Cont.Onchoc- - - Contrib.natio.BND
18	Min. Public Health	Health	Building-Energy	Pjt.Santé nut- - -Contrib.natio.BND
18	Min. Public Health	Health	Health	Pjt.Santé nut- - -Contrib.natio.BND
18	Min. Public Health	Health	Institution	Pjt.Santé nut- - -Contrib.natio.BND
18	Min. Public Health	Health	Economy	Pjt.Santé nut- - -Contrib.natio.BND
18	Min. Public Health	Health	Education	Pjt.Santé nut- - -Contrib.natio.BND
18	Min. Public Health	Health	Institution	Renf.Syst.Santé-Ens.N.V.--- Contrib.natio.BND

CD_SECTION	LB_CHAPTER	MAIN FUNCTIONS	SECONDARY FUNCTIONS	LB_SUB-CHAPTER
18	Min. Public Health	Health	Health	Renf.Syst.Santé-Ens.N.V.---Contrib.natio.BND
18	Min. Public Health	Health	Building-Energy	Renf.Syst.Santé-Ens.N.V.---Contrib.natio.BND
18	Min. Public Health	Health	Health	Renf.Syst.Santé-Ens.N.V.---Contrib.natio.BND
18	Min. Public Health	Health	Institution	Min.Health Pub.-Déconc.Cky---FdC eventual.h.pjt
18	Min. Public Health	Health	Health	Min.Health Pub.-Déconc.Cky---FdC eventual.h.pjt
18	Min. Public Health	Health	Professional network	Pjt.Santé nut- - -Contrib.natio.BND
18	Min. Public Health	Health	Economy	Pjt.Santé nut- - -Contrib.natio.BND
18	Min. Public Health	Health	Institution	Pjt.Santé nut- - -Contrib.natio.BND

Appendix 2: Classification by Secondary Functions

CD_SECTION	LB_CHAPTER	MAIN FUNCTIONS	SECONDARY FUNCTIONS	LB_SUB-CHAPTER
18	Min. Public Health	Health	Education	Lut.Cont.Onchoc- - - Contrib.natio.BND
18	Min. Public Health	Health	Health	Lut.Cont.Onchoc- - - Contrib.natio.BND
18	Min. Public Health	Health	Institution	Lut.Cont.Onchoc- - - Contrib.natio.BND
18	Min. Public Health	Health	Health	Réh.Hop. -Ens.N.V.- - Contrib.natio.BND-
18	Min. Public Health	Health	Health	SMI/Plan Fam.- - -Contrib.natio.BND
18	Min. Public Health	Health	Building-Energy	SMI/Plan Fam.- - -Contrib.natio.BND
18	Min. Public Health	Health	Health	Renf.Syst.Santé-Ens.N.V.--- Contrib.natio.BND
18	Min. Public Health	Health	Building-Energy	Min.Health Pub.-Déconc.Cky---FdC eventual.h.pjt

CD_SECTION	LB_CHAPTER	MAIN FUNCTIONS	SECONDARY FUNCTIONS	LB_SUB-CHAPTER
18	Min. Public Health	Health	Health	Renf.Syst.Santé-Ens.N.V.---Contrib.natio.BND
18	Min. Public Health	Health	Health	Réh.Hop.- - -Contrib.natio.BND
18	Min. Public Health	Health	Education	Pjt.Santé nut- - -Contrib.natio.BND
18	Min. Public Health	Health	Health	Renf.Syst.Santé-Ens.N.V.---Contrib.natio.BND
18	Min. Public Health	Health	Health	Lute. Cont. pal.- - -Contrib.natio.BND
18	Min. Public Health	Health	Institution	Lute. Cont. pal.- - -Contrib.natio.BND
18	Min. Public Health	Health	Building-Energy	Lute. Cont. pal.- - -Contrib.natio.BND
18	Min. Public Health	Health	Institution	SMI/Plan Fam.- - -Contrib.natio.BND
18	Min. Public Health	Health	Education	Renf.Syst.Santé-Ens.N.V.---Contrib.natio.BND

Appendix 2: Classification by Secondary Functions

CD_SECTION	LB_CHAPTER	MAIN FUNCTIONS	SECONDARY FUNCTIONS	LB_SUB-CHAPTER
18	Min. Public Health	Health	Institution	Renf.Syst.Santé-Ens.N.V.---Contrib.natio.BND
18	Min. Public Health	Health	Economy	Lut.Cont.Onchoc- - -Contrib.natio.BND
18	Min. Public Health	Health	Building-Energy	Lut.Cont.Onchoc- - -Contrib.natio.BND
18	Min. Public Health	Health	Professional network	SMI/Plan Fam.- - -Contrib.natio.BND
18	Min. Public Health	Health	Economy	SMI/Plan Fam.- - -Contrib.natio.BND
18	Min. Public Health	Health	Health	Centr santé urb-Déconc.Cky---FdC eventual.h.pjt
18	Min. Public Health	Health	Health	Fonds d'indigen-Ens. N.V.---Excluding proj.init. HIPC
18	Min. Public Health	Health	Institution	Serv.Administ.-Déconc.Cky- -FdC eventual.h.pjt

CD_SECTION	LB_CHAPTER	MAIN FUNCTIONS	SECONDARY FUNCTIONS	LB_SUB-CHAPTER
18	Min. Public Health	Health	Health	Serv.Administ.-Déconc.Cky- -FdC eventual.h.pjt
18	Min. Public Health	Health	Building-Energy	Serv.Administ.-Déconc.Cky- -FdC eventual.h.pjt
18	Min. Public Health	Health	Institution	Serv.Administ.-Déconc.Cky- -FdC eventual.h.pjt
18	Min. Public Health	Health	Health	Serv.Administ.-Déconc.Cky- -FdC eventual.h.pjt
18	Min. Public Health	Health	Institution	Serv.Administ.-Déconc.Cky- -FdC eventual.h.pjt
18	Min. Public Health	Health	Education	Serv.Administ.-Déconc.Cky- -FdC eventual.h.pjt
18	Min. Public Health	Health	Building-Energy	Centr santé urb-Déconc.Cky---FdC eventual.h.pjt

Appendix 2: Classification by Secondary Functions

CD_SECTION	LB_CHAPTER	MAIN FUNCTIONS	SECONDARY FUNCTIONS	LB_SUB-CHAPTER
18	Min. Public Health	Health	Economy	Renf.Syst.Santé-Ens.N.V.---Contrib.natio.BND
18	Min. Public Health	Health	Health	Renf.Syst.Santé-Ens.N.V.---Contrib.natio.BND
18	Min. Public Health	Health	Institution	Renf.Syst.Santé-Ens.N.V.---Contrib.natio.BND
18	Min. Public Health	Health	Health	Renf.Syst.Santé-Ens.N.V.---Contrib.natio.BND
18	Min. Public Health	Health	Building-Energy	Renf.Syst.Santé-Ens.N.V.---Contrib.natio.BND
18	Min. Public Health	Health	Building-Energy	Serv.Administ.-Déconc.Cky- -FdC eventual.h.pjt
18	Min. Public Health	Health	Professional network	Renf.Syst.Santé-Ens.N.V.---Contrib.natio.BND

CD_SECTION	LB_CHAPTER	MAIN FUNCTIONS	SECONDARY FUNCTIONS	LB_SUB-CHAPTER
18	Min. Public Health	Health	Health	Renf.Syst.Santé-Ens.N.V.---Contrib.natio.BND
18	Min. Public Health	Health	Economy	Renf.Syst.Santé-Ens.N.V.---Contrib.natio.BND
18	Min. Public Health	Health	Education	Renf.Syst.Santé-Ens.N.V.---Contrib.natio.BND
18	Min. Public Health	Health	Institution	Renf.Syst.Santé-Ens.N.V.---Contrib.natio.BND
18	Min. Public Health	Health	Health	Renf.Syst.Santé-Ens.N.V.---Contrib.natio.BND
18	Min. Public Health	Health	Institution	Opér.équip.imag-Ens.N.V.---Hors proj.init. HIPC
18	Min. Public Health	Health	Building-Energy	Serv.Administ.-Déconc.Cky- -FdC eventual.h.pjt

Appendix 2: Classification by Secondary Functions

CD_SECTION	LB_CHAPTER	MAIN FUNCTIONS	SECONDARY FUNCTIONS	LB_SUB-CHAPTER
18	Min. Public Health	Health	Health	Prog.N.L.Buruli-Ens.N.V.- - Contrib.natio.BND-
18	Min. Public Health	Health	Institution	Prog.N.L.Buruli-Ens.N.V.- - Contrib.natio.BND-
18	Min. Public Health	Health	Professional network	Prog.N.L.Buruli-Ens.N.V.- - Contrib.natio.BND-
18	Min. Public Health	Health	Economy	Prog.N.L.Buruli-Ens.N.V.- - Contrib.natio.BND-
18	Min. Public Health	Health	Building-Energy	Prog.N.L.Buruli-Ens.N.V.- - Contrib.natio.BND-
18	Min. Public Health	Health	Education	Prog.N.L.Buruli-Ens.N.V.- - Contrib.natio.BND-
18	Min. Public Health	Health	Health	Prog.fight SIDA-Ens.N.V.- - Contrib.natio.BND-

CD_SECTION	LB_CHAPTER	MAIN FUNCTIONS	SECONDARY FUNCTIONS	LB_SUB-CHAPTER
18	Min. Public Health	Health	Institution	Prog.fight SIDA-Ens.N.V.- - Contrib.natio.BND-
18	Min. Public Health	Health	Education	Prog.fight SIDA-Ens.N.V.- - Contrib.natio.BND-
18	Min. Public Health	Health	Professional network	Prog.fight SIDA-Ens.N.V.- - Contrib.natio.BND-
18	Min. Public Health	Health	Economy	Prog.fight SIDA-Ens.N.V.- - Contrib.natio.BND-
18	Min. Public Health	Health	Building-Energy	Prog.fight SIDA-Ens.N.V.- - Contrib.natio.BND-
18	Min. Public Health	Health	Health	PNDS Support---
18	Min. Public Health	Health	Institution	PNDS Support---
18	Min. Public Health	Health	Building-Energy	PNDS Support---

Appendix 2: Classification by Secondary Functions

CD_SECTION	LB_CHAPTER	MAIN FUNCTIONS	SECONDARY FUNCTIONS	LB_SUB-CHAPTER
18	Min. Public Health	Health	Health	Med. du Travail-Déconc.Cky---Ress.propres h.pjt
18	Min. Public Health	Health	Institution	Nati Day. Vacc-Sces centrx---FdC eventual.h.pjt
18	Min. Public Health	Health	Health	Centr santé urb-Déconc.Cky---FdC eventual.h.pjt
18	Min. Public Health	Health	Building-Energy	Centr santé urb-Déconc.Cky---FdC eventual.h.pjt
18	Min. Public Health	Health	Building-Energy	Reproductive Health-Ens.N.V.- -Contrib.natio.BND-
18	Min. Public Health	Health	Health	Med. du Travail-Déconc.Cky---Ress.propres h.pjt
18	Min. Public Health	Health	Health	INSE Fd.D'Indi.-Déconc.Cky---Hors proj.init. HIPC
18	Min. Public Health	Health	Institution	Dead.Childish---

CD_SECTION	LB_CHAPTER	MAIN FUNCTIONS	SECONDARY FUNCTIONS	LB_SUB-CHAPTER
18	Min. Public Health	Health	Health	Dead.Childish---
18	Min. Public Health	Health	Health	Prog.N.L.Buruli-Ens.N.V.- - Contrib.natio.BND-
18	Min. Public Health	Health	Institution	Prog.N.L.Buruli-Ens.N.V.- - Contrib.natio.BND-
18	Min. Public Health	Health	Health	Renf.Syst.Santé-Ens.N.V.--- Contrib.natio.BND
18	Min. Public Health	Health	Economy	Renf.Syst.Santé-Ens.N.V.--- Contrib.natio.BND
18	Min. Public Health	Health	Building-Energy	Prog.N.L.Buruli-Ens.N.V.- - Contrib.natio.BND-
18	Min. Public Health	Health	Health	Reproductive Health-Ens.N.V.- - Contrib.natio.BND-
18	Min. Public Health	Health	Institution	Reproductive Health-Ens.N.V.- - Contrib.natio.BND-

Appendix 2: Classification by Secondary Functions

CD_SECTION	LB_CHAPTER	MAIN FUNCTIONS	SECONDARY FUNCTIONS	LB_SUB-CHAPTER
18	Min. Public Health	Health	Economy	Reproductive Health-Ens.N.V.- - Contrib.natio.BND-
18	Min. Public Health	Health	Building-Energy	Reproductive Health-Ens.N.V.- - Contrib.natio.BND-
18	Min. Public Health	Health	Health	CS SIDA-Ens.N.V.- - Contrib.natio.BND-
18	Min. Public Health	Health	Institution	CS SIDA-Ens.N.V.- - Contrib.natio.BND-
18	Min. Public Health	Health	Health	CS SIDA-Ens.N.V.- - Contrib.natio.BND-
18	Min. Public Health	Health	Education	CS SIDA-Ens.N.V.- - Contrib.natio.BND-
18	Min. Public Health	Health	Professional network	CS SIDA-Ens.N.V.- - Contrib.natio.BND-

CD_SECTION	LB_CHAPTER	MAIN FUNCTIONS	SECONDARY FUNCTIONS	LB_SUB-CHAPTER
18	Min. Public Health	Health	Economy	CS SIDA-Ens.N.V.- - Contrib.natio.BND-
18	Min. Public Health	Health	Health	CS SIDA-Ens.N.V.- - Contrib.natio.BND-
18	Min. Public Health	Health	Building-Energy	CS SIDA-Ens.N.V.- - Contrib.natio.BND-
18	Min. Public Health	Health	Education	CS SIDA-Ens.N.V.- - Contrib.natio.BND-
18	Min. Public Health	Health	Institution	Mental health---
18	Min. Public Health	Health	Education	Mental health---
18	Min. Public Health	Health	Professional network	Mental health---
18	Min. Public Health	Health	Economy	Mental health---
18	Min. Public Health	Health	Building-Energy	Mental health---

Appendix 2: Classification by Secondary Functions

CD_SECTION	LB_CHAPTER	MAIN FUNCTIONS	SECONDARY FUNCTIONS	LB_SUB-CHAPTER
71	Min.Del.Sant	Health	Institution	Cab MDSP-Sces centrx---Ress.propres h.pjt
71	Min.Del.Sant	Health	Education	Cab MDSP-Sces centrx---FdC eventual.h.pjt
71	Min.Del.Sant	Health	Health	Cab MDSP-Sces centrx---FdC eventual.h.pjt
71	Min.Del.Sant	Health	Building-Energy	Cab MDSP-Sces centrx---FdC eventual.h.pjt
71	Min.Del.Sant	Health	Institution	Serv.Administ.-Déconc.int---FdC eventual.h.pjt
71	Min.Del.Sant	Health	Health	Serv.Administ.-Ens.N.V.---Ress.Own h.pjt
71	Min.Del.Sant	Health	Education	Serv.Administ.-Ens.N.V.---Ress.Own h.pjt

CD_SECTION	LB_CHAPTER	MAIN FUNCTIONS	SECONDARY FUNCTIONS	LB_SUB-CHAPTER
71	Min.Del.Sant	Health	Building-Energy	Serv.Administ.-Ens.N.V.---FdC eventual.h.pjt
71	Min.Del.Sant	Health	Health	Cab MDSP-Sces centrx---FdC eventual.h.pjt
71	Min.Del.Sant	Health	Building-Energy	Cab MDSP-Sces centrx---FdC eventual.h.pjt
71	Min.Del.Sant	Health	Health	Serv.Administ.-Ens.N.V.---FdC eventual.h.pjt
71	Min.Del.Sant	Health	Institution	Serv.Administ.-Ens.N.V.---Ress.Own h.pjt
71	Min.Del.Sant	Health	Building-Energy	Cab MDSP-Sces centrx---FdC eventual.h.pjt
71	Min.Del.Sant	Health	Institution	Cab MDSP-Sces centrx---FdC eventual.h.pjt

Appendix 2: Classification by Secondary Functions

CD_SECTION	LB_CHAPTER	MAIN FUNCTIONS	SECONDARY FUNCTIONS	LB_SUB-CHAPTER
71	Min.Del.Sant	Health	Health	Cab MDSP-Sces centrx---FdC eventual.h.pjt
71	Min.Del.Sant	Health	Economy	Cab MDSP-Sces centrx---FdC eventual.h.pjt
71	Min.Del.Sant	Health	Institution	Aut servi.centr-Sces centrx---FdC eventual.h.pjt
80	Ministry of Hydraulics and Sanitation	Health	Health	GIR/ Upper River Basin L-Inland Decentralised Services
80	Ministry of Hydraulics and Sanitation	Health	Health	National Agency for Sanitation and Public Health
80	Ministry of Hydraulics and Sanitation	Health	Health	Sanitation City of Conakry-Déc-Ckry

CD_SECTION	LB_CHAPTER	MAIN FUNCTIONS	SECONDARY FUNCTIONS	LB_SUB-CHAPTER
80	Ministry of Hydraulics and Sanitation	Health	Health	AEP of the 5 Cities (Gaou, Toug, Lélou, Lola and Yom)-Dec-Int
80	Ministry of Hydraulics and Sanitation	Health	Health	Prog. Gest. Integr. Res. Eau fl. Sénég. II-Dec-Int
80	Ministry of Hydraulics and Sanitation	Health	Health	Prog Accelerate. Water Access/All-Dec-Int
80	Ministry of Hydraulics and Sanitation	Health	Health	Hydrau. Villag. N'zérékoré-Lola-Yomou-Dec-Int
80	Ministry of Hydraulics and Sanitation	Health	Building-Energy	Rehabilitation of the City of Kankan-Dec-Int

Appendix 2: Classification by Secondary Functions

CD_SECTION	LB_CHAPTER	MAIN FUNCTIONS	SECONDARY FUNCTIONS	LB_SUB-CHAPTER
80	Ministry of Hydraulics and Sanitation	Health	Health	Water/Sanitation Boké - Télémélé-Déc-Int
80	Ministry of Hydraulics and Sanitation	Health	Building-Energy	Completion of 500 boreholes in HA. G-Dec-Int
80	Ministry of Hydraulics and Sanitation	Health	Building-Energy	Completion of 400 boreholes in G.MA-Dec-Int
80	Ministry of Hydraulics and Sanitation	Health	Health	4th Pj Eau de Ckry (1st phase)-Dec-Ckry
80	Ministry of Hydraulics and Sanitation	Health	Building-Energy	4th Pj Eau de Ckry (1st phase)-Dec-Ckry

CD_SECTION	LB_CHAPTER	MAIN FUNCTIONS	SECONDARY FUNCTIONS	LB_SUB-CHAPTER
80	Ministry of Hydraulics and Sanitation	Health	Health	4th Pj Eau de Ckry (1st phase)-Dec-Ckry
80	Ministry of Hydraulics and Sanitation	Health	Education	Renf. Cap. Prod/dist Drinking Water.-Dec-Int
80	Ministry of Hydraulics and Sanitation	Health	Building-Energy	Guinea-Dec-Int Water Urban Project
80	Ministry of Hydraulics and Sanitation	Health	Health	Prog Sanitation and Water for All-TTC
80	Ministry of Hydraulics and Sanitation	Health	Building-Energy	Prog Sanitation and Water for All-TTC

Appendix 2: Classification by Secondary Functions

CD_SECTION	LB_CHAPTER	MAIN FUNCTIONS	SECONDARY FUNCTIONS	LB_SUB-CHAPTER
80	Ministry of Hydraulics and Sanitation	Health	Building-Energy	Hydraupur Phase II-Dec-Int
80	Ministry of Hydraulics and Sanitation	Health	Health	Fouta Djallon-Dec-Int Massive Development Program
80	Ministry of Hydraulics and Sanitation	Health	Health	Sanitation City of Conakry-Déc-Ckry
80	Ministry of Hydraulics and Sanitation	Health	Institution	Fouta Djallon-Dec-Int Massive Development Program
80	Ministry of Hydraulics and Sanitation	Health	Economy	Fouta Djallon-Dec-Int Massive Development Program

CD_SECTION	LB_CHAPTER	MAIN FUNCTIONS	SECONDARY FUNCTIONS	LB_SUB-CHAPTER
80	Ministry of Hydraulics and Sanitation	Health	Health	Fouta Djallon-Dec-Int Massive Development Program
80	Ministry of Hydraulics and Sanitation	Health	Education	Fouta Djallon-Dec-Int Massive Development Program
80	Ministry of Hydraulics and Sanitation	Health	Institution	Fouta Djallon-Dec-Int Massive Development Program
80	Ministry of Hydraulics and Sanitation	Health	Institution	Sanitation City of Conakry-Déc-Ckry
80	Ministry of Hydraulics and Sanitation	Health	Health	Payroll Processing Service - Central Services

Appendix 2: Classification by Secondary Functions

CD_SECTION	LB_CHAPTER	MAIN FUNCTIONS	SECONDARY FUNCTIONS	LB_SUB-CHAPTER
80	Ministry of Hydraulics and Sanitation	Health	Social Network	Payroll Processing Service - Central Services
80	Ministry of Hydraulics and Sanitation	Health	Economy	AEP of the 5 Cities (Gaou, Toug, Lélou, Lola and Yom)-Dec-Int
80	Ministry of Hydraulics and Sanitation	Health	Institution	AEP of the 5 Cities (Gaou, Toug, Lélou, Lola and Yom)-Dec-Int
80	Ministry of Hydraulics and Sanitation	Health	Economy	AEP of the 5 Cities (Gaou, Toug, Lélou, Lola and Yom)-Dec-Int
80	Ministry of Hydraulics and Sanitation	Health	Building-Energy	AEP of the 5 Cities (Gaou, Toug, Lélou, Lola and Yom)-Dec-Int

CD_SECTION	LB_CHAPTER	MAIN FUNCTIONS	SECONDARY FUNCTIONS	LB_SUB-CHAPTER
80	Ministry of Hydraulics and Sanitation	Health	Institution	4th Pj Eau de Ckry (1st phase)-Dec-Ckry
80	Ministry of Hydraulics and Sanitation	Health	Economy	4th Pj Eau de Ckry (1st phase)-Dec-Ckry
80	Ministry of Hydraulics and Sanitation	Health	Education	4th Pj Eau de Ckry (1st phase)-Dec-Ckry
80	Ministry of Hydraulics and Sanitation	Health	Institution	Fouta Djallon-Dec-Int Massive Development Program
80	Ministry of Hydraulics and Sanitation	Health	Institution	National Directorate of Hydraulics-SCE Centrx

Appendix 2: Classification by Secondary Functions

CD_SECTION	LB_CHAPTER	MAIN FUNCTIONS	SECONDARY FUNCTIONS	LB_SUB-CHAPTER
80	Ministry of Hydraulics and Sanitation	Health	Institution	Regional Bases of the Na-Central Services Service
80	Ministry of Hydraulics and Sanitation	Health	Institution	Cabinet-Sce Centrx
80	Ministry of Hydraulics and Sanitation	Health	Institution	National Directorate of Hydraulics-SCE Centrx
80	Ministry of Hydraulics and Sanitation	Health	Institution	Regional Bases of the Na-Central Services Service
80	Ministry of Hydraulics and Sanitation	Health	Institution	Regional Bases of the Na-Central Services Service

CD_SECTION	LB_CHAPTER	MAIN FUNCTIONS	SECONDARY FUNCTIONS	LB_SUB-CHAPTER
80	Ministry of Hydraulics and Sanitation	Health	Health	GIR/ Upper River Basin L-Inland Decentralised Services
80	Ministry of Hydraulics and Sanitation	Health	Health	P/Integr. Dv. Adapt. Chang. Cl - Interior decentralised services
80	Ministry of Hydraulics and Sanitation	Health	Health	Assmt 4 Capitals/Reg and Ckry-Central Services
80	Ministry of Hydraulics and Sanitation	Health	Health	Hydraupur Phase II-Dec-Int
80	Ministry of Hydraulics and Sanitation	Health	Health	National Agency for Sanitation and Public Health

Appendix 2: Classification by Secondary Functions

CD_SECTION	LB_CHAPTER	MAIN FUNCTIONS	SECONDARY FUNCTIONS	LB_SUB-CHAPTER
80	Ministry of Hydraulics and Sanitation	Health	Health	P/Integr. Dv. Adapt. Chang. Cl - Interior decentralised services
80	Ministry of Hydraulics and Sanitation	Health	Health	Assmt 4 Capitals/Reg and Ckry-Central Services
80	Ministry of Hydraulics and Sanitation	Health	Health	Hydraupur Phase II-Dec-Int
80	Ministry of Hydraulics and Sanitation	Health	Health	AEP of the 5 Cities (Gaou, Toug, Lélou, Lola and Yom)-Dec-Int
80	Ministry of Hydraulics and Sanitation	Health	Health	4th Pj Eau de Ckry (1st phase)-Dec-Ckry

CD_SECTION	LB_CHAPTER	MAIN FUNCTIONS	SECONDARY FUNCTIONS	LB_SUB-CHAPTER
80	Ministry of Hydraulics and Sanitation	Health	Health	Fouta Djallon-Dec-Int Massive Development Program
80	Ministry of Hydraulics and Sanitation	Health	Health	Fouta Djallon-Dec-Int Massive Development Program
80	Ministry of Hydraulics and Sanitation	Health	Institution	National Planning Service-Central Services
80	Ministry of Hydraulics and Sanitation	Health	Economy	Hydraulics Fund-Central Services
80	Ministry of Hydraulics and Sanitation	Health	Health	AEP of the 5 Cities (Gaou, Toug, Lélou, Lola and Yom)-Dec-Int

Appendix 2: Classification by Secondary Functions

CD_SECTION	LB_CHAPTER	MAIN FUNCTIONS	SECONDARY FUNCTIONS	LB_SUB-CHAPTER
80	Ministry of Hydraulics and Sanitation	Health	Health	Prog. Gest. Integr. Res. Eau fl. Sénég. II-Dec-Int
80	Ministry of Hydraulics and Sanitation	Health	Health	Prog Accelerate. Water Access/All-Dec-Int
80	Ministry of Hydraulics and Sanitation	Health	Health	Hydrau. Villag. N'zérékoré-Lola-Yomou-Dec-Int
80	Ministry of Hydraulics and Sanitation	Health	Health	4th Pj Eau de Ckry (1st phase)-Dec-Ckry
80	Ministry of Hydraulics and Sanitation	Health	Building-Energy	4th Pj Eau de Ckry (1st phase)-Dec-Ckry

CD_SECTION	LB_CHAPTER	MAIN FUNCTIONS	SECONDARY FUNCTIONS	LB_SUB-CHAPTER
80	Ministry of Hydraulics and Sanitation	Health	Health	4th Pj Eau de Ckry (1st phase)-Dec-Ckry
80	Ministry of Hydraulics and Sanitation	Health	Health	4th Pj Eau de Ckry (1st phase)-Dec-Ckry
80	Ministry of Hydraulics and Sanitation	Health	Building-Energy	Guinea-Dec-Int Water Urban Project
80	Ministry of Hydraulics and Sanitation	Health	Institution	Sanitation City of Conakry-Déc-Ckry
80	Ministry of Hydraulics and Sanitation	Health	Health	Sanitation City of Conakry-Déc-Ckry

Appendix 2: Classification by Secondary Functions

CD_SECTION	LB_CHAPTER	MAIN FUNCTIONS	SECONDARY FUNCTIONS	LB_SUB-CHAPTER
80	Ministry of Hydraulics and Sanitation	Health	Health	Sanitation City of Conakry-Déc-Ckry
80	Ministry of Hydraulics and Sanitation	Health	Health	Sanitation City of Conakry-Déc-Ckry
80	Ministry of Hydraulics and Sanitation	Health	Health	Sanitation City of Conakry-Déc-Ckry
80	Ministry of Hydraulics and Sanitation	Health	Health	Payroll Processing Service - Central Services
80	Ministry of Hydraulics and Sanitation	Health	Health	Action Riposte covid-19-Sce Centrx

CD_SECTION	LB_CHAPTER	MAIN FUNCTIONS	SECONDARY FUNCTIONS	LB_SUB-CHAPTER
80	Ministry of Hydraulics and Sanitation	Health	Health	P/Integr. Dv. Adapt. Chang. Cl Niger-Sce Centrx
80	Ministry of Hydraulics and Sanitation	Health	Institution	Cabinet-Sce Centrx
80	Ministry of Hydraulics and Sanitation	Health	Education	Cabinet-Sce Centrx
80	Ministry of Hydraulics and Sanitation	Health	Professional Network	Cabinet-Sce Centrx
80	Ministry of Hydraulics and Sanitation	Health	Social Network	Cabinet-Sce Centrx

Appendix 2: Classification by Secondary Functions

CD_SECTION	LB_CHAPTER	MAIN FUNCTIONS	SECONDARY FUNCTIONS	LB_SUB-CHAPTER
80	Ministry of Hydraulics and Sanitation	Health	Health	Cabinet-Sce Centrx
80	Ministry of Hydraulics and Sanitation	Health	Building-Energy	Cabinet-Sce Centrx
80	Ministry of Hydraulics and Sanitation	Health	Institution	Cabinet-Sce Centrx
80	Ministry of Hydraulics and Sanitation	Health	Institution	National Directorate of Hydraulics-SCE Centrx
80	Ministry of Hydraulics and Sanitation	Health	Institution	National Directorate of Assai-Central Services

CD_SECTION	LB_CHAPTER	MAIN FUNCTIONS	SECONDARY FUNCTIONS	LB_SUB-CHAPTER
80	Ministry of Hydraulics and Sanitation	Health	Health	Sustainable Urban Development Support Program
80	Ministry of Hydraulics and Sanitation	Health	Health	National Agency for Sanitation and Public Health
80	Ministry of Hydraulics and Sanitation	Health	Institution	National Planning Service-Central Services
80	Ministry of Hydraulics and Sanitation	Health	Economy	Hydraulics Fund-Central Services
80	Ministry of Hydraulics and Sanitation	Health	Building-Energy	Rehabilitation of the City of Kankan-Dec-Int

Appendix 2: Classification by Secondary Functions

CD_SECTION	LB_CHAPTER	MAIN FUNCTIONS	SECONDARY FUNCTIONS	LB_SUB-CHAPTER
80	Ministry of Hydraulics and Sanitation	Health	Health	Sanitation City of Conakry-Déc-Ckry
80	Ministry of Hydraulics and Sanitation	Health	Health	Sanitation City of Conakry-Déc-Ckry
80	Ministry of Hydraulics and Sanitation	Health	Building-Energy	Sanitation City of Conakry-Déc-Ckry
80	Ministry of Hydraulics and Sanitation	Health	Health	Water/Sanitation Boké - Télémélé-Déc-Int
80	Ministry of Hydraulics and Sanitation	Health	Health	Guinea-Dec-Int Water Urban Project

CD_SECTION	LB_CHAPTER	MAIN FUNCTIONS	SECONDARY FUNCTIONS	LB_SUB-CHAPTER
80	Ministry of Hydraulics and Sanitation	Health	Health	Payroll Processing Service - Central Services
80	Ministry of Hydraulics and Sanitation	Health	Social Network	Payroll Processing Service - Central Services
80	Ministry of Hydraulics and Sanitation	Health	Institution	Regional Bases of the Na-Central Services Service
80	Ministry of Hydraulics and Sanitation	Health	Health	Sanitation City of Conakry-Déc-Ckry

APPENDIX 3: Explanatory Note to Appendices 1 and 2

Appendices 1 and 2 present extracts from the functional budget after the classification of the budget lines according to main and secondary functions. The State budget is drawn up and managed by the Budget Directorate of the Ministry in charge of Economy and Finance according to the nomenclature of public accounting. This nomenclature makes it possible to classify the budget appropriations by heading. This classification distinguishes between two main headings of the budget, namely: revenue and expenditure. Indeed, Finance Law establishes the legal framework for the mobilization of revenues and the commitment of public expenditure.

In the context of the functional transformation of the traditional State budget, it is the regulation law that is used. This law is preferred because, unlike the initial programmatic finance law, it reflects the actual actions of the State during the financial year. However, in the absence of the availability of the settlement law during certain budgetary transformation operations, it is possible to have recourse to the authorized budget.

The use of the expenditure heading for the budget transformation is based on the principle of balanced budgets, according to which all revenue must be equal to all expenditure during a budget year. A country's executed budget file for the period under analysis is usually in Excel format, with hundreds or thousands of rows depending on the size of the budget. In columns, the elements of the budget classification of expenditure are generally observed. On the one hand, we have the elements of the classification by destination (Section, chapter or sub-chapter) and those of the classification by type of expenditure (Title, Article, Paragraph and Economic nature).

The section designates the ministries or State institutions that receive the budget appropriations. The chapter includes the services or groups of services that manage or receive the endowment, within the same department or institution. The sub-chapter being a more detailed codification of the chapter.

The title groups expenditure operations into three categories: ordinary expenditure, capital expenditure, ancillary budgets and special accounts. The article breaks down the appropriations at the level of the subdivisions of the section, while the paragraph specifies the expenditure for each chapter.

The classification used in Appendix 1 is based on the section column of the budget, based on a cross-analysis between the purpose of the engagement letter of the department or institution concerned and the eight economic functions of the DDMI. The classification of the secondary function in Appendix 2 is a bit more complex. It is generally based on chapters and sub-chapters. However, there may be times when elements such as the article or paragraph provide relevant information to determine the secondary function, especially when the wording of the chapter or subchapter is unclear. Appendix 2 shows an excerpt from the secondary classification for institutions in the health sector.

KEYWORD GLOSSARY

Assets: Fixed assets are tangible or intangible assets that arise from one production process and are used repeatedly in other production processes. Significant improvements to an asset corresponding to an investment decision, and which significantly increase the performance or production capacity of the existing asset, are recorded in Gross Fixed Capital Formation (GFCF).

Algorithm: this is a set of operating rules whose application makes it possible to solve a problem stated by means of a finite number of operations. An algorithm can be translated, through a programming language, into a program that can be executed by a computer.

Altruism: this is a set of operating rules whose application makes it possible to solve a problem stated by means of a finite number of operations.

Analysis of covariance: An analytical procedure in which the effects of one or more exogenous variables (called covariates) are removed from the analysis before an analysis of variance is conducted.

Regression analysis: A technique for analyzing multivariate data aimed at explaining variations in an endogenous variable (or explained variable) by exogenous (or explanatory) variables.

Analysis of variance: A data analysis technique that reveals the relationships between a quantitative dependent variable and one or more non-metric exogenous variable(s) (nominal or ordinal).

Bivariate analyses: Statistical techniques consisting of studying the relationships between two variables; the study of the relationship between two variables may lead to the calculation of indicators of association between the two variables (the formulation and methods of calculating these indicators vary according to the measurements of the variables concerned).

Multivariate analyses: Analysis of data developed to allow the simultaneous processing of several variables. There are two groups of multivariate methods depending on whether one seeks to structure or summarize a group of variables (descriptive methods) or to study the relationships between groups of variables (so-called "explanatory" methods, which are also descriptive).

Univariate analyses: Data analysis that consists of examining the distribution of a variable.

Exploratory approach: A research approach aimed at generating or selecting dimensions or hypotheses.

Linkage: this is a step of the BSDD that allows the analysis of budget sensitivity to judge budget elasticities and auxiliary functions for optimal budget allocation.

Self-employment: this term gives access to the reflexive dimension where the employee and the employer designate the same natural person. Self-employment is also referred to as "self-employment" or "self-employment."

Other Taxes on production are those related to economic activity, such as net taxes on factors of production.

Frame: An exhaustive list of individuals in a population.

Benchmarking: a management and marketing technique that consists of comparing your company to one or more others that are benchmarks in a specific field.

Budgeting Sensitive to Demographic Dividend (BSDD): This is a process for assessing whether the demographic dividend (DD) is considered in budget allocations. It is an approach to integrate DD and gender capture concerns into the design, implementation, monitoring and evaluation of policies and programs. The term "sensitive" refers to the fact that budget execution must be able to produce positive changes in the sectors involved in capturing the demographic dividend.

Model calibration: This is any procedure that allows information on the value of the model's parameters to be obtained from the observations that this model synthesizes. Depending on the objectives pursued, statistical, econometric or simply subjective methods are used.

Human capital: all the skills, talents, qualifications, experience accumulated by an individual and which partly determine his or her ability to work or produce for himself or for others

Natural unemployment: this is the unemployment rate to which the economy fluctuates in the long term.

Functional budget classification: This is the classification of expenditure transactions according to the purpose for which these transactions are carried out. A functional classification does not depend on the units that carry out the activities concerned.

Internal coherence: The quality of an instrument or scale of measurement, the different questions of which are supposed to contribute to measuring the same phenomenon or the same dimensions of this phenomenon.

National accounts: it provides a simplified, aggregated and quantified representation of the national economy.

Concept (or Construct or trait): Building of the mind to organize perceptions and knowledge. Examples of constructs: attitude, involvement, perceived risk, emotions.

Consumption of fixed capital (CCF): this is the additional investment necessary to maintain the initial capital at the end of the financial year. It is the cost of production that represents the normal wear and tear of the stock of fixed capital held by the producer.

Market final consumption: these are the purchases of goods and services by households (in the strict sense). It excludes stored goods and Building goods classified as Gross Fixed Capital Formation (GFCF).

Non-market final consumption: it is equal to the non-market output of the general government and to the consumption of final households in non-market products (self-consumption).

Final consumption: the expenditure actually incurred by resident households to acquire goods and services to meet their needs. The corresponding products are not stored but considered to be consumed at the time of purchase, even if they are durable (cars, appliances, furniture, etc.).

Intermediate consumption: It corresponds to the value of goods and services consumed as inputs during a production process, excluding fixed assets. Consumption Interim includes leases of fixed assets as well as royalties on assets, products, commissions and other to be paid under the licensing agreement. Intermediate consumption is calculated using technical coefficients or standard accounts.

Fuel consumption (CF): it is the value of goods and services used to satisfy needs. It breaks down into consumption intermediate and final consumption

World prices: the selling price of an agricultural or mining commodity on the world market at a given time.

Economic growth: a positive change in the production of goods and services in an economy over a reference period, usually a one-year period.

Inclusive growth: growth that benefits all segments of society, including the poor, the relatively poor with low incomes, the middle class, and even the rich.

Budget deficit: A situation in which government spending is higher than its revenues.

Life Cycle Deficit: Situation in which consumption of an individual is greater than his or her income from work.

Demand for labor: the amount of labor that firms need to be able to produce goods and services

Demand for the composite goods: the composite good is then called the goods, considered as the currency of the economy.

Hypothetico-deductive approach: An approach consisting of starting from the knowledge acquired – theories – concepts to formulate hypotheses that will then be tested to the test of facts (on the other hand, a purely deductive approach consists in drawing the logical consequences of a system of axioms and rules).

Inductive approach: An approach that consists of building schemas based on limited observations that claim to be a certain generality.

Density (of the population): This is the average number of people who occupy a given unit of geographical area, usually the square kilometer.

Economic dependence: The situation of an individual with little or no income, who is forced to resort to public and/or private transfers to meet his or her consumption needs.

Sustainable development: Sustainable development is a new vision of economic growth, designed from the outset with a long-term perspective and which integrates the constraints linked to the environment and the functioning of society.

Economic development: Economic development is about expanding the opportunities for success to those who want to escape the balance of poverty development implies an increase in social well-being, changes in the structures and mentalities of society. It involves urbanization, industrialization, literacy and training, and the destruction of rural societies.

Demographic dividend: Accelerating economic growth that can result from a rapid decline in fertility of a country and the subsequent evolution of the age structure of the population

Qualitative data: Data corresponding to variables measured on nominal and ordinal scales. Not to be confused with qualitative studies.

Quantitative data: Data corresponding to variables measured on cardinal scales (real or integer). Not to be confused with quantitative studies.

Scale of measure: An ordered set of references in which a variable takes value.

Nominal scale: A scale of measurement that only identifies the belonging of the object under study to a class (hence the expression often used of class or group variable), i.e. expresses a characteristic that distinguishes it from others, of "naming" it (hence the expression nominal variable).

Ordinal scale: A scale of measurement that establishes an order relationship between response modalities. The gendarmes are classified by rank, from the most senior to the lowest ranked.

Employment: It is "the set of tasks and functions performed, or intended to be performed, by a person, whether for an employer or as a self-employed person"

Employment independent: it is a job whose remuneration is directly linked to profits and whose holder makes management decisions affecting the company or is held responsible for the good health of the company"

Enterprises: it is an organizational unit to produce goods and services enjoying a certain autonomy of decision based on the allocation of current resources.

Generational equity: more specifically equity intergenerational is the new consideration of the intrinsic dilemma that characterizes the relationship between generations. On the one hand, equity between living generations is jeopardized by the fact that they are not bound to each other by any contract that would ensure that the older generations have a claim on the future resources of their offspring, in return for the efforts made for their education: even if altruistic, the oldest are therefore inclined to seek to maintain their acquired rights. Equity between present and future generations, on the other hand, is affected by temporal irreversibility which hinders the action of successors, who are unable to modify the decisions taken today or to claim their due after the fact. CG: refers to generational accounting, which considers the relationships between different generations in public policies

ERE or Resource-Use Equilibrium: show that, for a group of products or for all products, total resources are equal to total uses (uses). ERAs relate to different quantities.

Exports of goods: these are defined as the outflow of goods from the economic territory to the rest of the world. They are counted at FOB (free on board) prices. The FOB price expresses the value of leaving the territory excluding the cost of transport and insurance.

Gross fixed capital formation (GFCF): it records the value of acquisitions minus disposals of fixed assets. It concerns goods whose life cycle lasts longer than one year.

Gross fixed capital formation: flow investment in the country. It is the sum of the investments, mainly material, made during the year in a territory.

GRG: The Reduced Gradient Method (also called Generalized Reduced Gradient or GRG) is an optimization technique that allows us to find solutions to optimization problems with nonlinear inequality constraints.

Hypothesis: A proposition obtained by induction or observation and intended to be verified or invalidated by experimentation. Research in the Social Sciences frequently consists of the verification of hypotheses, propositions deduced from the scientific literature (or induced by observation) on the subject studied and whose choice is based on the possibility of measurement.

Imports of goods: these represent the value of goods entering economic territory. They are recorded in CIF value (freight insurance cost). CIF value is the value of entry into the economic territory. It includes the costs of getting to the border.

Taxes on production and imports: Taxes are unrequited payments, in kind or in cash, made by institutional units serving the administrations. They include taxes on products and other taxes on production.

Taxes on products are payable on goods and services when they are produced, supplied, transferred or otherwise made available by producers. They include duties and taxes on imports. They include VAT-type taxes, import taxes and duties (excluding VAT), export taxes, and product taxes excluding VAT and taxes on imports and exports.

Synthetic indicator: an index that measures the change in the value of a complex quantity defined as the aggregation of a set of elementary quantities.

Statistical inference: Extrapolation of results obtained on a sample (50% of people in the sample prefer A to B) to the characteristics of the entire parent population (50% of people in the entire population prefer A to B). Inference is only a logical operation, but a probabilistic one. It is based on the notion of plausibility.

Investment: The action of acquiring new means of production, improving their yield or investing capital in an economic activity, in a company, etc.

Foreign direct investment: international investment by which entities resident in an economy acquire or have acquired a lasting interest in an entity resident in an economy other than that of the investor.

The unemployment rate prospecting: it is a voluntary unemployment rate that is the result of an individual strategy. It is an incompressible unemployment that corresponds to the time it takes for a worker to look for another job who voluntarily leaves his job in search of another.

Non-market services: this is the output of government and is measured at the cost of production.

Law: A rule specifying the relationship between concepts (or quantities). For example, Weber's law, which explains that the stronger the initial intensity of a stimulus, the greater the increase in this stimulus must be to be perceived by a subject.

Rent charged to owners: notional rent calculated from the rental value of dwellings occupied by their own owners.

Household: it consists of a person living alone or a group of people not necessarily related by a family relationship residing at the same address and collectively consuming certain goods or services, i.e. sharing at least one meal per day or sharing a living room or living room.

Households: All occupants of the same housing without these people necessarily being related (in the case of cohabitation, for example). A household can be composed of one person.

Modalities: Possible values of a variable. Example of possible modalities of a variable: the different possible answers to a question – yes, no, don't know – constitute the different modalities of the variable measured by the question "do you have a business card?".

Model: simplified representation of reality relating explanatory variables and variables to be explained, allowing us to understand a complex phenomenon.

Descriptive model: A model whose purpose is to simplify the structure of a system to facilitate its understanding and communication.

Prescriptive or prescriptive model: A model that includes a recommendation for action and/or identifies the best solution(s).

Predictive model: A model that allows the user to anticipate the evolution of a system, based on different assumptions about the explanatory variables.

Infant mortality: Deaths of children under one year of age.

Nonparametric (tests and analyses): Analyses and tests that do not impose constraints on the distribution of the data, adapted when the data are non-metric (nominal or ordinal) and/or the sample sizes are small.

Labor supply: The amount of work that workers provide, in exchange for remuneration

A distinction is made between the dependency ratio of young people (individuals under 20 years of age) and the dependency ratio of the elderly (65 years of age and over), both calculated in relation to the number of individuals aged 20 to 64. Together, these ratios provide information on the demographic trends of countries and future trends.

Operationalization of a concept: The passage of this concept from the abstract universe to the empirical world through variables allowing measurements.

Transactions with the rest of the world: Trade in goods and services is the various transactions with the rest of the world. These exchanges are either exported or imported.

Optimization of the allocation of the state budget: Optimizing budget allocation means determining the functional structure of the budget that maximizes the production function of public goods and services in an economy or in a country, under budgetary constraints.

Foreign trade payments: this is the sum of all trade between residents and the rest of the world. They are reproduced in the balance of payments and relate to current account accounts (relating to goods, services and income), capital, financial and monetary transactions.

Paradigm: A corpus of problems and techniques specific to their study. Entire constellation of beliefs, values, etc. Shared by members of a given community. For example, the cognitive paradigm explains the process of persuasion by an articulation of two phases (reception and acceptance) and a hierarchy of effects (modification of the cognitive structure--mediating role of beliefs--behavior).

Parametric (tests and analyses): Inference techniques adopted in case variables follow parametric distributions.

Poverty: An individual (or household) is considered poor when he or she lives in a household whose Standard of living is below the poverty line.

Process: The unfolding of a phenomenon in time with stages related to each other.

Self-consumed production: This is production for own use. It is consumed by the producer himself.

Production of domestic services is equal to the remuneration of domestic staff.

Production of real estate services is equal to the amount of rents on offices and housing.

Insurance production: It is equal to the difference between the premiums earned and the indemnities due, adjusted for changes in technical reserves.

Total domestic production: the production carried out within households, and which is not remunerated. It includes the self-consumption of households and individual businesses.

Trade market production: It is measured by the total value of trade margins generated by resale as is. Margin is the difference between the actual sale price and the purchase price at the time the asset is sold or used.

Market production: it comes from the branches of market activities. These branches are made up of production units whose main resources come from the sale of goods and services on a market at an economically significant price.

Non-market production: it comes from non-market branches of activity made up of units producing public services free of charge or almost free of charge. Production is determined for each branch and sub-branch of activity.

Production on own account: in addition to self-consumption production in the traditional sense, there is the production of goods and services by households for themselves.

Production: it is defined as the activity that consists of using Inputs (inputs) to produce Outputs (finished products).

Productivity: The ratio, in volume, between production and the resources used to obtain it. Productivity measures the effectiveness of a process in turning one or more input factors into an outcome

Gross domestic product at market prices (GDP): This is the sum of total gross value added and net taxes on products. This method of determining GDP corresponds to the production approach.

Demographic dependency ratio: The demographic dependency ratio is a function of the age structure of the population. It is the ratio of the number of individuals who are supposed to be "dependent" on others for their daily lives – young and old – and the number of individuals able to bear this burden. In this sense, this ratio represents potential. Because by introducing the problem of child labor and senior labor in developing countries, we quickly realize that this ratio can lead to confusion in detailed analyses.

Economic Support Ratio: Ratio between the number of actual producers and the number of actual consumers. It is a synthetic measure of the structure of production and consumption depending on age. There is also the **Intrinsic Support Ratio** which is calculated on a subnational geographical entity considering that it is self-sufficient.

State revenues: These are non-grant revenues composed of tax and non-tax revenues from the central government, public administrations and local authorities. This includes levies from social organizations, revenues from the exploitation of natural resources and collected by the State, whether fiscal or non-fiscal. Tax revenue is the sum of revenue from the different categories of taxes and duties in force in the country (direct taxes, consumption taxes). and taxes on international trade). Non-tax revenue is mainly income from the State's assets, the product of various user fees for the use of the State public domain and the proceeds of fines.

Residence: an institutional unit is resident when it has a center of interest in the country's economic territory. This means that it carries out economic activities there for a period exceeding the year.

Business income: Business income represents all economic, commercial, industrial or financial activities that are capable of generating a profit and that are more than ownership or passive ownership. Not to be confused with income.

Household income: this is the set of rights to available resources that are allocated to households during a given period without deduction from their assets.

Income from the capital factor: it corresponds to the remuneration in kind, in cash for all securities assets, land or real estate assets, cash that goes into the production of goods and services.

Income from the labour factor: it corresponds to remuneration in kind, in cash without taking from the patrimony the physical or intellectual effort that must be made to do something in production. It can be an allowance, a gain, a pension, a product, an annuity, a reward, or wages.

Science: a classified, systematic body of knowledge, composed of one or more central theories and a number of general principles, usually in quantitative terms; this body of knowledge allows for the prediction and, under certain circumstances, the control of future events.

Agricultural sector: In the broadest sense, this sector of the economy includes crops, livestock, hunting, fishing and forestry.

Formal sector: it is made up of officially declared companies, which comply with laws and regulations, and pay their taxes. It is composed of the trade sector, the Building sector, the industry sector and the service sector.

Informal sector: this is the set of economic activities that are carried out outside of criminal, social and tax legislation or that are not covered by the National Accounts.

Informal sector: Defined as enterprises that are not registered at the level of a chamber of commerce and therefore have no NINEA.

Modern sector: A sector of the economy that includes enterprises that are incorporated and operate in accordance with the law. It is a legal sector, declared and accounted for in the statistics that are subject to tax and social obligations

Private sector: A field of activity made up of companies, associations or organizations that do not depend directly on the State, its administration and/or local authorities and where public funds are not invested or only minimally.

Subsidies: Subsidies are unrequited payments made by administrations, possibly non-resident, to companies. They include subsidies on local or import products exclusively on products at the level of balance on goods and services. They therefore exclude balancing subsidies to public companies.

Supply and Use Table (TAR): The TAR describes the structure of national production. It offers a summary presentation of the production and operating accounts of the branches on the one hand and the resource-use balances of products on the other.

Banking rate: Percentage of the population with access to banking services

Theory: A set of abstract concepts more or less organized applied to a particular field. The place of theory in the dynamics of research can be appreciated by the words of Claude Bernard "Theory is the hypothesis verified after it has been subjected to the control of reasoning and experimental criticism." For example, the theory of surveys, a statistical theory that links the concepts of random choice of subjects in a sample, precision and significance of the results obtained.

Theory of investments in forms: it states that the qualification of employees plays a preponderant role in the functioning of the labor market, but within the framework of institutions that forge systems of vertical hierarchies and horizontal equivalences.

Budget transformation: this is a process that aims to reorganize the data of the national budget and make it correspond to a structure defined by the BSDD (08 functions related to DDMI): Education, Health, Security, Institution, Professional Network, Social Network, Building/ Energy and Economic Affairs.

A "sharing" economy: which establishes a relationship between employees' remuneration and the results of their companies. Thus, the workers' salary will be divided into two parts: one that is fixed and the other that depends on the performance of the company.

Gross value added is defined as the difference between the output of the branch and the amount of intermediate consumption used.

Convergent validity: Quality of a measurement instrument where the indicators that are supposed to measure the same phenomenon are effectively correlated.

Trait (or constructed) validity: Quality of a measurement instrument where the constructed indicators are a good representation of the phenomenon studied.

Discriminant validity: Quality of a measurement instrument where indicators measuring different and independent phenomena must be weakly correlated with each other.

External validity: The ability to extrapolate the results and conclusions of the research to the entire field that was investigated or, possibly, to a larger field.

Facial (or content) validity: Quality of a measuring instrument that gives results accepted by intuition.

Internal validity: Assurance that changes in the response variable (or dependent variable or variable to be explained) are caused solely by changes in the independent variable.

Predictive validity (nomological validity): The quality of a measuring instrument such that the relationship between the measurements of one concept and that of other concepts is consistent with the predictions from theory based on previous research.

Variables: Building of the mind, which can take on values, used to measure a concept (a variable is often apprehended by a question). Example of a simple variable: the age of a person; of composite variable: his socio-professional category.

Changes in inventories: this is the difference between inventories at the end of the year and inventories at the beginning of the fiscal year. The products concerned are goods with the exception of capital goods classified as Gross Fixed Capital Formation (GFCF) or associated services.

Vulnerability: Low ability to protect against the high risk of experiencing poverty status.

KEYWORD INDEXING

AFTERWORD

DEMOGRAPHIC DIVIDEND-SENSITIVE BUDGETING FOR A PROSPEROUS FUTURE

As we conclude this book, it is necessary to reflect on the scope of the subject we have explored: budgeting sensitive to the demographic dividend. This hopeful concept invites us to reconsider the way in which public resources are allocated to increase the benefits that demographic dynamics can offer. More than just a budget management tool, it is a real strategy to turn challenges into opportunities and build more equitable and resilient societies.

The demographic dividend, with its promises related to an increase in the number of effective workers compared to dependent people, represents an unprecedented lever for development. However, as this book has demonstrated, maximizing this potential requires careful planning and strategic policies. This implies investing in education, health, employment and well-being while promoting an economic framework conducive to inclusive growth.

By taking a demographic-dividend-sensitive approach, economic and policy makers can align their fiscal priorities with long-term outcomes. How can we ignore the impact that well-educated and healthy youth can have on a country's prosperity? Or the importance of a robust health system to ensure productivity durable? These questions, which have run through the various chapters, highlight the direct implications of budgeting centered on this concept.

However, it would be illusory to think that this model does not present major challenges. One of the main obstacles remains budget management, which is often constrained by limited resources and competing priorities. How many times have we observed promising initiatives run out of steam due to a lack of resources?

It is also essential to adopt a gender perspective, rurality and access to basic services. Inequalities if they are not Reduced, could undermine the expected benefits of the demographic dividend, by limiting the participation of entire segments of the population to economic and social life.

This book stressed that the fulfilment of the promises of the demographic dividend is based on a collective effort. Governments obviously play a central role, but they cannot act alone. The private sector, international organizations and civil society must join forces to create an ecosystem conducive to transformative transformation.

Reading the pages of this book, it becomes clear that demographic dividend-sensitive budgeting is not a one-size-fits-all solution, but a dynamic framework for action. Each country, with its historical, economic and cultural particularities, will have to adapt the principles set out to its own reality.

This book represents a call to action, a reminder that the budget choices made today will define the opportunities of tomorrow. By investing strategically, promoting equity and anticipating the needs of future generations, we have the power to transform the current demographic structure into an engine of prosperity and sustainable development.

As we turn the final page, one question remains: how are we, as an international, national and local community, going to make the most of this precious window of opportunity that is the demographic dividend? This book has provided tools, ideas, and concrete examples, but the responsibility for implementing them rests with each one of us.

May this afterword serve as a catalyst for further discussions, policy innovation and, above all, action. Demographic dividend-sensitive budgeting is not just a technical approach. It embodies a vision of justice, progress and hope for a better future. It's up to us to make it a reality.

Prof. Barthélémy BIAO
Rector of the African University of Cooperative Development in Benin

BIOGRAPHIES OF AUTHORS AND CONTRIBUTORS

Prof. Latif DRAMANI

Associate Professor in Economics and holder of a PhD in Economics from the Cheikh Anta Diop University of Dakar, Senegal, Latif Dramani is Full Professor of Economics at the Iba Der Thiam University of Thiès and Coordinator of the Center for Research in Economics and Applied Finance of Thiès (CREFAT). He is the Africa representative of the NTA network and the Coordinator of the Regional Consortium for Research in Generational Economics (CREG). He is the Africa representative of the NTA network and present chair of the said network. Affiliated with several universities around the world (University of Manchester, University of Berkeley, University of Parakou, University of Cape Town, University of Hawaii at Manoa). Author of several scientific and programmatic books, Prof Latif Dramani conducts his research in the following main areas: the issue of sustainable development through the prism of the Demographic Dividend and the Generational Economy; Poverty dynamics; the Care Economy, unpaid domestic work and women's contribution to GDP; and finally the national and local integration of economies.

Mrs. Oumy LAYE

Ms. Oumy Laye, an economist, has been a member of the CREG research team for ten years. She has contributed to the work on the Demographic Dividend and on the evaluation and valuation of women's unpaid domestic work in the economy. Before working at CREG, she was working at ANSD as head of the Regional Service of Statistics and Demography of the Thiès region, bringing to her credit 10 years of experience in development economics at the regional level. She published with Professor Dramani in 2011 in the journal of Science, technology, innovation & development vol 3: "link between ICT investments, growth and job creation in Senegal".

Mr. Edem Kossi AKPO

Mr. Edem Kossi AKPO is a statistical engineer and economist (ISE) who graduated from the National School of Statistics and Economic Analysis (ENSAE) in Dakar. He currently leads the Knowledge and

Policy (KPD) at CREG. He has extensive experience in supporting countries in the implementation of public policies that promote the capture of demographic dividend and more generally sustainable development.

Mrs. Mame Coura NDIAYE KAMA

Mrs. Mame Coura NDIAYE KAMA is Chief of Staff to the Coordinating President of the Regional Consortium for Research in Generational Economy (CREG) where she has brought 12 years of experience in the field of administrative management. She holds a master's degree in foreign Languages Applied-Option Business and Commerce. She also holds a master's degree in business administration (MBA). She is also a trainer in Business English, Marketing and Hospitality Techniques. PhD student in Management Sciences, she is particularly interested in the practice of marketing communication in public organizations in general and Public Health Establishments in particular. She worked at ISM Dakar and ISM Thiès respectively. She has significantly contributed to the influence of the ISM in Thiès. She has visited more than 12 countries in Africa, the United States, which greatly strengthened his cultural experience.

Dr Camille Dètondji GUIDIME

Dr. Camille Dètondji GUIDIME is Assistant Professor of Economics and Teacher-Researcher at the University of Parakou in Benin. He is an associate researcher member at the Regional Center of Excellence for Research in Generational Economics (CREG). He is a member of the research team of the National Transfer Accounts network, the Feminist Economics network and the International Trade Research Unit. He conducts research in population economics, an international economy with a focus on developing countries.

Monsieur Seukap Roger

Seukap Roger, CREG's Director of Programs, originally a nutrition engineer, is a high-performing, visionary senior leader in population, development and reproductive health, with extensive experience in developing health programs in government organizations and various non-governmental organizations at the national and international levels. Analytical professional skilled in successfully leading teams to excellence in conducting health, population, and development activities for diverse populations, including data for strategic decision-making.

Dr Jean-Baptiste OGA

Jean-Baptiste OGA, a Beninese national, is a lecturer and researcher at the Faculty of Economics and Management of the University of Parakou in Benin. He obtained a PhD in Economics from the Mohammed V University of Rabat (Morocco) in 2017 and a Research master's degree in development economics from the Centre d'Etudes et de Recherches sur le Développement International (CERDI, France), in 2008. He is a member of the Laboratory of Research in Economics and Management (LAREG) of the University of Parakou and an associate researcher at the Regional Consortium for Research in Generational Economics (CREG), based in Thiès, Senegal. He is also a lecturer in the master's program in Generational Economics and Public Policy (EGPP) at CREG and the Doctoral Program at the African University for Cooperative Development (UADC) based in Cotonou, Benin.

Mrs. Edmée Ndoye

Edmée Ndoye is an Economist at the Regional Consortium for Research in Generational Economics (CREG). A graduate of the Interuniversity Postgraduate Program (PTCI), she has more than 5 years of experience in Demo-economic research, population dynamics, gender and social protection. A doctoral student at the end of her training at the Iba Der Thiam University in Thiès, she is the author and co-author of scientific articles, books and policy briefs as part of her research activities. She is also an Alumni in Policy Communication for the Population Reference Bureau (PRB) Policy Advocacy and Communication Enhanced for Population and Reproductive Health (PACE) project and is part of the Partnership for Economic Policy (PEP) Researchers Network for the Modeling Policy and Impact Analysis program. His interests are mainly in research, music, reading and travel.

Dr Mame Sangoné DIOP

Mame Sangoné DIOP is currently a research assistant at CREG (Centre of Excellence for Research in Generational Economics). He holds a PhD in Economic and Social Sciences from the Iba Der Thiam University in Thiès since February 2023 and a master's degree in Territorial Development Engineering from the Alioune Diop University in Bambey in 2016. He works on human capital issues and uses micro and macroeconomic approaches to understand well-being.

Dr Faoziatou G. TOSSOUNON

Faoziatou G. TOSSOUNON: Economist – researcher affiliated with the Regional Consortium for Research in Generational Economics (CREG). I am a member of the Economic Commission for Africa's (ECA) Africa Youth Network. Alumni of the African Economic Research Consortium (AERC) in Nairobi and the Inter-University Postgraduate Programme (PTCI). I hold a PhD from the Cheikh Anta Diop University in Dakar, Senegal, which focuses on "ESSAYS ON SOCIAL PROTECTION IN BENIN". My research focuses mainly on public economics and development issues, including the demographic dividend, human capital, the Care Economy, social protection and gender within the CREG. In addition, work on market integration and the international economy is the subject of investigation and reflection by the author within the CREG.

Dr Boubacar DIALLO

Doctor in economics from the Doctoral School of Sustainable Development and Society (ED2DS) of the Iba Der Thiam University of Thiès, I devoted my thesis to the analysis of profiling and the determinants of the poverty in Senegal. Previously, I obtained a DEA in Applied Macroeconomics, with a specialization in Monetary Economics, Banking and Public Finance, as part of the Inter-University Postgraduate Programme (PTCI). Currently, I am a researcher affiliated with the Regional Consortium for Research in Generational Economics (CREG), and my work focuses mainly on issues of poverty, inequality and inequality. social protection.

Dr Rachidou YOROU

Dr. Rachidou YOROU is a Beninese economist who did his thesis at the Thomas Sankara University in Burkina Faso. Economist at the Regional Consortium for Research in Generational Economics (CREG) in Senegal since 2019 and Associate Teacher-Researcher at the Faculty of Economics and Management of the University of Parakou in Benin since 2016. He is involved in the drafting of the Country Reports on the Demographic Dividend. He is the author of several published works in the field of development economics.

Dr Pierre Aloyse Mundor NDIAYE

Pierre Aloyse Mundor NDIAYE is an economist/researcher currently affiliated with CREG (Centre of Excellence for Research in Generational Economics). He holds a PhD in Economic and Social

Sciences from the Iba Der Thiam University in Thiès since April 2025 and has worked on the effect of bank financing as a lever for the development of Senegal's economy. He is a specialist in development economics.

Mr. Olaniran Franck BALOGOUN

Olaniran Franck BALOGOUN is a financial economist and PhD student at the Iba Der Thiam University in Thiès, Senegal. He holds a master's degree in Banking and Financial Markets and is currently a Research Economist at the Regional Consortium for Research in Generational Economics (CREG). He is actively involved in research projects on the generational economy and public policy, as well as on the financial economics of climate change for the formulation and evaluation of economic policies in African Union countries.

Mr. Ibrahima MBALLO

Ibrahima MBALLO is currently a research assistant at the Regional Consortium for Research in Generational Economics (CREG), and a doctoral student at the Doctoral School of Sustainable Development and society (ED2DS). He works on issues of evaluation of economic policies and programs. He is also a teaching assistant and lecturer at the Iba Der Thiam University in Thiès.

TABLE OF CONTENTS

Structures éditoriales du groupe L'Harmattan

L'Harmattan Italie
Via degli Artisti, 15
10124 Torino
harmattan.italia@gmail.com

L'Harmattan Hongrie
Kossuth l. u. 14-16.
1053 Budapest
harmattan@harmattan.hu

L'Harmattan Sénégal
10 VDN SICAP AMITIE 3
BP 45034 Dakar-Fann
direction@senharmattan.com

L'Harmattan Cameroun
Tsinga/Derrière polyclinique FECAFOOT
BP 11486 Yaoundé
Jacques.koukam@harmattan.fr

L'Harmattan Burkina Faso
Villa 281, secteur 23 623, rue 14.32
Ouagadougou
zagbie@outlook.fr

L'Harmattan Guinée
Almamya, rue KA 028 OKB Agency
BP 3470 Conakry
harmattanguinee@yahoo.fr

L'Harmattan RDC
185, avenue Nyangwe
Commune de Lingwala – Kinshasa
matangilamusadila@yahoo.fr

L'Harmattan Congo
219, avenue Nelson Mandela
BP 2874 Brazzaville
deunovmikhael@gmail.com

L'Harmattan Mali
Immeuble Mgr Jean Marie Cissé
Aci Hamadallaye
BP 145 Bamako
syllaka@yahoo.fr

L'Harmattan Togo
Djidjole – Maison Amela
face EPP BATOME
02 BP 20680 Lomé
didieramela11@gmail.com

L'Harmattan Côte d'Ivoire
Résidence Karl – Cité des Arts
Abidjan-Cocody
03 BP 1588 Abidjan
harmattan.ivoire@gmail.com

L'Harmattan Bénin
Rue 604, (Immeuble à l'entrée
de la rue UCAO- Cite de Saint-Jean)
Cotonou
stepcorpus@gmail.com

Nos librairies en France

Librairie internationale
16, rue des Écoles
75005 Paris
librairie.internationale@harmattan.fr
01 40 46 79 11
www.librairieharmattan.com

Librairie des savoirs
21, rue des Écoles
75005 Paris
librairie.sh@harmattan.fr
01 46 34 13 71
www.librairieharmattansh.com

www.ingramcontent.com/pod-product-compliance
Lightning Source LLC
Chambersburg PA
CBHW071422230926
51846CB00001B/106

* 9 7 8 2 3 3 6 5 6 6 2 0 7 *